GUITAR CHORDS ENCYCLOPEDIA

Fast Reference for the Chords You Need in Every Key

ANDY SCHNEIDER

SEEING MUSIC
METHOD BOOKS

This book is dedicated to Sharon Schneider,
who gave me my first music lessons and made
sure I could enjoy a lifetime of making music.

CONTENTS

SEEING MUSIC
METHOD BOOKS

GUITAR
CHORDS
ENCYCLOPEDIA

HOW TO USE THIS BOOK

|||||||||||||||||||||||||||||||||||||||||||||||||||||||||||||||||||||||||||

READ THIS FIRST

Not all guitarists need the same chords for every situation. If you've reached for this book, it's probably because you have a question. You know what you want to get done, like play a chord for certain song or set of songs, and you are looking for answers as to how to play that chord.

If only the answer to your question were simple. For any given chord type, say C Major, there are so many ways to play that chord that it boggles the mind. Now there is a way to get your answers, faster.

Generally in the guitar universe, guitarists are of a few basic types. Those types use different families of chords which satisfy their jobs-at-hand. Imagine a folk guitarist by the campfire and a jazz guitarist at a club in New York City. Both might play a C Major, but probably wouldn't play the exact same chord.

|||||||||||||||||||||||||||||||||||||||||||||||||||||||||||||||||||||||||||

IMAGINE THREE DIFFERENT GUITARISTS

At the risk..no, *certainty*, of oversimplfying musical genre and style, imagine there are three basic groups to which a guitarist might belong at a given moment.

BIG — In the first group are those guitarists who need big chords with 4, 5 or 6 notes to play rhythm. Acoustic soloists and rock guitarists fall generally into this group.

COMPACT — Other players like smaller chords with fewer notes. They usually are in an ensemble that doesn't require such a full sound from the guitar. Two or three note chords, voiced in the middle of the fretboard will work quite well. Imagine Rock, Blues or Rhythm & Blues players and place them in this second group.

VIVID — Then in the third group are guitarists who don't need to carry the full rhythm of the song, nor the full harmonic structure. The have the freedom to choose very colorful chords that may not even carry the chord's root. These guitarists might be Soul or Jazz players and many of these voicings are sometimes called *drop* voicings because of their unusual sequence of chord tones.

Of course, this is quite an oversimplification of the world of music, but you probably can identify with one or two of these very broad groups. When discussing guitar chords, it really is necessary to consider the setting of the music before making chordal recommendations. That's how this book is organized.

CHORD FAMILIES

So, to take you to the chord you seek, this book is designed with your type of music in mind. Whether you're looking for big, rooted chords, or smaller chords for ensemble work, or for extended chords for sophisticated harmonic settings, this book has you covered.

Chords are presented first by root or key. Next, they are grouped by the family type. For a general descriptive category name, they're termed Big, Compact and Vivid. Inside of each of those family types, you'll find chords in major, minor, dominant, diminished, augmented and suspended or power chord types.

Whatever your style of music, you'll find fast answers and ideas for chords. Maybe chords you never thought possible. You'll probably find one of the broad categories that works well for you, but check out the other chord family types as well. Maybe you'll find a sound in one of those areas that surprises you and ignites a fire of creativity. If you love, use it!

CHORD PRIORITIES

If you're experienced with guitar chords you may not enjoy or agree with some of the voicings presented here. For example, a chord with the 7th degree as its lowest note may be considered a bad voicing - one that is harmonically confusing. Or maybe a chord you'll see here has a tight note group across the lowest three strings which might ordinarily be considered muddy sounding.

Chords presented in this book are meant to be a creative guide for everyone. Some guitarists work in the avant-garde fields of music, or compose soundtracks for motion pictures. The conventional rules of voice leading and arrangement become much more fluid in those musical areas and so chords which may interest them are presented here, as well.

If a chord voicing doesn't strike you as pleasing, just move on to find one that does work for you. Or just maybe it will spark a new idea, arrangement or song.

READING CHORD DIAGRAMS

The chord diagrams in this book are kind of like pictures of what you'll see when you look at your guitar.

Hold your guitar upright in front of you and look at fretboard. The strings run up and down, the frets run horizontally. That is the view used in fretboard diagrams.

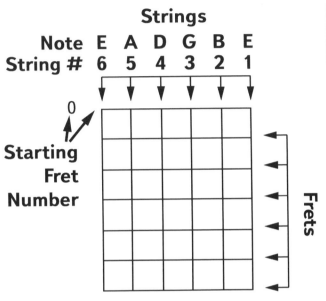

FIG.1 - FRET NOTATION

FIG.2 - FRETBOARD

In the chord diagram at right, the root and type of chord are indicated at the top. In this case, C Major.

In the next row are the names of the notes used. Below that row is the suggested fingering.

The number at the top left of the diagram is the fret at which the drawing begins. In this diagram, the first finger is placed just behind (or to the left) of the 8th fret.

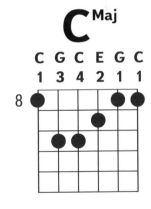

FIG.3 - C MAJOR CHORD DIAGRAM

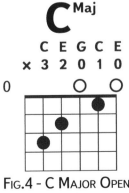

In the chord at left, the black dots indicate fretted notes and the open dots indicate open-strings. An "X" indicates an unplayed string.

FIG.4 - C MAJOR OPEN-
STRING CHORD

A Note About Page Layout

The layout of chord diagrams across the page is meant to speed your chord search. Generally, chords which are predominantly voiced on the bass strings (4, 5 and 6) are see on the left side of the page. Treble voicings (across 1, 2 and 3) are found toward the right side.

If a diagram appears missing from a row of chord diagrams, it is usually because that voicing is not available or too difficult to reach with the fretting fingers.

GUITAR
CHORDS
ENCYCLOPEDIA

SPELLING CHORDS

WHAT IS CHORD "SPELLING"?

All chords are comprised of particular notes or degrees of their associated scale. Selection and combination of a set of those notes creates a chord. Chords then provide the harmonic framework of music.

Some chords are quite complex harmonically, while others very simple. The more complex chords are generally simple chords with the addition of one or a few extra notes added. Understanding the construction of chords enables the musician to make good choices when arranging their part.

IT ALL STARTS WITH A SCALE

It's impossible to really understand chords without first understanding scales. All music comes from scales: Melodies come from scales and so do triads and chords. Scales produce triads, triads produce chords.

Scales → Triads → Chords

TRIADS

A triad is a collection of three notes of a scale and they are the building blocks of chords. Scales produce triads, triads produce chords. Have a look.

Each note of a scale can be given a number name, or degree. Using C Major as an example: C, D, E, F, G, A, B and C have scale degrees 1, 2, 3, 4, 5, 6, 7 and 1, again. While the last note, C, is the 8th note, it's still called the 1st degree, because although it's one octave higher, its still the same note name, as the 1st degree, or root of the scale.

Interval	1	2	3	4	5	6	7	1
Note	C	D	E	F	G	A	B	C

Fig.5 - C Major Scale Degrees

A triad contains the 1st, 3rd and 5th degrees of the scale. So a C Major triad is spelled C, E, G.

Interval	**1**	2	**3**	4	**5**	6	7	1
Note	**C**	D	**E**	F	**G**	A	B	C

FIG.6 - C MAJOR TRIAD

CHORDS

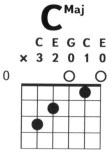

FIG.7 - C MAJOR CHORD

Chords are built from triads. Take the notes from a triad—played together, they make a chord. Optionally, rearrange them or combine them with the same notes in another octave and you'll have another way to play the chord.

EXTENDING TRIADS

The concept of triads is one of taking a root note, adding the scale tone two notes above and adding another note again, two notes higher. Scale tones: 1, 3 and 5. It's like counting by odd numbers, skipping the even numbers.

Some chords include the first 3 notes of the triad, 1, 3 and 5, then add the 7th. These are 7th chords. The triad is then extended beyond its basic form.

Continuing in this manner, it's possible to add more triadic scale degrees. The next extension of chords is the 9th chord and it includes the 1st, 3rd, 5th, 7th and 9th scale degrees.

But wait a minute! There are only 7 notes in a scale, with the root being repeated an octave above as the 8th note. Then how can there be a note called the 9th?

Great point! In a set of 7 notes, how *can* there be a 9th note? Have a look.

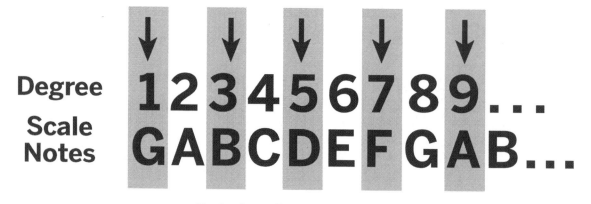

FIG.8 - SCALE DEGREES OF G MIXOLYDIAN

Gently combining scales and math, one more than eight is nine, right? Since scales repeat themselves at the 8th note (the octave of the root), the note after the 8th note of a scale would be the 9th note. Since the scale's 8th note is the octave of the root—or 1st degree—the next degree could be called either the 9th or the 2nd degree.

When spelling chords, the 2nd degree is called the 9th because chords work well when built by stacking 3rds, or rather extending triads. From the basic triad (1, 3 and 5), the 7th is added to make a 7th chord, just like counting by odd numbers. Continuing to count by odd numbers then, the 9th is added to make a 9th chord.

GUIDELINES FOR BUILDING CHORDS

Remember, what follows are just guidelines. In music, there are few rules. Like, unbreakable, never-ever can be broken rules. There are some good guidelines though that can help you make great music.

Generally in guitar playing, guitarists are somewhat limited because of the physical reach of hands and just the general design and tuning of the instrument. However, there are a LOT of combinations for any given chord that are still in range for you. Feel free to experiment.

WHAT TO LEAVE OUT, BY SCALE DEGREES

In a given situation, there are some notes that are too important to ever omit and there are other notes that may be less important. Remember, this is situational depending on the music style and whether you're playing solo or with other musicians. Again, there are no iron-clad rules, no laws to abide, but there are some good guidelines to consider.

Imagine a song calls for a pretty complicated chord, say a major 9th chord. You'll need to identify what notes are contained in the chord. Then, you'll look for a way to play arrange them on the fretboard so they're playable. If an easy and suitable solution doesn't present itself, you'll probably want to simplify the chord by leaving out a note or two. After all, you've only got 4 fingers!

The Root

When playing solo, always include the root of every chord. It's grounding and generally considered very necessary. In musical groups, there may be a bass player or other instrument playing the root note. That's generally the job of the bass instrument. If you're in a group, you may consider omitting the root.

After you've placed the root on the bottom, you're free to order the notes of the chord anywhere you like.

The 3rd

Unless you're making Rock music, include the 3rd in every chord. If you're making Rock, you may want just the root and 5th. Play it loud and proud!

The 5th

This note is pretty easily omitted from most chords. True, Rock music uses many chords built from only the root and 5th. They're called "Power Chords" because the 3rd is omitted. As such, they sound great and powerful when played really loudly. But, for more conventional chords, consider the 5th a good candidate for omission.

7ths and 9ths

These are the most colorful notes and really define the flavor fully. However, they are the most ornamental and while pretty, aren't functionally necessary.Consider them like dessert after a nice meal: very enjoyable, but probably not 100% necessary.

So, if at all possible, include 7th or 9th extensions if you can, but don't feel too bad if you need to leave them out.

OVERVIEW OF CHORD TYPES

Extending triads is a manner of building chords using the interval of thirds. Thirds, either major or minor, are stacked on top of each other creating unique combinations.

One example of a minor third is C to E flat. A major third would be C to E natural. Stacking various combinations of these third intervals produces the most familiar chord types. Notice how each chord type has a unique combination of intervals.

	Major	Minor	Dominant	Augmented	Half-Diminished	Full Diminished
5th-7th	Major	minor	minor	--	Major	minor
3rd-5th	minor	Major	minor	Major	minor	minor
Root-3rd	Major	minor	Major	Major	minor	minor

Fig.9 - Chord Types and Triadic Construction

14 Guitar Chords Encyclopedia: A Seeing Music Method Book

DOUBLE-SHARPS AND DOUBLE-FLATS

Without going too deep into music theory, contrapuntal voice leading and arrangement, suffice it to say that note names have a great meaning apart from telling the musician what pitch they should play. They also inform arrangers and, in classical settings the conductors, what the *function* of each pitch is. In the key of C, the third is always an E and the fifth is always a G. Now, if the key is C Minor, the third will be E flat and if the key is C Major the third will be E natural, but the third will always be some variety named "E-something".

That convention of giving the chord tones names that are indicative of their function in the chord is really quite helpful. Understanding music without that bit of subtext would be difficult given that the same note can have several names.

Again without going too deeply into music theory, just know that A sharp, B flat and C double-flat are three different names for the same note. They are *enharmonically* equivalent. You may be saying, "*Double*-flat?" Yes, just as a sharp raises the natural note one half-step and a flat lowers it, the double-sharp raises the natural note two half-steps and the double-flat lowers it two half-steps. Just to keep the basic note name meaningful, sometimes it's necessary to use such nomenclature.

So, if you see a G double-flat, you'll know that the note is two half-steps below G natural. G double-flat is equivalent to F natural (or E sharp). Don't let these multiple names of notes stop you from learning the chords. It's just a bit of fun chord spelling and music theory in action.

Utilize Scales and Modes Common to Genres
Apply Major and Minor Pentatonics Creatively
Learn the Shortcuts to Memorizing Scales
Includes Scale/Chord/Genre Styleguide
Apply Scales with Loads of Exercises

SEEING MUSIC
METHOD BOOKS

Master the Universe of Scales in Every Style and Genre

GUITAR
SCALES
INFINITY

ANDY SCHNEIDER

INTERMEDIATE TO ADVANCED

A universe of scales is waiting.
SeeingMusicBooks.com

SEEING MUSIC
METHOD BOOKS

16 GUITAR CHORDS ENCYCLOPEDIA: A SEEING MUSIC METHOD BOOK

BIG
MAJOR

A^Maj
A E A C# E
× 0 1 2 3 0
0
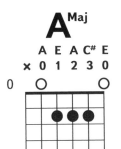

A^Maj
A E A C#
× 0 1 1 1 ×
0
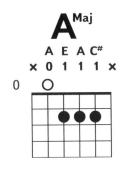

A^Maj
A E A C# E A
1 3 4 2 1 1
5
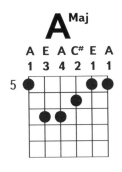

A^Maj
A E A C#
× 0 1 1 1 ×
0
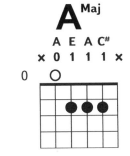

A^△7
A E G# C# E
× 0 2 1 3 0
0
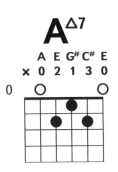

A^△7
A E G# C#
× 0 2 1 3 ×
0
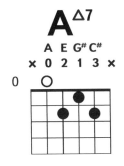

A^△7#11
A D# G# C# E
× 0 1 2 3 0
0
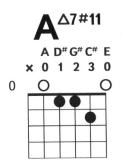

A^△9
A C# G# B
× 2 1 4 3 ×
11
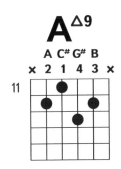

A^6/9
A   C# G♭ B
1 × × 2 4 4
5
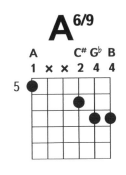

A^6/9
A C# F# B
× 2 1 1 3 ×
11
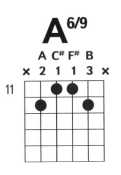

A^6/9
A E B C# F#
× 0 1 3 1 1
0
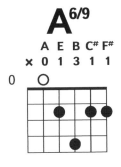

A^add9
A   C# E B
1 × × 2 1 4
5
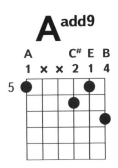

BIG
MINOR

Amin
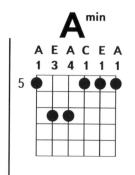
A E A C E A
1 3 4 1 1 1
5

Amin
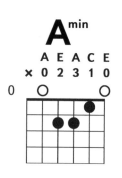
A E A C E
× 0 2 3 1 0
0

Amin7
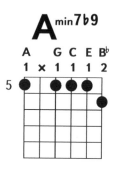
A E G C E
× 0 2 0 1 0
0

Amin7
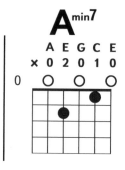
A E G C E A
1 3 1 1 1 1
5

Amin7♭5
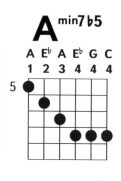
A E♭ A E♭ G C
1 2 3 4 4 4
5

Amin7♭9
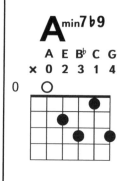
A E B♭ C G
× 0 2 3 1 4
0

Amin7♭9
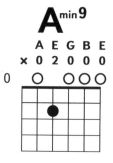
A G C E B♭
1 × 1 1 1 2
5

Amin9
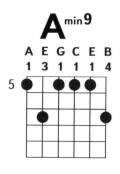
A E G B E
× 0 2 0 0 0
0

Amin9
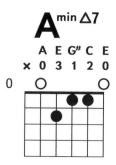
A E G C E B
1 3 1 1 1 4
5

Amin△7
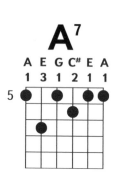
A E G# C E
× 0 3 1 2 0
0

BIG
DOMINANT

A7
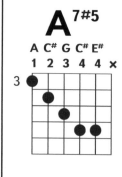
A E G C# E
× 0 2 0 3 0
0

A7
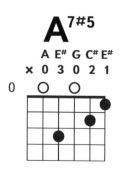
A E G C# E A
1 3 1 2 1 1
5

A7♭5
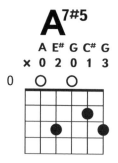
A E♭ G C# G
× 0 1 0 3 4
0

A7♭5
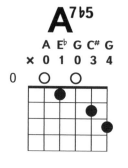
A E♭ G C#
× × 1 2 2 4
7

A7#5
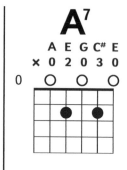
A C# G C# E#
1 2 3 4 4 ×
3

A7#5
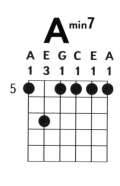
A E# G C# E#
× 0 3 0 2 1
0

A7#5
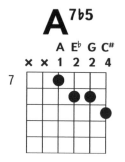
A E# G C# G
× 0 2 0 1 3
0

18 GUITAR CHORDS ENCYCLOPEDIA: A SEEING MUSIC METHOD BOOK

BIG
DOMINANT (CONT.)

A^{7♭9}

A   G C# E B♭
1 × 1 2 1 3

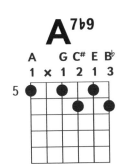

A⁹

A E G C# E B
1 3 1 2 1 4

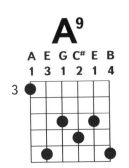

A⁹

A C# G B
× 2 1 3 4 ×

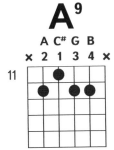

A^{7#9}

A   G C# G B#
1 × 1 2 4 4

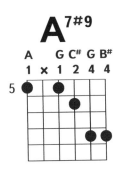

A^{7#9}

A   G C# E B#
1 × 1 2 1 4

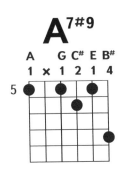

A^{7#9}

A C# G B#
× 2 1 3 4 ×

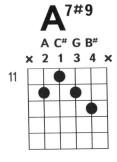

A^{7#9}

A C# G B#
× × 2 1 4 4

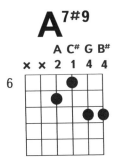

BIG
AUGMENTED

A^{Aug}

A E# A C#
× 0 2 1 1 ×

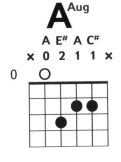

A^{Aug}

A C# E# A
4 3 2 1 × ×

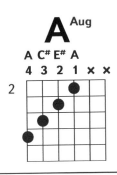

A^{Aug}

A C# E# A
× 3 2 1 1 ×

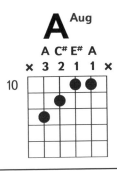

A^{Aug}

A   A C# E# A
1 × 4 2 3 1

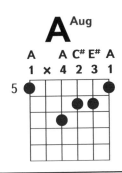

A^{Aug}

E# A C# E#
× 3 2 1 1 ×

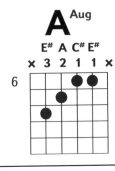

A^{Aug}

C# E# A C#
× 3 2 1 1 ×

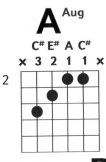

BIG
DIMINISHED

A^ø

A E♭ G C
× 0 2 0 3 ×

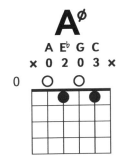

A^ø

A E♭ A E♭ G C
1 2 3 4 4 4

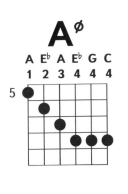

A^{dim}

A E♭ A C G♭
× 0 1 2 1 3

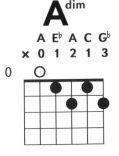

A^{dim}

A G♭ C E♭
× 0 1 2 1 ×

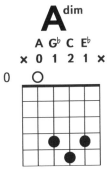

A^{dim}

A   G♭ C E♭ A
2 × 1 3 1 4

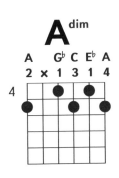

CHORDS WITH ROOT A 19

BIG
STACKED 5THS

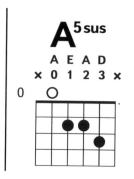

A5sus
A E A D
× 0 1 2 3 ×
0

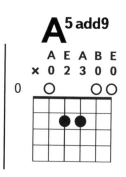

A5add9
A E A B E
× 0 2 3 0 0
0

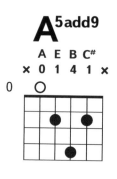

A5add9
A E B C#
× 0 1 4 1 ×
0

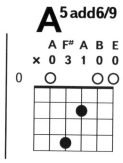

A5add6/9
A F# A B E
× 0 3 1 0 0
0

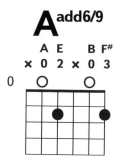

Aadd6/9
A E B F#
× 0 2 × 0 3
0

COMPACT
MAJOR

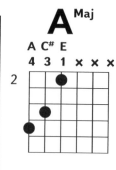

AMaj
A C# E
4 3 1 × × ×
2

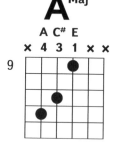

AMaj
A C# E
× 4 3 1 × ×
9

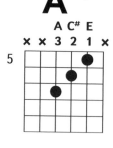

AMaj
A C# E
× × 3 2 1 ×
5

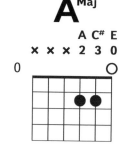

AMaj
A C# E
× × × 2 3 0
0

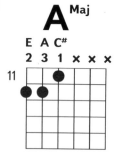

AMaj
E A C#
2 3 1 × × ×
11

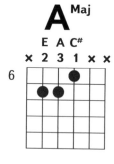

AMaj
E A C#
× 2 3 1 × ×
6

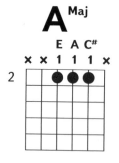

AMaj
E A C#
× × 1 1 1 ×
2

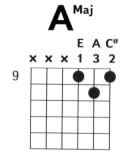

AMaj
E A C#
× × × 1 3 2
9

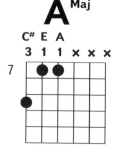

AMaj
C# E A
3 1 1 × × ×
7

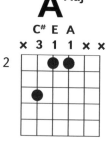

AMaj
C# E A
× 3 1 1 × ×
2

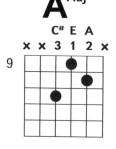

AMaj
C# E A
× × 3 1 2 ×
9

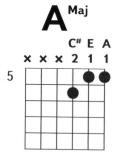

AMaj
C# E A
× × × 2 1 1
5

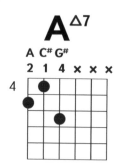

A△7
A C# G#
2 1 4 × × ×
4

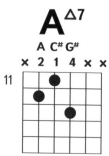

A△7
A C# G#
× 2 1 4 × ×
11

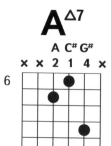

A△7
A C# G#
× × 2 1 4 ×
6

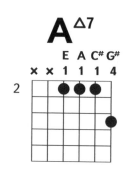

A△7
E A C# G#
× × 1 1 1 4
2

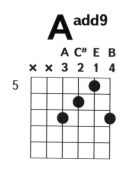

Aadd9
A C# E B
× × 3 2 1 4
5

20 GUITAR CHORDS ENCYCLOPEDIA: A SEEING MUSIC METHOD BOOK

A COMPACT *MINOR*

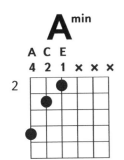 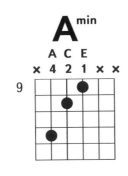 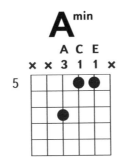 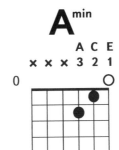

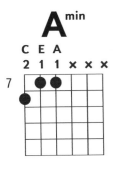 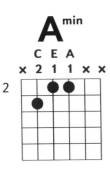 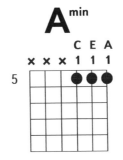 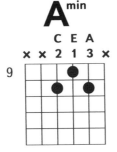

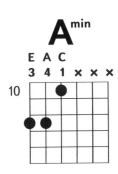 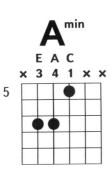 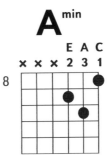 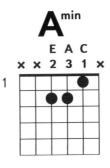

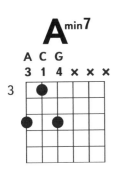 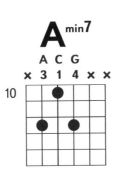 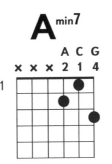 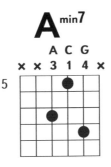

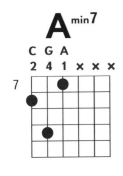 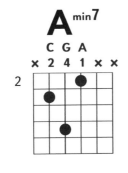 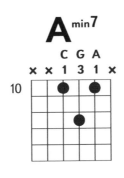 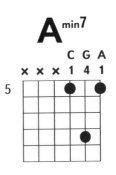 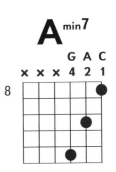

COMPACT
MINOR (CONT.)

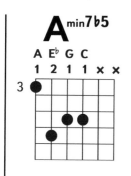

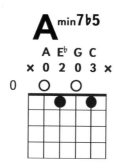

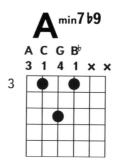

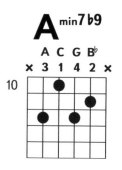

COMPACT
DOMINANT

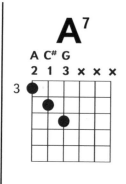

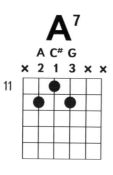

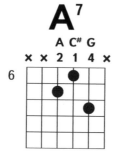

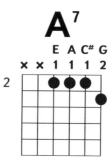

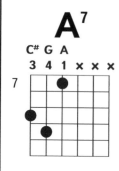

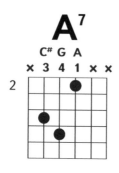

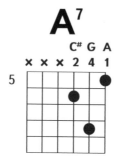

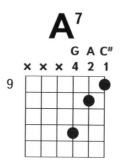

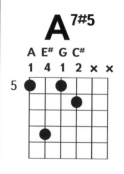

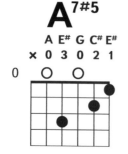

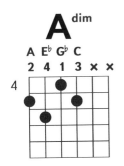

A^{dim}

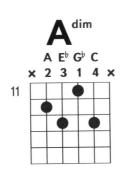

A^{dim}

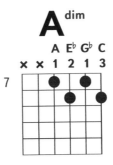

A^{dim}

COMPACT
DIMINISHED

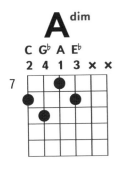

A^{dim}

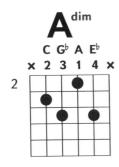

A^{dim}

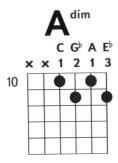

A^{dim}

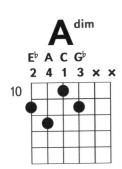

A^{dim}

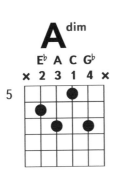

A^{dim}

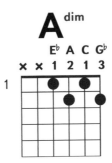

A^{dim}

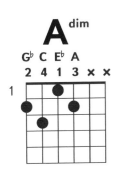

A^{dim}

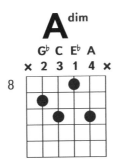

A^{dim}

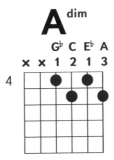

A^{dim}

COMPACT
DIMINISHED (CONT.)

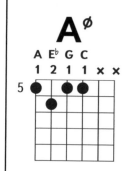

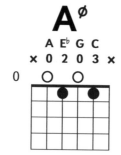

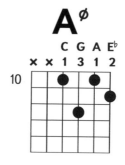

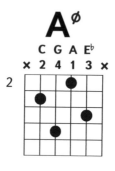

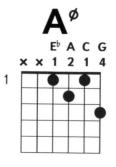

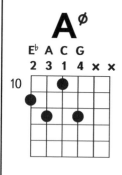

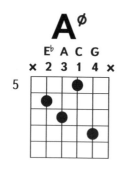

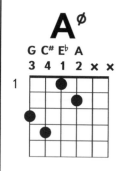

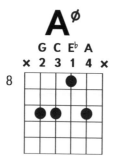

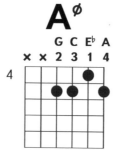

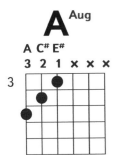

A^{Aug}

A C# E#
3 2 1 × × ×
3

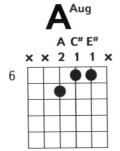

A^{Aug}

A C# E#
× 3 2 1 × ×
10

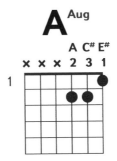

A^{Aug}

A C# E#
× × 2 1 1 ×
6

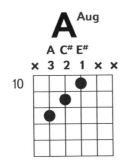

A^{Aug}

A C# E#
× × × 2 3 1
1

A
COMPACT
AUGMENTED

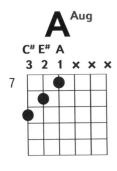

A^{Aug}

C# E# A
3 2 1 × × ×
7

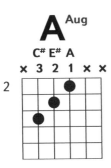

A^{Aug}

C# E# A
× 3 2 1 × ×
2

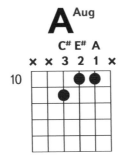

A^{Aug}

C# E# A
× × 3 2 1 ×
10

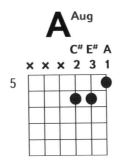

A^{Aug}

C# E# A
× × × 2 3 1
5

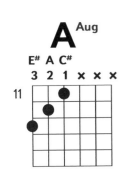

A^{Aug}

E# A C#
3 2 1 × × ×
11

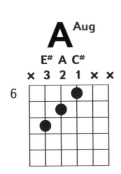

A^{Aug}

E# A C#
× 3 2 1 × ×
6

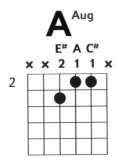

A^{Aug}

E# A C#
× × 2 1 1 ×
2

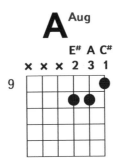

A^{Aug}

E# A C#
× × × 2 3 1
9

COMPACT
STACKED 5THS

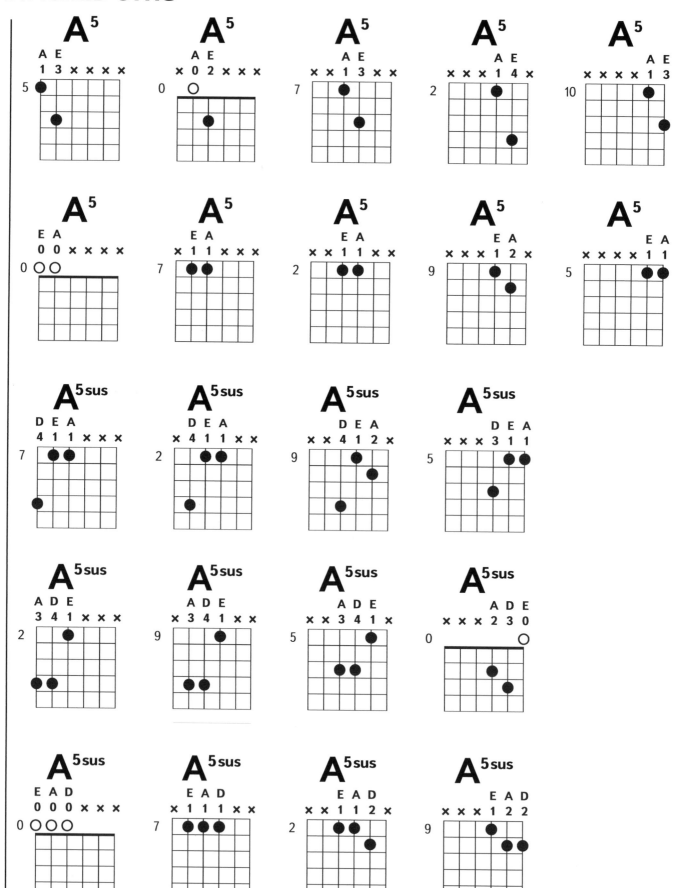

A ^{5add9}

B A E
1 × 1 4 × ×
7
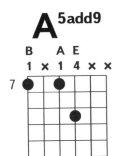

A ^{5add9}

× B × A E
1 × 1 4 ×
2
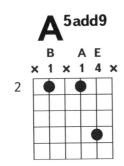

A ^{5add9}

× × B × A E
1 × 2 4
9
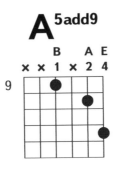

A ^{5add9}

B E A
1 1 1 × × ×
7
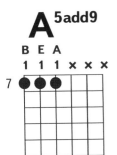

A ^{5add9}

× B E A
1 1 1 × ×
2
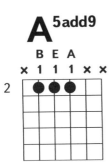

A ^{5add9}

× × B E A
1 1 2 ×
9
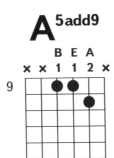

A ^{5add9}

× × × B E A
1 2 3
4
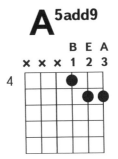

A ^{5add9}

A E B
1 3 4 × × ×
5
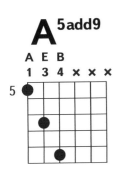

A ^{5add9}

A E B
× 0 1 3 × ×
0 ○
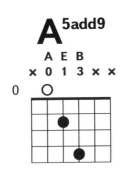

A $^{5add6/9}$

B G♭ A E
1 3 1 4 × ×
7
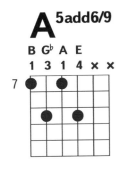

A $^{5add6/9}$

× B F# A E
1 3 1 4 ×
2
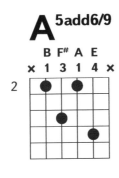

A $^{5add6/9}$

× × B F# A E
1 3 2 4
9
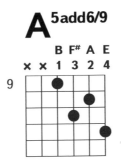

A $^{5add6/9}$

F# B E A
1 1 1 1 × ×
2
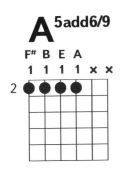

A $^{5add6/9}$

× F# B E A
1 1 1 2 ×
9
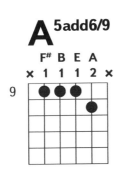

A $^{5add6/9}$

× × F# B E A
1 1 2 3
4
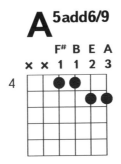

VIVID
MAJOR

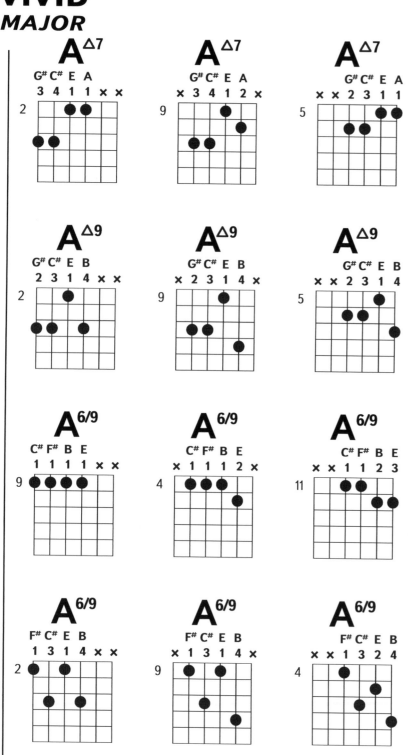

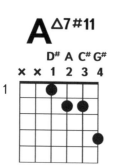

VIVID
MAJOR (CONT.)

VIVID
MINOR

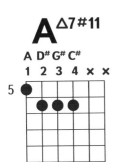
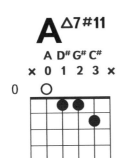
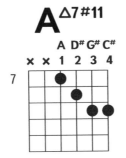
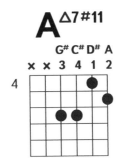

$A^{\triangle 7\#11}$ — A D# G# C#, 1 2 3 4 × ×, 5
$A^{\triangle 7\#11}$ — A D# G# C#, × 0 1 2 3 ×, 0
$A^{\triangle 7\#11}$ — A D# G# C#, × × 1 2 3 4, 7
$A^{\triangle 7\#11}$ — G# C# D# A, × × 3 4 1 2, 4

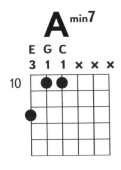
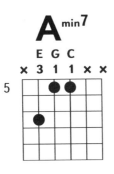
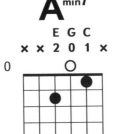
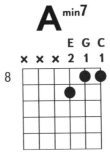

A^{min7} — E G C, 3 1 1 × × ×, 10
A^{min7} — E G C, × 3 1 1 × ×, 5
A^{min7} — E G C, × × 2 0 1 ×, 0
A^{min7} — E G C, × × × 2 1 1, 8

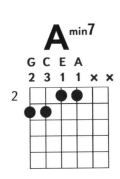
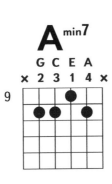
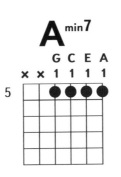
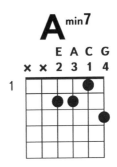

A^{min7} — G C E A, 2 3 1 1 × ×, 2
A^{min7} — G C E A, × 2 3 1 4 ×, 9
A^{min7} — G C E A, × × 1 1 1 1, 5
A^{min7} — E A C G, × × 2 3 1 4, 1

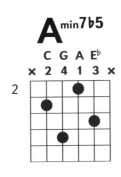
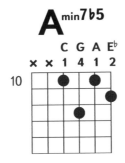

A^{min7b5} — C G A E♭, × 2 4 1 3 ×, 2
A^{min7b5} — C G A E♭, × × 1 4 1 2, 10

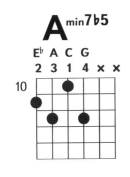
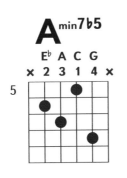
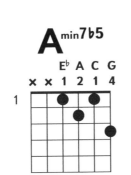
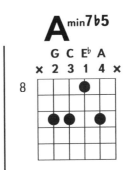
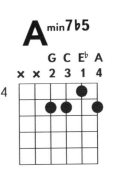

A^{min7b5} — E♭ A C G, 2 3 1 4 × ×, 10
A^{min7b5} — E♭ A C G, × 2 3 1 4 ×, 5
A^{min7b5} — E♭ A C G, × × 1 2 1 4, 1
A^{min7b5} — G C E♭ A, × 2 3 1 4 ×, 8
A^{min7b5} — G C E♭ A, × × 2 3 1 4, 4

CHORDS WITH ROOT A 29

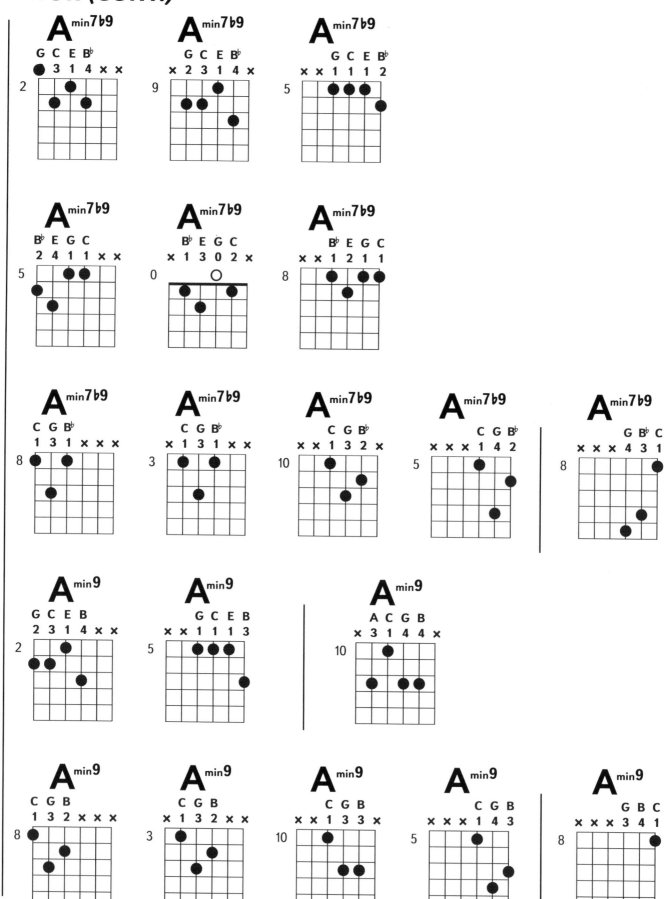

VIVID
MINOR (CONT.)

Amin9

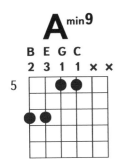

B E G C
2 3 1 1 × ×
5

Amin9

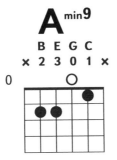

B E G C
× 2 3 0 1 ×
0

Amin9

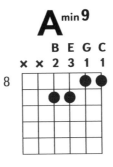

B E G C
× × 2 3 1 1
8

Amin△7

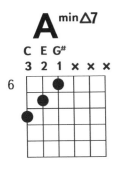

C E G#
3 2 1 × × ×
6

Amin△7

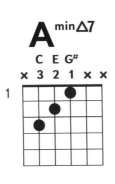

C E G#
× 3 2 1 × ×
1

Amin△7

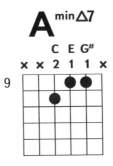

C E G#
× × 2 1 1 ×
9

Amin△7

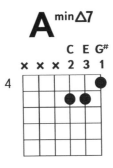

C E G#
× × × 2 3 1
4

Amin△7

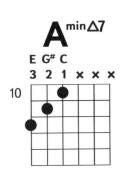

E G# C
3 2 1 × × ×
10

Amin△7

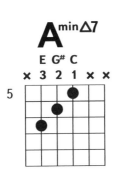

E G# C
× 3 2 1 × ×
5

Amin△7

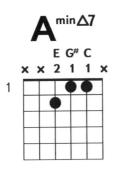

E G# C
× × 2 1 1 ×
1

Amin△7

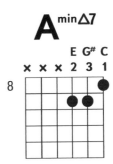

E G# C
× × × 2 3 1
8

Amin△7

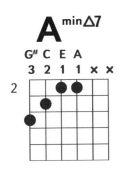

G# C E A
3 2 1 1 × ×
2

Amin△7

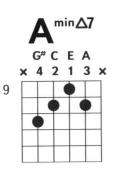

G# C E A
× 4 2 1 3 ×
9

Amin△7

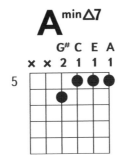

G# C E A
× × 2 1 1 1
5

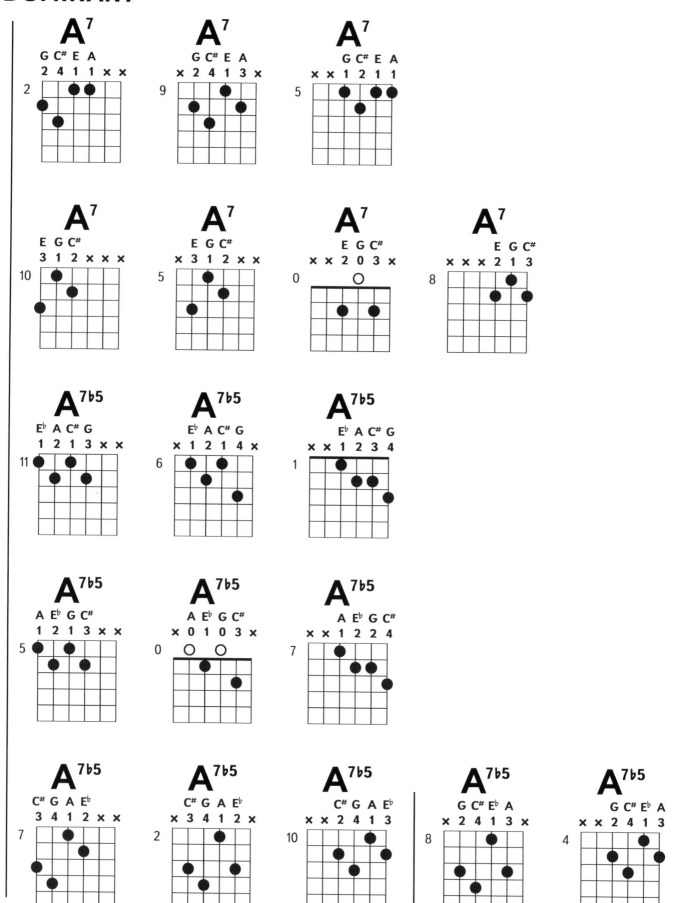

A^{7#5}

E# A C# G
4 2 1 3 × ×
11
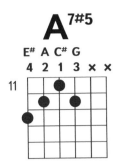

A^{7#5}

F A C# G
× 3 2 1 4 ×
4
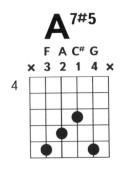

A^{7#5}

E# A C# G
× × 2 1 1 3
2
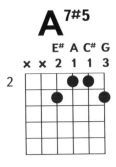

A^{7#5}

G C# E# A
2 4 3 1 × ×
2
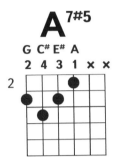

A^{7#5}

G C# E# A
× 1 2 1 1 ×
10
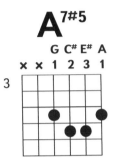

A^{7#5}

G C# E# A
× × 1 2 3 1
3
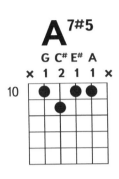

A^{7b9}

G C# E Bb
2 4 1 3 × ×
2
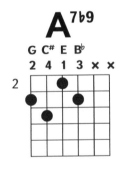

A^{7b9}

G C# E Bb
× × 1 2 1 3
5
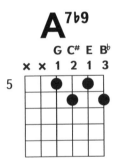

A^{7b9}

A C# G Bb
× 2 1 3 1 ×
11
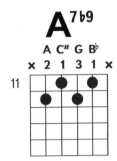

A^{7b9}

A C# G Bb
× × 2 1 3 1
6
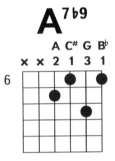

A^{7b9}

Bb E G Db
2 4 1 3 × ×
5
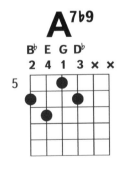

A^{7b9}

Bb E G Db
× 2 3 1 4 ×
10
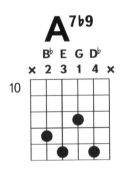

A^{7b9}

Bb E G C#
× × 2 3 1 4
8
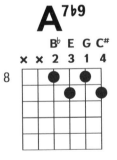

A^{7b9}

C# G Bb
2 3 1 × × ×
8
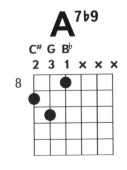

A^{7b9}

C# G Bb
× 2 4 1 × ×
3
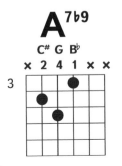

A^{7b9}

C# G Bb
× × × 2 4 1
6

A^{7b9}

G Bb C#
× × × 4 3 1
9

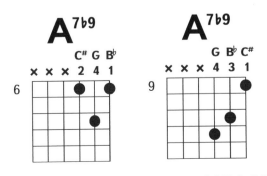

VIVID
DOMINANT

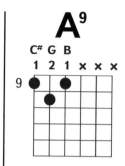

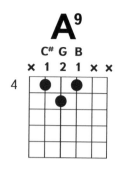

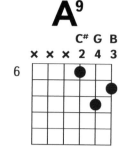

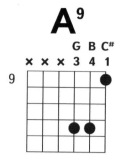

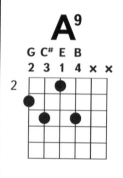

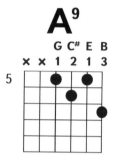

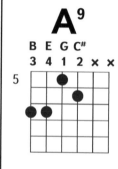

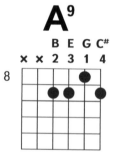

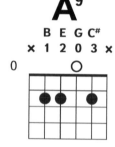

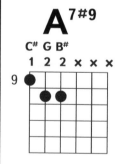

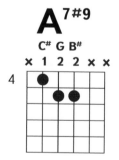

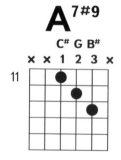

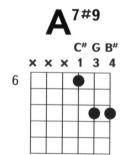

34 GUITAR CHORDS ENCYCLOPEDIA: A SEEING MUSIC METHOD BOOK

VIVID
DIMINISHED

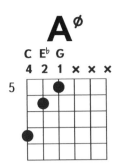
$A^{\emptyset}$
C E♭ G
4 2 1 × × ×
5

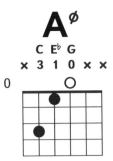
$A^{\emptyset}$
C E♭ G
× 3 1 0 × ×
0

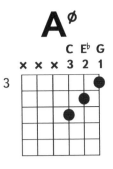
$A^{\emptyset}$
C E♭ G
× × 3 1 1 ×
8

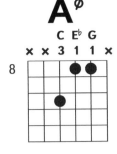
$A^{\emptyset}$
C E♭ G
× × × 3 2 1
3

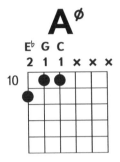
$A^{\emptyset}$
E♭ G C
2 1 1 × × ×
10

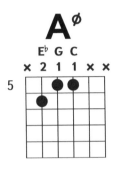
$A^{\emptyset}$
E♭ G C
× 2 1 1 × ×
5

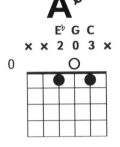
$A^{\emptyset}$
E♭ G C
× × 2 0 3 ×
0

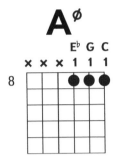
$A^{\emptyset}$
E♭ G C
× × × 1 1 1
8

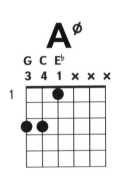
$A^{\emptyset}$
G C E♭
3 4 1 × × ×
1

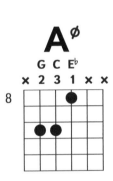
$A^{\emptyset}$
G C E♭
× 2 3 1 × ×
8

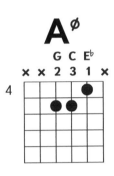
$A^{\emptyset}$
G C E♭
× × 2 3 1 ×
4

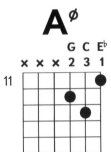
$A^{\emptyset}$
G C E♭
× × × 2 3 1
11

36 GUITAR CHORDS ENCYCLOPEDIA: A SEEING MUSIC METHOD BOOK

BIG *MAJOR*

A#/Bb Maj
Bb F Bb D F Bb
A# E# A# C## E# A#
1 3 4 2 1 1
6

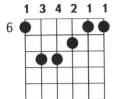

A#/Bb Maj
Bb F Bb D
A# E# A# C##
× 1 3 3 3 ×
1

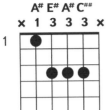

A#/Bb △7
Bb F A D
A# E# G## C##
× 1 3 2 4 ×
1

A#/Bb △7#11
Bb E A D F
A# D## G## C## E#
× 1 2 3 4 1
1

A#/Bb 6/9
Bb   D G C
A#   C## F## B#
1 × × 2 4 4
6

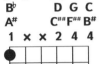

A#/Bb 6/9
Bb D G C
A# C## F## B#
× 1 0 0 2 ×
0

A#/Bb add9
Bb   D F C
A#   C## E# B#
1 × × 2 1 4
6

BIG *MINOR*

A#/Bb min
Bb F Bb Db F Bb
A# E# A# C# E# A#
1 3 4 1 1 1
6

A#/Bb min
Bb F Bb Db F
A# E# A# C# E#
× 1 3 4 2 1
1

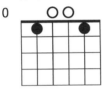

A#/Bb min7
Bb F Ab Db F Bb
A# E# G# C# E# A#
1 3 1 1 1 1
6

A#/Bb min7b5
Bb Fb Bb Fb Ab Db
A# E A# E G# C#
1 2 3 4 4 4
6

A#/Bb min7b9
Bb   Ab Db F Cb
A#   G# C# E# B
1 × 1 1 1 2
6

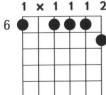

A#/Bb min9
Bb F Ab Db F C
A# E# G# C# E# B#
1 3 1 1 1 4
6

A#/Bb min △7
Bb F A Db F
A# E# G## C# E#
× 1 4 2 3 1
1

A#/Bb⁷

B♭ F A♭ D F B♭
A# E# G# C## E# A#
1 3 1 2 1 1
6

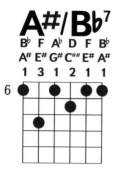

A#/Bb⁷

B♭ F A♭ D F
A# E# G# C## E#
× 1 3 1 4 1
1

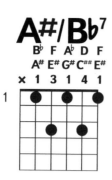

A#/Bb⁷♭⁵

B♭ F♭ A♭ D
A# E G# C##
× × 1 2 2 4
8

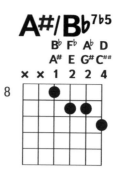

A#/Bb⁷#⁵

B♭ D A♭ D F#
A# C## G# C## E##
1 2 3 4 4 ×
5

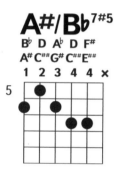

A#/Bb⁷#⁵

B♭ F# A♭ D F#
A# E## G# C## E##
× 1 4 1 3 2
1

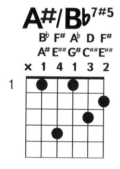

A#/Bb⁷♭⁹

B♭ A♭ D F C♭
A# G# C## E# B
1 × 1 2 1 3
6

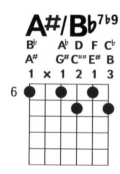

A#/Bb⁹

B♭ F A♭ D F C
A# E# G# C## E# B#
1 3 1 2 1 4
6

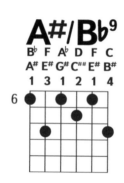

A#/Bb⁹

B♭ D A♭ C
A# C## G# B#
× 1 0 2 3 ×
0

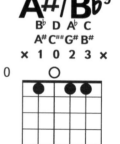

A#/Bb⁷#⁹

B♭ A♭ D A♭ C#
A# G# C## G# B##
1 × 1 2 4 4
6

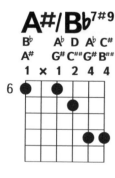

A#/Bb⁷#⁹

B♭ A♭ D F C#
A# G# C## E# B##
1 × 1 2 1 4
6

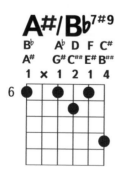

A#/Bb⁷#⁹

B♭ D A♭ C#
A# C## G# B##
× 1 0 2 3 ×
0

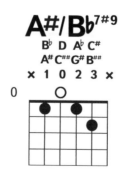

A#/Bb⁷#⁹

B♭ D A♭ C#
A# C## G# B##
× × 2 1 4 4
7

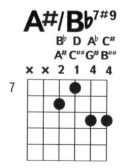

BIG
AUGMENTED

A#/Bb^{Aug}
B♭ D F# B♭
A# C## E## A#
4 3 2 1 × ×
3
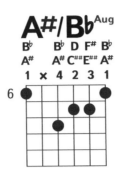

A#/Bb^{Aug}
B♭ D F# B♭
A# C## E## A#
× 3 2 1 1 ×
11

A#/Bb^{Aug}
B♭ B♭ D F# B♭
A# A# C## E## A#
1 × 4 2 3 1
6
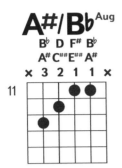

A#/Bb^{Aug}
F# B♭ D F#
E## A# C## E##
× 3 2 1 1 ×
7
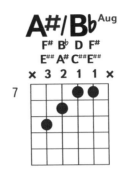

A#/Bb^{Aug}
D F# B♭ D
C## E## A# C##
× 3 2 1 1 ×
3
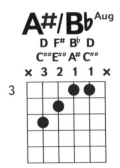

BIG
DIMINISHED

A#/Bb^ø
B♭ F♭ B♭ F♭ A♭ D♭
A# E A# E G# C#
1 2 3 4 4 4
6
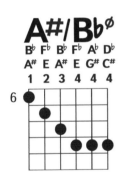

A#/Bb^{dim}
B♭ A♭♭ D♭ F♭ B♭
A# G C# E A#
2 × 1 3 1 4
5
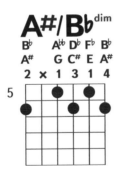

BIG
STACKED 5THS

A#/Bb^{5 sus}
B♭ F B♭ E♭
A# E# A# D#
× 1 3 4 1 ×
1
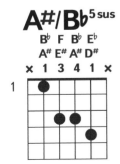

A#/Bb^{5 add9}
B♭ F B♭ C F
A# E# A# B# F
× 1 3 4 1 1
1
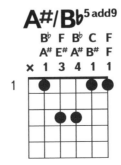

A#/Bb^{add6/9}
B♭ F C G
A# E# B# G
× 1 3 × 1 4
1
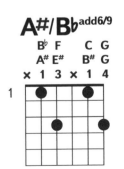

A#/Bb^{Maj}
Bb D F
A# C## E#
4 3 1 × × ×
3
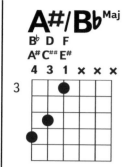

A#/Bb^{Maj}
Bb D F
A# C## E#
× 4 3 1 × ×
10
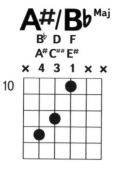

A#/Bb^{Maj}
Bb D F
A# C## E#
× × 3 2 1 ×
6
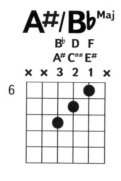

A#/Bb^{Maj}
Bb D F
A# C## E#
× × × 2 3 1
1
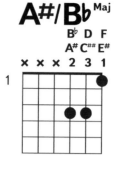

A#/Bb^{Maj}
F Bb D
E# A# C##
1 2 0 × × ×
0
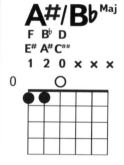

A#/Bb^{Maj}
F Bb D
E# A# C##
× 2 3 1 × ×
7
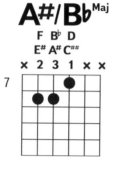

A#/Bb^{Maj}
F Bb D
E# A# C##
× × 1 1 1 ×
3
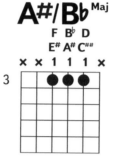

A#/Bb^{Maj}
F Bb D
E# A# C##
× × × 1 3 2
10
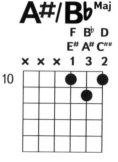

A#/Bb^{Maj}
D F Bb
C## E# A#
3 1 1 × × ×
8
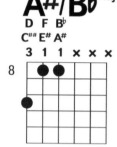

A#/Bb^{Maj}
D F Bb
C## E# A#
× 3 1 1 × ×
3
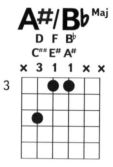

A#/Bb^{Maj}
D F Bb
C## E# A#
× × 3 1 2 ×
10
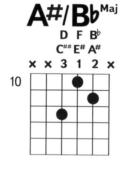

A#/Bb^{Maj}
D F Bb
C## E# A#
× × × 2 1 1
6
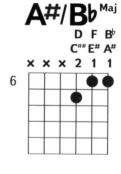

A#/Bb^{△7}
Bb D A
A# C## G##
2 1 4 × × ×
5
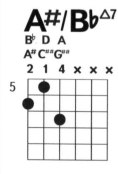

A#/Bb^{△7}
Bb D A
A# C## G##
× 1 0 3 × ×
0
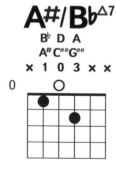

A#/Bb^{△7}
Bb D A
A# C## G##
× × 2 1 4 ×
7
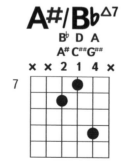

A#/Bb^{△7}
F Bb D A
E# A# C## G##
× × 1 1 1 4
3
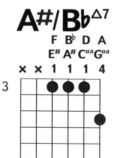

A#/Bb^{add9}
Bb D F C
A# C## E# B#
× × 3 2 1 4
6
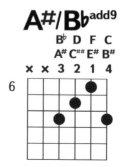

COMPACT
MINOR

A#/Bbmin
Bb Db F
A# C# E#
4 2 1 × × ×
3
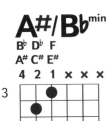

A#/Bbmin
Bb Db F
A# C# E#
× 4 2 1 × ×
10
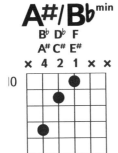

A#/Bbmin
Bb Db F
A# C# E#
× × 3 1 1
6

A#/Bbmin
Bb Db F
A# C# E#
× × × 3 2 1
1
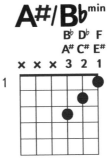

A#/Bbmin
Db F Bb
C# E# A#
2 1 1 × × ×
8
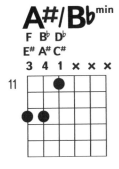

A#/Bbmin
Db F Bb
C# E# A#
× 2 1 1 × ×
3
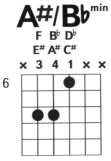

A#/Bbmin
Db F Bb
C# E# A#
× × 2 1 3 ×
10
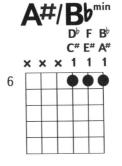

A#/Bbmin
Db F Bb
C# E# A#
× × 1 1 1
6
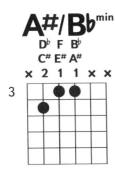

A#/Bbmin
F Bb Db
E# A# C#
3 4 1 × × ×
11
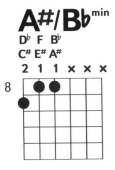

A#/Bbmin
F Bb Db
E# A# C#
× 3 4 1 × ×
6
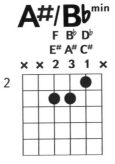

A#/Bbmin
F Bb Db
E# A# C#
× × 2 3 1 ×
2
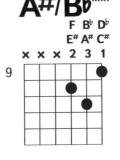

A#/Bbmin
F Bb Db
E# A# C#
× × × 2 3 1
9
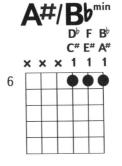

A#/Bbmin7
Bb Db Ab
A# C# G#
3 1 4 × × ×
4
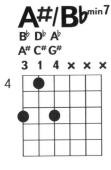

A#/Bbmin7
Bb Db Ab
A# C# G#
× 3 1 4 × ×
11
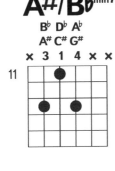

A#/Bbmin7
Bb Db Ab
A# C# G#
× × 3 1 4
6
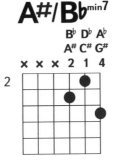

A#/Bbmin7
Bb Db Ab
A# C# G#
× × × 2 1 4
2
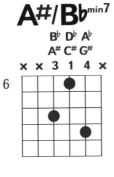

A#/Bbmin7
Db Ab Bb
C# G# A#
2 4 1 × × ×
8
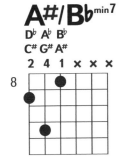

A#/Bbmin7
Db Ab Bb
C# G# A#
× 2 4 1 × ×
3
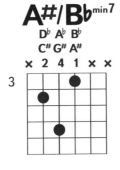

A#/Bbmin7
Db Ab Bb
C# G# A#
× × 1 3 1 ×
11
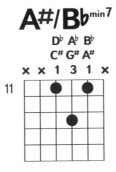

A#/Bbmin7
Db Ab Bb
C# G# A#
× × × 1 4 1
6
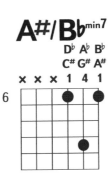

A#/Bbmin7
Ab Bb Db
G# A# C#
× × × 4 2 1
9
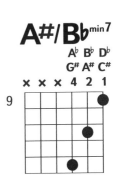

CHORDS WITH ROOT A SHARP - B FLAT 41

COMPACT
MINOR (CONT.)

A#/Bbmin7b5
Bb Fb Ab Db
A# E G# C#
1 2 1 1 × ×
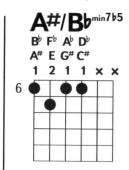
6

A#/Bbmin7b5
Bb E Ab Db
A# D## G# B##
× 1 2 1 3 ×
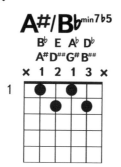
1

A#/Bbmin7b9
Bb Db Ab Cb
A# C# G# B
3 1 4 1 × ×
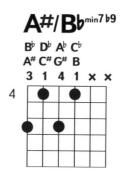
4

A#/Bbmin7b9
Bb Db Ab Cb
A# C# G# B
× 3 1 4 2 ×
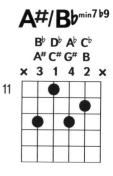
11

COMPACT
DOMINANT

A#/Bb7
Bb D Ab
A# C## G#
2 1 3 × × ×
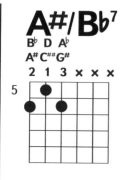
5

A#/Bb7
Bb D Ab
A# C## G#
× 1 0 2 × ×
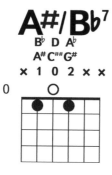
0

A#/Bb7
Bb D Ab
A# C## G#
× × 2 1 4 ×
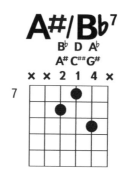
7

A#/Bb7
F Bb D Ab
E# A# C## G#
× × 1 1 1 2
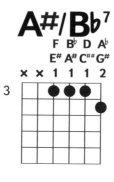
3

A#/Bb7
D Ab Bb
C## G# A#
3 4 1 × × ×
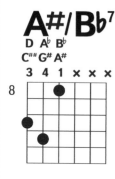
8

A#/Bb7
D Ab Bb
C## G# A#
× 3 4 1 × ×
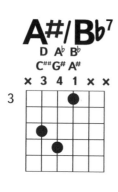
3

A#/Bb7
D Ab Bb
C## G# A#
× × × 2 4 1
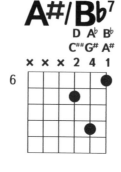
6

A#/Bb7
Ab Bb D
G# A# C##
× × × 4 2 1
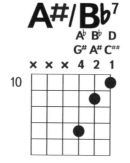
10

A#/Bb7#5
Bb F# Ab D
A# E## G# C##
1 4 1 2 × ×
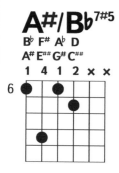
6

A#/Bb7#5
Bb F# Ab D F#
A# E## G# C## E##
× 1 4 1 3 2
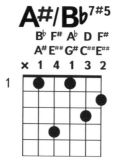
1

42 GUITAR CHORDS ENCYCLOPEDIA: A SEEING MUSIC METHOD BOOK

COMPACT
DIMINISHED

A#/Bbdim
Bb Fb Abb Db
A# E G C#
2 4 1 3 × ×
5
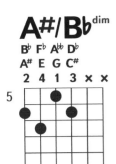

A#/Bbdim
Bb Fb Abb Db
A# E G C#
× 1 2 0 3 ×
0
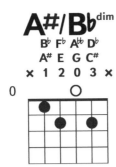

A#/Bbdim
Bb Fb Abb Db
A# E G C#
× × 1 2 1 3
8
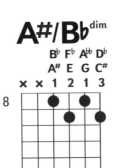

A#/Bbdim
Db Abb Bb Fb
C# G A# E
2 4 1 3 × ×
8
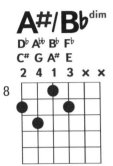

A#/Bbdim
Db Abb Bb Fb
C# G A# E
× 2 3 1 4 ×
3
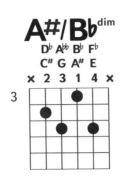

A#/Bbdim
Db Abb Bb Fb
C# G A# E
× × 1 2 1 3
11
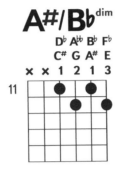

A#/Bbdim
Fb Bb Db Abb
E A# C# G
2 4 1 3 × ×
11
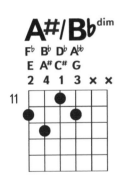

A#/Bbdim
Fb Bb Db Abb
E A# C# G
× 2 3 1 4 ×
6
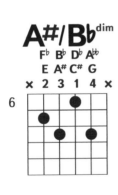

A#/Bbdim
Fb Bb Db Abb
E A# C# G
× × 1 2 1 3
2
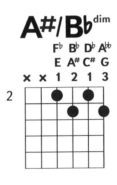

A#/Bbdim
Abb Db Fb Bb
G C# E A#
2 4 1 3 × ×
2
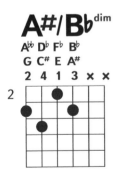

A#/Bbdim
Abb Db Fb Bb
G C# E A#
× 2 3 1 4 ×
9
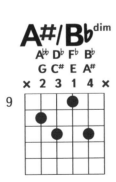

A#/Bbdim
Abb Db Fb Bb
G C# E A#
× × 1 2 1 3
5
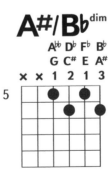

COMPACT
DIMINISHED (CONT.)

A#/Bb°
Bb Fb Ab Db
A# E G# C#
1 2 1 1 × ×
6
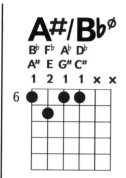

A#/Bb°
Bb Fb Ab Db
A# E G# C#
× 1 2 1 3 ×
1
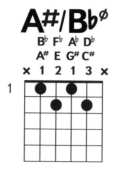

A#/Bb°
Bb Fb Ab Db
A# E G# C#
× × 1 3 3 3
8
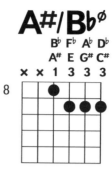

A#/Bb°
Db Ab Bb Fb
C# G# A# E
× 2 4 1 3 ×
3
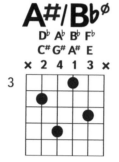

A#/Bb°
Db Ab Bb Fb
C# G# A# E
× × 1 3 1 2
11
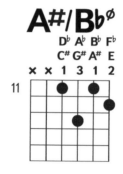

A#/Bb°
Fb Bb Db Ab
E A# C# G#
2 3 1 4 × ×
11
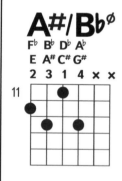

A#/Bb°
Fb Bb Db Ab
E A# C# G#
× 2 3 1 4 ×
6
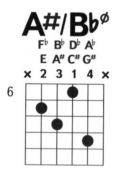

A#/Bb°
Fb Bb Db Ab
E A# C# G#
× × 1 2 1 4
2
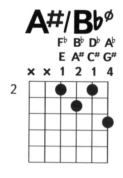

A#/Bb°
Ab D Fb Bb
G# C## E A#
3 4 1 2 × ×
2
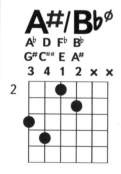

A#/Bb°
Ab D Fb Bb
G# C# E A#
× 2 3 1 4 ×
9
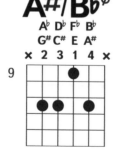

A#/Bb°
Ab D Fb Bb
G# C# E A#
× × 2 3 1 4
5
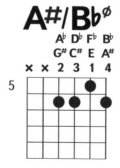

COMPACT
AUGMENTED

A#/Bb^Aug
Bb D F#
A# C## E##
3 2 1 × × ×
4
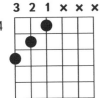

A#/Bb^Aug
Bb D F#
A# C## E##
× 3 2 1 × ×
11
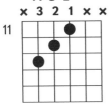

A#/Bb^Aug
Bb D F#
A# C## E##
× × 2 1 1 ×
7
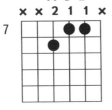

A#/Bb^Aug
Bb D F#
A# C## E##
× × × 2 3 1
2

A#/Bb^Aug
D F# Bb
C## E## A#
3 2 1 × × ×
8
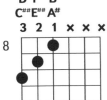

A#/Bb^Aug
D F# Bb
C## E## A#
× 3 2 1 × ×
3
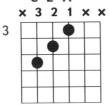

A#/Bb^Aug
D F# Bb
C## E## A#
× × 3 2 1 ×
11
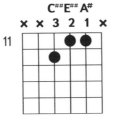

A#/Bb^Aug
D F# Bb
C## E## A#
× × × 2 3 1
6
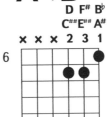

A#/Bb^Aug
F# Bb D
E## A# C##
3 2 1 × × ×
0

A#/Bb^Aug
F# Bb D
E## A# C##
× 3 2 1 × ×
7
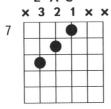

A#/Bb^Aug
F# Bb D
E## A# C##
× × 2 1 1 ×
3
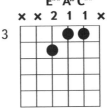

A#/Bb^Aug
F# Bb D
E## A# C##
× × × 2 3 1
10
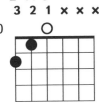

COMPACT
STACKED 5THS

A#/Bb⁵
Bb F
A# E#
1 3 × × × ×
6
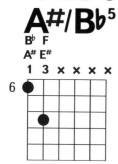

A#/Bb⁵
Bb F
A# E#
× 1 3 × × ×
1
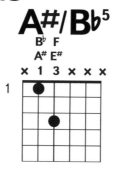

A#/Bb⁵
Bb F
A# E#
× × 1 3 × ×
8
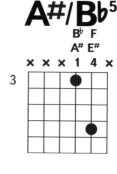

A#/Bb⁵
Bb F
A# E#
× × × 1 4 ×
3
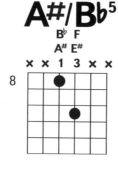

A#/Bb⁵
Bb F
A# E#
× × × 1 3
11
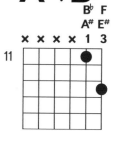

A#/Bb⁵
F Bb
E# A#
1 1 × × × ×
1
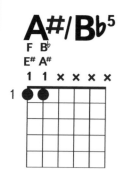

A#/Bb⁵
F Bb
E# A#
× 1 1 × × ×
8
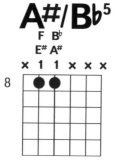

A#/Bb⁵
F Bb
E# A#
× × 1 1 × ×
3
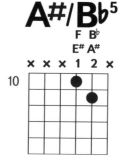

A#/Bb⁵
F Bb
E# A#
× × × 1 2 ×
10
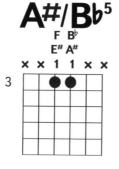

A#/Bb⁵
F Bb
E# A#
× × × 1 1
6
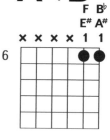

A#/Bb⁵ˢᵘˢ
Eb F Bb
D# F A#
4 1 1 × × ×
8
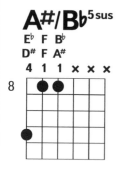

A#/Bb⁵ˢᵘˢ
Bb Eb F
A# D# E#
× × × 2 4 1
1
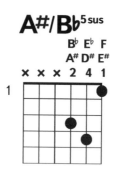

A#/Bb⁵ˢᵘˢ
Eb F Bb
D# E# A#
× × 4 1 2 ×
10
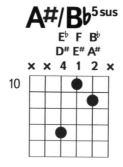

A#/Bb⁵ˢᵘˢ
Eb F Bb
D# E# A#
× × × 3 1 1
6
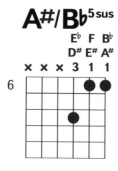

A#/Bb⁵ˢᵘˢ
Bb Eb F
A# D# E#
3 4 1 × × ×
3
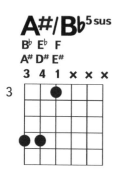

A#/Bb⁵ˢᵘˢ
Bb Eb F
A# D# E#
× 3 4 1 × ×
10
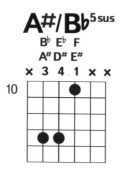

A#/Bb⁵ˢᵘˢ
Bb Eb F
A# D# E#
× × 3 4 1 ×
6
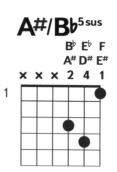

A#/Bb⁵ˢᵘˢ
Bb Eb F
A# D# E#
× × × 2 4 1
1
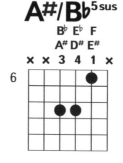

A#/Bb⁵ˢᵘˢ
F Bb Eb
F A# D#
1 1 1 × × ×
1
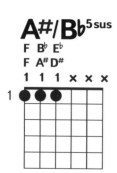

A#/Bb⁵ˢᵘˢ
F Bb Eb
E# A# D#
× 1 1 1 × ×
8
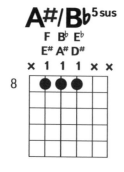

A#/Bb⁵ˢᵘˢ
F Bb Eb
E# A# D#
× × 1 1 2 ×
3
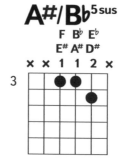

A#/Bb⁵ˢᵘˢ
F Bb Eb
E# A# D#
× × × 1 2 2
10
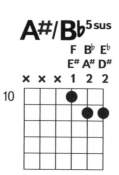

46 GUITAR CHORDS ENCYCLOPEDIA: A SEEING MUSIC METHOD BOOK

A#/Bb

COMPACT
STACKED 5THS
(CONT.)

A#/Bb⁵ᵃᵈᵈ⁹
C   Bb   F
B#   A# E#
1 × 1 4 × ×
8
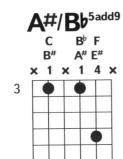

A#/Bb⁵ᵃᵈᵈ⁹
C   Bb   F
B#   A# E#
× 1 1 4 ×
3
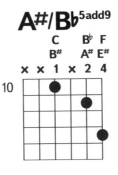

A#/Bb⁵ᵃᵈᵈ⁹
C   Bb   F
B#   A# E#
× × 1 × 2 4
10

A#/Bb⁵ᵃᵈᵈ⁹
C F Bb
B# E# A#
1 1 1 × × ×
8
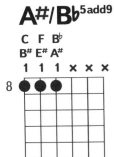

A#/Bb⁵ᵃᵈᵈ⁹
C F Bb
B# E# A#
× 1 1 1 × ×
3
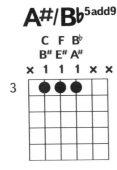

A#/Bb⁵ᵃᵈᵈ⁹
C F Bb
B# E# A#
× × 1 1 2 ×
10
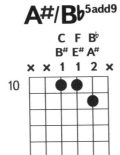

A#/Bb⁵ᵃᵈᵈ⁹
C F Bb
B# E# A#
× × × 1 2 3
5
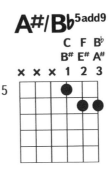

A#/Bb⁵ᵃᵈᵈ⁹
Bb F C
A# E# B#
1 3 4 × × ×
6
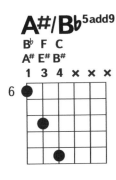

A#/Bbᵃᵈᵈ⁹
Bb F C
A# E# B#
× 1 3 4 × ×
1
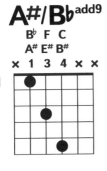

A#/Bb⁵ᵃᵈᵈ⁶/⁹
C G Bb F
B# F## A# E#
1 3 1 4 × ×
8
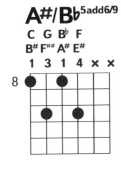

A#/Bb⁵ᵃᵈᵈ⁶/⁹
C G Bb F
B# F## A# E#
× 1 3 1 4 ×
3
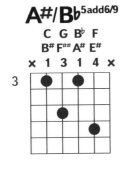

A#/Bb⁵ᵃᵈᵈ⁶/⁹
C G Bb F
B# F## A# E#
× × 1 3 2 4
10
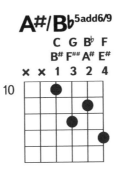

A#/Bb⁵ᵃᵈᵈ⁶/⁹
G C F Bb
F## B# E# A#
1 1 1 1 × ×
3
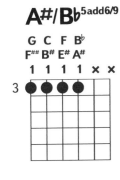

A#/Bb⁵ᵃᵈᵈ⁶/⁹
G C F Bb
F## B# E# A#
× 1 1 1 2 ×
10
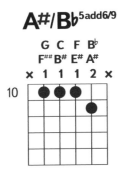

A#/Bb⁵ᵃᵈᵈ⁶/⁹
G C F Bb
F## B# E# A#
× × 1 1 2 3
5
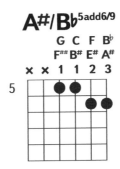

VIVID
MAJOR

A#/Bb$^{\triangle 7}$
A D F Bb
G## C## E# A#
3 4 1 1 × ×
3
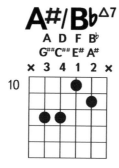

A#/Bb$^{\triangle 7}$
A D F Bb
G## C## E# A#
× 3 4 1 2 ×
10
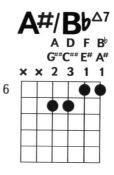

A#/Bb$^{\triangle 7}$
A D F Bb
G## C## E# A#
× × 2 3 1 1
6
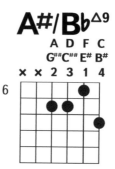

A#/Bb$^{\triangle 9}$
A D F C
G## C## E# B#
2 3 1 4 × ×
3
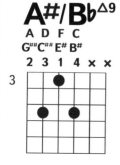

A#/Bb$^{\triangle 9}$
A D F C
G## C## E# B#
× 2 3 1 4 ×
10
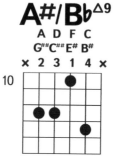

A#/Bb$^{\triangle 9}$
A D F C
G## C## E# B#
× × 2 3 1 4
6
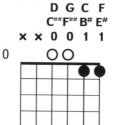

A#/Bb$^{6/9}$
D G C F
C## F## B# E#
1 1 1 1 × ×
10
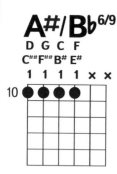

A#/Bb$^{6/9}$
D G C F
C## F## B# E#
× 1 1 1 2 ×
5
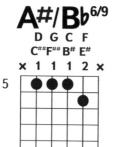

A#/Bb$^{6/9}$
D G C F
C## F## B# E#
× × 0 0 1 1
0
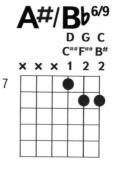

A#/Bb$^{6/9}$
D G C
C## F## B#
× × × 1 2 2
7

A#/Bb$^{6/9}$
G D F C
F## C## E# B#
1 3 1 4 × ×
3
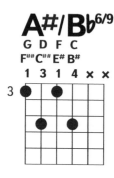

A#/Bb$^{6/9}$
G D F C
F## C## E# B#
× 1 3 1 4 ×
10
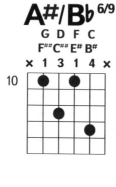

A#/Bb$^{6/9}$
G D F C
F## C## E# B#
× × 1 3 2 4
5
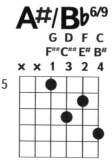

A#/Bb$^{\triangle 7\#11}$
E Bb D A
D## A# C## G##
0 1 0 3 × ×
0
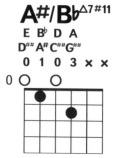

A#/Bb$^{\triangle 7\#11}$
E Bb D A
D## A# C## G##
× × 1 2 3 4
2
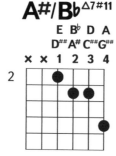

48 GUITAR CHORDS ENCYCLOPEDIA: A SEEING MUSIC METHOD BOOK

A#/Bb△7#11
Bb E A D
A# D## G## C##
1 2 3 4 × ×
6

A#/Bb△7#11
Bb E A D
A# D## G## C##
× 1 2 3 4 ×
1

A#/Bb△7#11
Bb E A D
A# D## G## C##
× × 1 2 3 4
8

A#/Bb△7#11
A D E Bb
G## C## D## A#
× × 3 4 1 2
5

A#/Bbmin7
F Ab Db
E# G# C#
3 1 1 × × ×
11

A#/Bbmin7
F Ab Db
E# G# C#
× 3 1 1 × ×
6

A#/Bbmin7
F Ab Db
E# G# C#
× × 3 1 2 ×
1

A#/Bbmin7
F Ab Db
E# G# C#
× × × 2 1 1
9

A#/Bbmin7
Ab Db F Bb
G# C# E# A#
2 3 1 1 × ×
3

A#/Bbmin7
Ab Db F Bb
G# C# E# A#
× 2 3 1 4 ×
10

A#/Bbmin7
Ab Db F Bb
G# C# E# A#
× × 1 1 1 1
6

A#/Bbmin7
F Bb Db Ab
E# A# C# G#
× × 2 3 1 4
2

A#/Bbmin7b5
Db Ab Bb Fb
C# G# A# E
× 2 4 1 3 ×
3

A#/Bbmin7b5
Db Ab Bb Fb
C# G# A# E
× × 1 4 1 2
11

A#/Bbmin7b5
Fb Bb Db Ab
E A# C# G#
2 3 1 4 × ×
11

A#/Bbmin7b5
Fb Bb Db Ab
E A# C# G#
× 2 3 1 4 ×
6

A#/Bbmin7b5
E Bb Db Ab
D## A# B## G#
× × 1 2 1 4
2

A#/Bbmin7b5
Ab Db Fb Bb
G# C# E A#
× 2 3 1 4 ×
9

A#/Bbmin7b5
Ab Db Fb Bb
G# C# E A#
× × 2 3 1 4
5

A#/Bbmin7b9
Ab Db F Cb
G# C# E# B
2 3 1 4 × ×
3
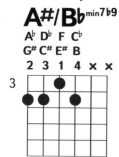

A#/Bbmin7b9
Ab Db F B
G# C# E# A##
× 2 3 1 4 ×
10
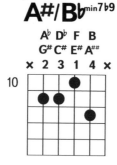

A#/Bbmin7b9
Ab Db F Cb
G# C# E# B
× × 1 1 1 2
6
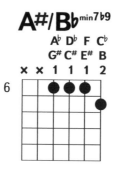

A#/Bbmin7b9
Cb F Ab Db
B E# G# C#
2 4 1 1 × ×
6
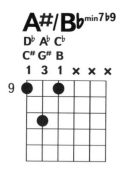

A#/Bbmin7b9
Cb F Ab Db
B E# G# C#
× 2 4 1 3 ×
1
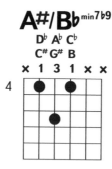

A#/Bbmin7b9
Cb F Ab Db
B E# G# C#
× × 1 2 1 1
9
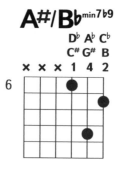

A#/Bbmin7b9
Db Ab Cb
C# G# B
1 3 1 × × ×
9
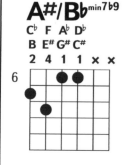

A#/Bbmin7b9
Db Ab Cb
C# G# B
× 1 3 1 × ×
4
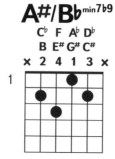

A#/Bbmin7b9
Db Ab Cb
C# G# B
× × 1 3 2 ×
11
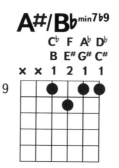

A#/Bbmin7b9
Db Ab Cb
C# G# B
× × × 1 4 2
6
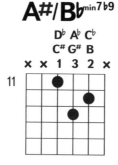

A#/Bbmin7b9
Ab Cb Db
G# B C#
× × × 4 3 1
9
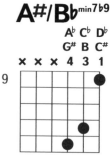

A#/Bbmin9
Ab Db F C
G# C# E# B#
2 3 1 4 × ×
3
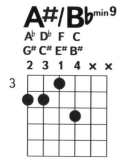

A#/Bbmin9
Ab Db F C
G# C# E# B#
× × 1 1 1 3
6
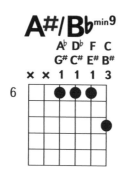

A#/Bb5sus
Eb F Bb
D# E# A#
× × × 3 1 1
6
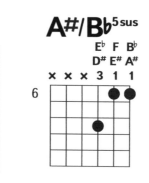

A#/Bbmin9
Db Ab C
C# G# B#
1 3 2 × × ×
9
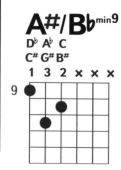

A#/Bbmin9
Db Ab C
C# G# B#
× 1 3 2 × ×
4
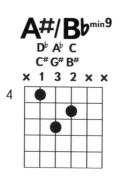

A#/Bbmin9
Db Ab C
C# G# B#
× × 1 3 3 ×
11
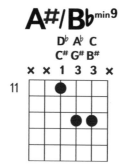

A#/Bbmin9
Db Ab C
C# G# B#
× × × 1 4 3
6
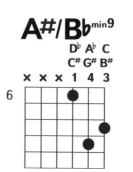

A#/Bbmin9
Ab C Db
G# B# C#
× × × 3 4 1
9
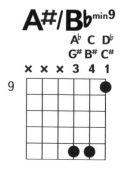

50 GUITAR CHORDS ENCYCLOPEDIA: A SEEING MUSIC METHOD BOOK

A#/Bb^{min9}
C F Ab Db
B# E# G# C#
2 3 1 1 × ×
6
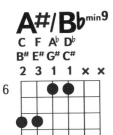

A#/Bb^{min9}
C F Ab Db
B# E# G# C#
× 3 4 1 2 ×
1
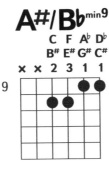

A#/Bb^{min9}
C F Ab Db
B# E# G# C#
× × 2 3 1 1
9
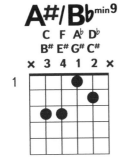

A#/Bb^{minΔ7}
Db F A
C# E# G##
3 2 1 × × ×
7
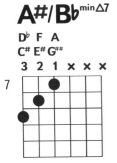

A#/Bb^{minΔ7}
Db F A
C# E# G##
× 3 2 1 × ×
2
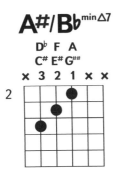

A#/Bb^{minΔ7}
Db F A
C# E# G##
× × 2 1 1 ×
10
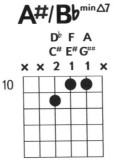

A#/Bb^{minΔ7}
Db F A
C# E# G##
× × × 2 3 1
5
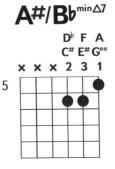

A#/Bb^{minΔ7}
F A Db
E# G## C#
3 2 1 × × ×
11
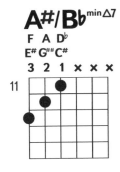

A#/Bb^{minΔ7}
F A Db
E# G## C#
× 3 2 1 × ×
6
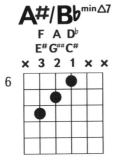

A#/Bb^{minΔ7}
F A Db
E# G## C#
× × 2 1 1 ×
2
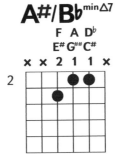

A#/Bb^{minΔ7}
F A Db
E# G## C#
× × 2 3 1
9
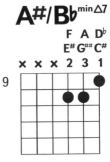

A#/Bb^{minΔ7}
A Db F Bb
G## C# E# A#
3 2 1 1 × ×
3
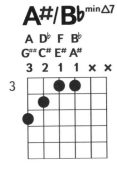

A#/Bb^{minΔ7}
A Db F Bb
G## C# E# A#
× 4 2 1 3 ×
10
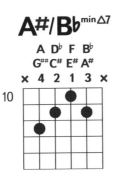

A#/Bb^{minΔ7}
A Db F Bb
G## C# E# A#
× × 2 1 1 1
6
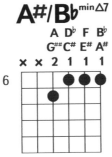

A#/Bb⁷
Ab D F Bb
G# C## E# A#
2 4 1 1 × ×

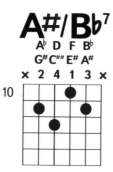
3

A#/Bb⁷
Ab D F Bb
G# C## E# A#
× 2 4 1 3 ×

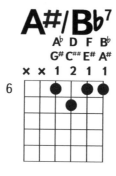
10

A#/Bb⁷
Ab D F Bb
G# C## E# A#
× × 1 2 1 1

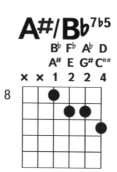
6

A#/Bb⁷
F Ab D
E# G# C##
3 1 2 × × ×

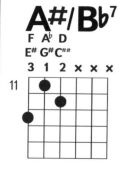
11

A#/Bb⁷
F Ab D
E# G# D
× 3 1 2 × ×

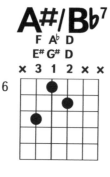
6

A#/Bb⁷
F Ab D
E# G# C##
× 3 1 4 ×

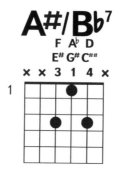
1

A#/Bb⁵ˢᵘˢ
Eb F Bb
D# E# A#
× × × 3 1 1

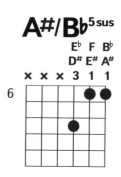
6

A#/Bb⁷
F Ab D
E# G# C##
3 1 2 × × ×

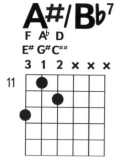
11

A#/Bb⁷ᵇ⁵
Fb Bb D Ab
E A# C## G#
× 1 2 1 4 ×

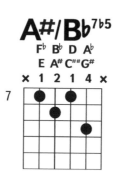
7

A#/Bb⁷
F Ab D
E# G# C##
× × 3 1 4 ×

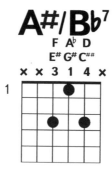
1

A#/Bb⁷ᵇ⁵
Bb Fb Ab D
A# E G# C##
1 2 1 3 × ×

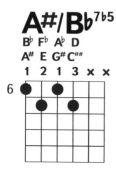
6

A#/Bb⁷ᵇ⁵
Bb Fb Ab D
A# E G# C##
× 1 2 1 4 ×

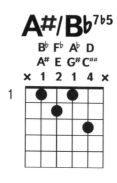
1

A#/Bb⁷ᵇ⁵
Bb Fb Ab D
A# E G# C##
× × 1 2 2 4

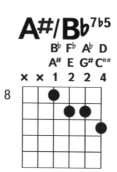
8

A#/Bb⁷ᵇ⁵
D Ab Bb Fb
C## G# A# E
3 4 1 2 × ×

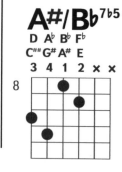
8

A#/Bb⁷ᵇ⁵
D Ab Bb Fb
D G# A# E
× 3 4 1 2 ×

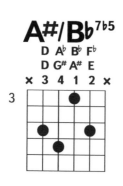
3

A#/Bb⁷ᵇ⁵
D Ab Bb Fb
C## G# A# E
× × 2 4 1 3

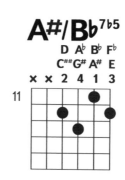
11

A#/Bb⁷ᵇ⁵
Ab D E Bb
G# C## E A#
2 4 1 3 ×

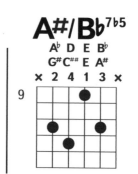
9

A#/Bb⁷
Ab D F Bb
G# D E# A#
× × 1 2 1 1

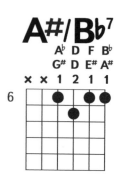
6

A#/Bb⁷#⁵
F# Bb D Ab
E## A# C## G#
3 2 0 1 × ×
0
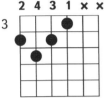

A#/Bb⁷#⁵
F# Bb D Ab
E## A# C## G#
× 3 2 1 4 ×
7

A#/Bb⁷#⁵
F# Bb D Ab
E## A# C## G#
× × 2 1 1 3
3
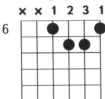

A#/Bb⁷#⁵
Ab D F# Bb
G# C## E## A#
2 4 3 1 × ×
3
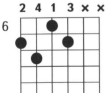

A#/Bb⁷#⁵
Ab D F# Bb
G# C## E## A#
× 1 2 1 1 ×
11
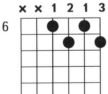

A#/Bb⁷#⁵
Ab D F# Bb
G# C## E## A#
× × 1 2 3 1
6

A#/Bb⁷ᵇ⁹
Ab D F Cb
G# C## E# B
2 4 1 3 × ×
3
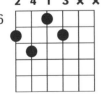

A#/Bb⁷ᵇ⁹
Ab D F Cb
G# C## E# B
× × 1 2 1 3
6
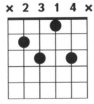

A#/Bb⁷ᵇ⁹
Bb D Ab Cb
A# C## G# B
× 1 0 2 0 ×
0

A#/Bb⁷ᵇ⁹
Bb D Ab Cb
A# C## G# B
× × 2 1 3 1
7

A#/Bb⁷ᵇ⁹
Cb F Ab D
B E# G# C##
2 4 1 3 × ×
6

A#/Bb⁷ᵇ⁹
Cb F Ab D
B E# G# C##
× 2 3 1 4 ×
1

A#/Bb⁷ᵇ⁹
Cb F Ab D
B E# G# C##
× × 2 3 1 4
9

A#/Bb⁷ᵇ⁹
D Ab Cb
C## G# B
2 3 1 × × ×
9
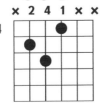

A#/Bb⁷ᵇ⁹
D Ab Cb
C## G# B
× 2 4 1 × ×
4

A#/Bb⁷ᵇ⁹
D Ab Cb
C## G# B
× × × 2 4 1
7
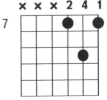

A#/Bb⁷ᵇ⁹
Ab Cb D
G# B C##
× × × 4 3 1
10
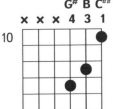

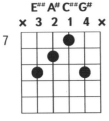

A#/Bb⁹
D Ab C
C## G# B#
1 2 1 × × ×
10

A#/Bb⁹
D Ab C
C## G# B#
× 1 2 1 × ×
5

A#/Bb⁹
D Ab C
C## G# B#
× × 0 1 1 ×
0

A#/Bb⁹
D Ab C
C## G# B#
× × × 2 4 3
7

A#/Bb⁹
Ab C D
G# B# C##
× × × 3 4 1
10

A#/Bb⁹
Ab D F C
G# C## E# B#
2 3 1 4 × ×
3

A#/Bb⁹
Ab D F C
G# C## E# B#
× × 1 2 1 3
6

A#/Bb⁹
C F Ab D
B# E# G# C##
3 4 1 2 × ×
6

A#/Bb⁹
C F Ab D
B# E# G# C##
× 2 3 1 4 ×
1

A#/Bb⁹
C F Ab D
B# E# G# C##
× × 2 3 1 4
9

A#/Bb⁷#⁹
D Ab C#
C## G# B##
1 2 2 × × ×
10

A#/Bb⁷#⁹
D Ab C#
C## G# B##
× 1 2 2 × ×
5

A#/Bb⁷#⁹
D Ab C#
C## G# B##
× × 0 1 2 ×
0

A#/Bb⁷#⁹
D Ab C#
C## G# B##
× × × 1 3 4
7

VIVID
DIMINISHED

A#/Bbø
Db E Ab
C# D## G#
4 2 1 × × ×
6

A#/Bbø
Db Fb Ab
C# E G#
× 4 2 1 × ×
1

A#/Bbø
Db Fb Ab
C# E G#
× × 3 1 1 ×
9

A#/Bbø
Db Fb Ab
C# E G#
× × × 3 2 1
4

A#/Bbø
Fb Ab Db
E G# C#
2 1 1 × × ×
11

A#/Bbø
Fb Ab Db
E G# C#
× 2 1 1 × ×
6

A#/Bbø
Fb Ab Db
E G# C#
× × 2 1 3 ×
1

A#/Bbø
Fb Ab Db
D## G# C#
× × × 1 1 1
9

A#/Bbø
Ab Db Fb
G# C# E
3 4 1 × × ×
2

A#/Bbø
Ab Db Fb
G# C# E
× 2 3 1 × ×
9

A#/Bbø
Ab Db Fb
G# C# E
× × 2 3 1 ×
5

A#/Bbø
Ab Db Fb
G# C# E
× × × 2 3 0
0

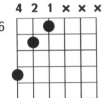
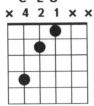
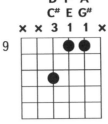
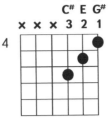
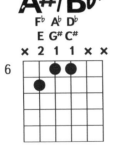
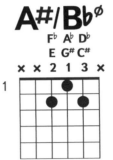
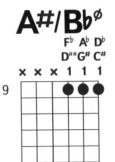
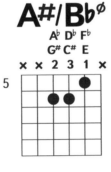
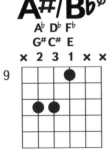

CHORDS WITH ROOT A SHARP - B FLAT 55

GUITAR
CHORDS
ENCYCLOPEDIA

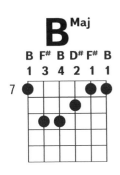

B^{Maj}

B F# B D# F# B
1 3 4 2 1 1

7

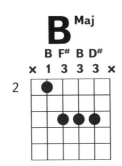

B^{Maj}

B F# B D#
× 1 3 3 3 ×

2

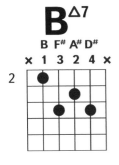

B^{△7}

B F# A# D#
× 1 3 2 4 ×

2

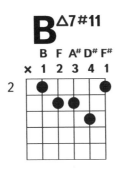

B^{△7#11}

B F A# D# F#
× 1 2 3 4 1

2

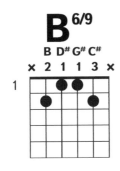

B^{△9}

B E♭ A# C#
× 2 1 4 3 ×

1

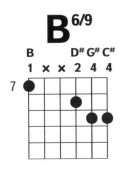

B^{6/9}

B   D# G# C#
1 × × 2 4 4

7

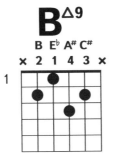

B^{6/9}

B D# G# C#
× 2 1 1 3 ×

1

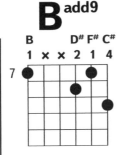

B^{add9}

B   D# F# C#
1 × × 2 1 4

7

BIG
MINOR

B^{min}

B F# B D F# B
1 3 4 1 1 1
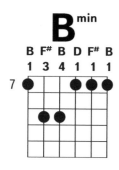
7

B^{min}

B F# B D F#
× 1 3 4 2 1
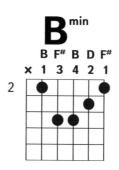
2

B^{min7}

B F# A D F# B
1 3 1 1 1 1
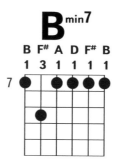
7

B^{min7♭5}

B F B F A D
1 2 3 4 4 4
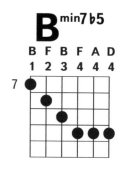
7

B^{min7♭9}

B A D F# C
1 × 1 1 1 2
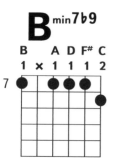
7

B^{min9}

B F# A D F# C#
1 3 1 1 1 4
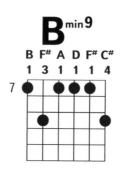
7

B^{min △7}

B F# A# D F#
× 1 4 2 3 1
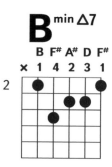
2

BIG
DOMINANT

B⁷

B G♭ A D# G♭ B
1 3 1 2 1 1
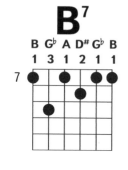
7

B⁷

B F# A D# F#
× 1 3 1 4 1
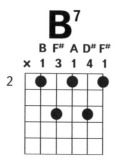
2

B^{7♭5}

B F A D#
× × 1 2 2 4
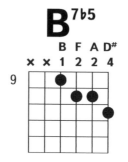
9

B^{7#5}

B D# A D# F##
1 2 3 4 4 ×
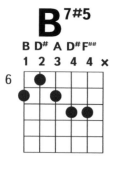
6

B^{7#5}

B F## A D# F##
× 1 4 1 3 2
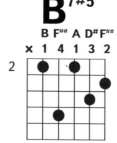
2

58 GUITAR CHORDS ENCYCLOPEDIA: A SEEING MUSIC METHOD BOOK

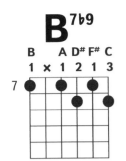

B$^{7\flat9}$
B　A D♯ F♯ C
1 × 1 2 1 3
7

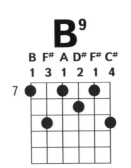

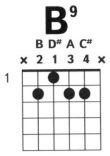

B^9
B F♯ A D♯ F♯ C♯
1 3 1 2 1 4
7

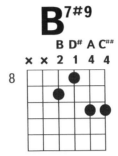

B^9
B D♯ A C♯
× 2 1 3 4 ×
1

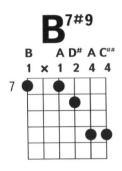

B$^{7\#9}$
B　A D♯ A C♯♯
1 × 1 2 4 4
7

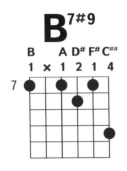

B$^{7\#9}$
B　A D♯ F♯ C♯♯
1 × 1 2 1 4
7

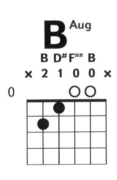

B$^{7\#9}$
B D♯ A C♯♯
× 2 1 3 4 ×
1

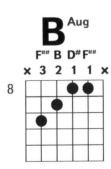

B$^{7\#9}$
B D♯ A C♯♯
× × 2 1 4 4
8

BIG
AUGMENTED

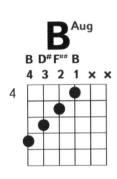

B^{Aug}
B D♯ F♯♯ B
4 3 2 1 × ×
4

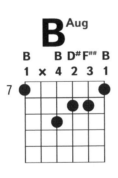

B^{Aug}
B D♯ F♯♯ B
× 2 1 0 0 ×
0

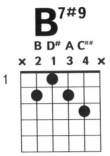

B^{Aug}
B　B D♯ F♯♯ B
1 × 4 2 3 1
7

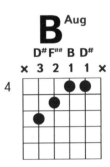

B^{Aug}
F♯♯ B D♯ F♯♯
× 3 2 1 1 ×
8

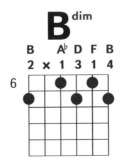

B^{Aug}
D♯ F♯♯ B D♯
× 3 2 1 1 ×
4

BIG
DIMINISHED

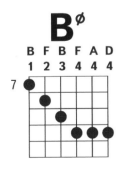

B^{ø}
B F B F A D
1 2 3 4 4 4
7

B^{dim}
B A♭ D F B
2 × 1 3 1 4
6

BIG
STACKED 5THS

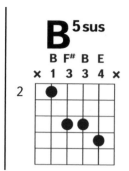

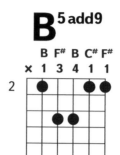

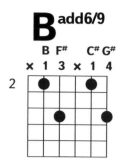

COMPACT
MAJOR

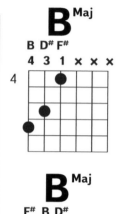

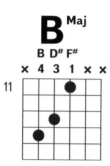

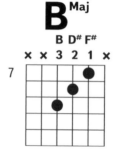

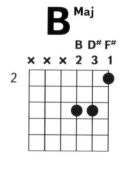

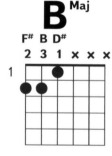

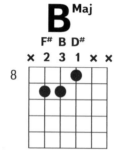

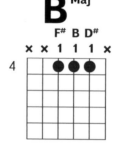

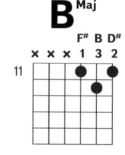

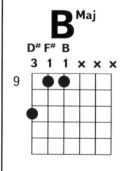

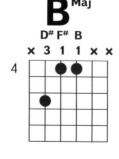

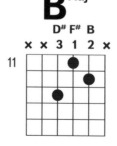

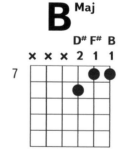

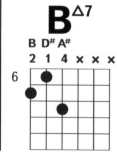

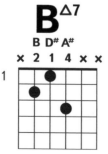

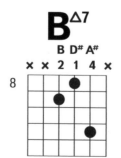

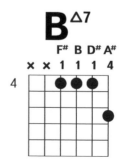

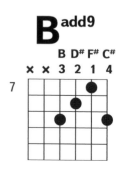

60 GUITAR CHORDS ENCYCLOPEDIA: A SEEING MUSIC METHOD BOOK

B
COMPACT
MINOR

Bmin   **B**min   **B**min   **B**min

B D F#   B D F#   B D F#   B D F#
4 2 1 × × ×   × 4 2 1 × ×   × × 3 1 1 ×   × × 3 2 1

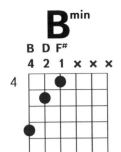 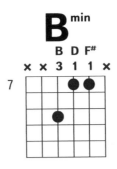 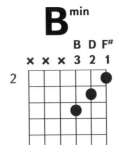 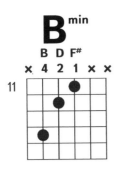

Bmin   **B**min   **B**min   **B**min

D F# B   D F# B   D F# B   D F# B
2 1 1 × × ×   × 2 1 1 × ×   × × 2 1 3 ×   × × × 1 1 1

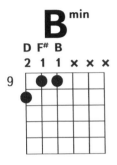 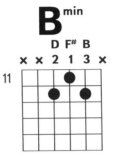 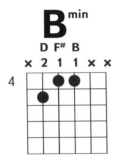 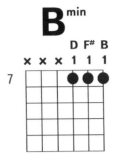

Bmin   **B**min   **B**min   **B**min

F# B D   F# B D   F# B D   F# B D
2 3 0 × × ×   × 3 4 1 × ×   × × 2 3 1 ×   × × × 2 3 1

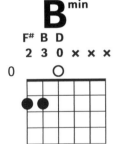 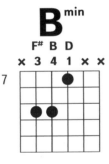 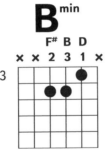 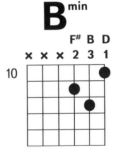

Bmin7   **B**min7   **B**min7   **B**min7

B D A   B D A   B D A   B D A
3 1 4 × × ×   × 2 0 3 × ×   × × 3 1 4 ×   × × × 2 1 4

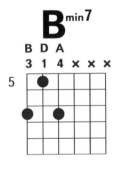 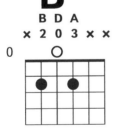 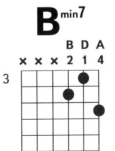 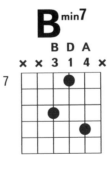

Bmin7   **B**min7   **B**min7   **B**min7   **B**min7

D A B   D A B   D A B   D A B   A B D
2 4 1 × × ×   × 2 4 1 × ×   × × 0 2 0 ×   × × × 1 4 1   × × × 4 2 1

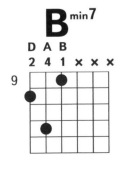 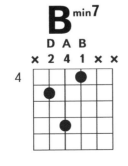 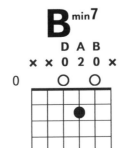 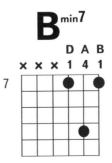 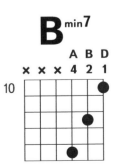

COMPACT
MINOR (CONT.)

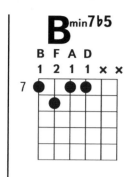

B^{min7b5}
B F A D
1 2 1 1 × ×
7

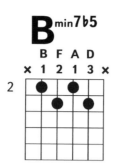

B^{min7b5}
B F A D
× 1 2 1 3 ×
2

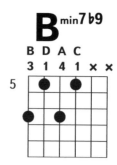

B^{min7b9}
B D A C
3 1 4 1 × ×
5

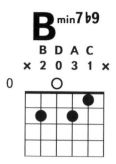

B^{min7b9}
B D A C
× 2 0 3 1 ×
0

COMPACT
DOMINANT

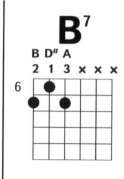

B⁷
B D# A
2 1 3 × × ×
6

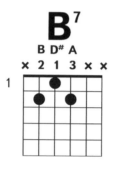

B⁷
B D# A
× 2 1 3 × ×
1

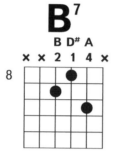

B⁷
B D# A
× × 2 1 4 ×
8

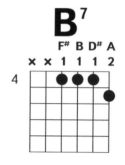

B⁷
F# B D# A
× × 1 1 1 2
4

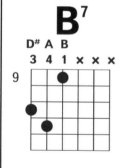

B⁷
D# A B
3 4 1 × × ×
9

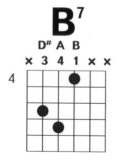

B⁷
D# A B
× 3 4 1 × ×
4

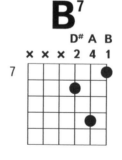

B⁷
D# A B
× × × 2 4 1
7

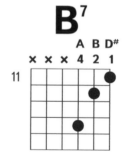

B⁷
A B D#
× × × 4 2 1
11

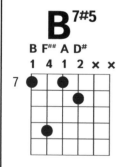

B^{7#5}
B F## A D#
1 4 1 2 × ×
7

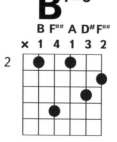

B^{7#5}
B F## A D#F##
× 1 4 1 3 2
2

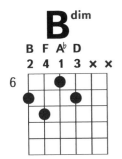

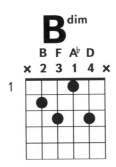

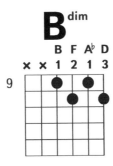

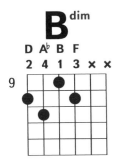

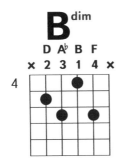

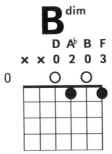

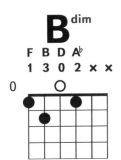

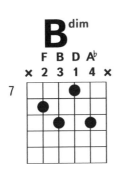

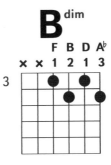

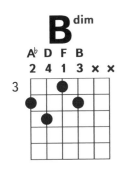

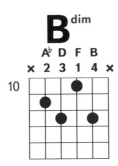

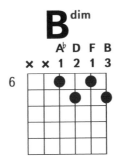

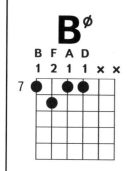

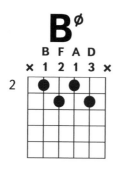

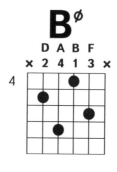

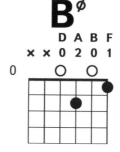

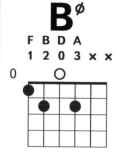

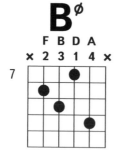

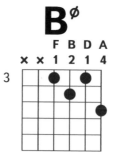

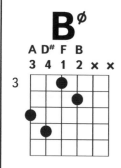

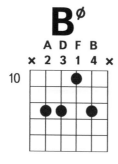

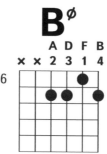

COMPACT
AUGMENTED

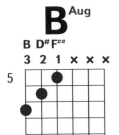

B^{Aug}
B D# F##
3 2 1 × × ×
5

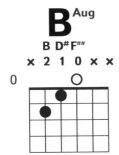

B^{Aug}
B D# F##
× 2 1 0 × ×
0

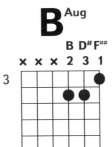

B^{Aug}
B D# F##
× × 2 1 1 ×
8

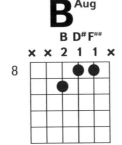

B^{Aug}
B D# F##
× × × 2 3 1
3

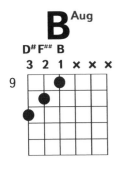

B^{Aug}
D# F## B
3 2 1 × × ×
9

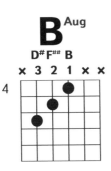

B^{Aug}
D# F## B
× 3 2 1 × ×
4

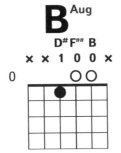

B^{Aug}
D# F## B
× × 1 0 0 ×
0

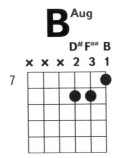

B^{Aug}
D# F## B
× × × 2 3 1
7

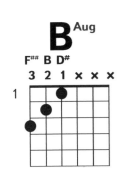

B^{Aug}
F## B D#
3 2 1 × × ×
1

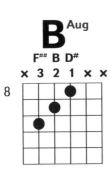

B^{Aug}
F## B D#
× 3 2 1 × ×
8

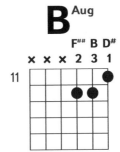

B^{Aug}
F## B D#
× × 2 1 1 ×
4

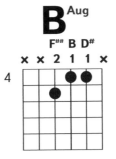

B^{Aug}
F## B D#
× × × 2 3 1
11

COMPACT
STACKED 5THS

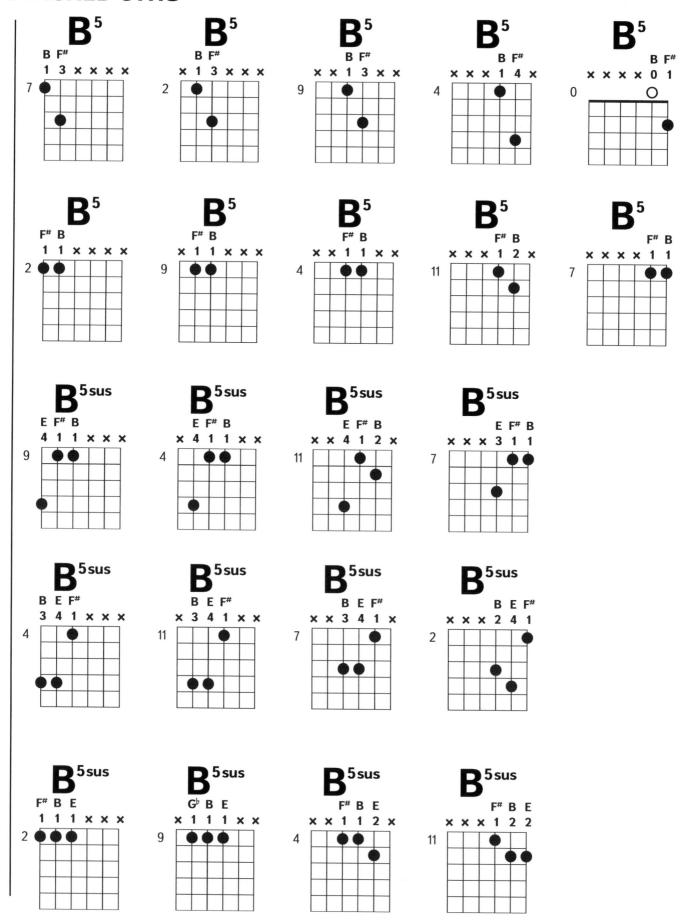

COMPACT
STACKED 5THS
(CONT.)

B^{5add9}

C# B F#
1 × 1 4 × ×
9
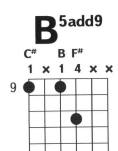

B^{5add9}

C# B G♭
× 1 × 1 4 ×
4
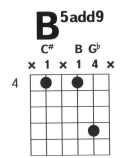

B^{5add9}

C# B F#
× × 1 × 2 4
11
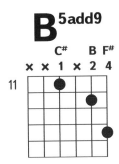

B^{5add9}

C# F# B
1 1 1 × × ×
9
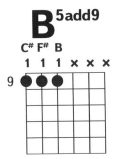

B^{5add9}

C# F# B
× 1 1 1 × ×
4
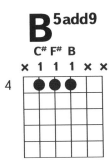

B^{5add9}

C# F# B
× × 1 1 2 ×
11
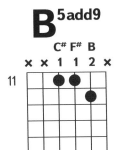

B^{5add9}

C# G♭ B
× × × 1 2 3
6
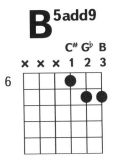

B^{5add9}

B F# C#
1 3 4 × × ×
7
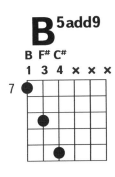

B^{5add9}

B F# C#
× 1 3 4 × ×
2
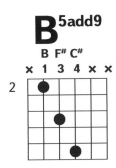

B^{5add6/9}

C# G# B F#
1 3 1 4 × ×
9
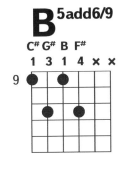

B^{5add6/9}

C# G# B F#
× 1 3 1 4 ×
4
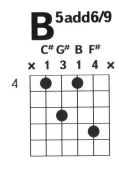

B^{5add6/9}

C# G# B F#
× × 1 3 2 4
11
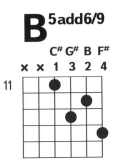

B^{5add6/9}

G# C# F# B
1 1 1 1 × ×
4
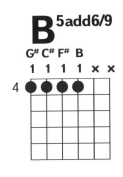

B^{5add6/9}

G# C# F# B
× 1 1 1 2 ×
11
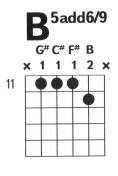

B^{5add6/9}

G# C# F# B
× × 1 1 2 3
6
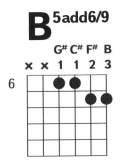

CHORDS WITH ROOT B 67

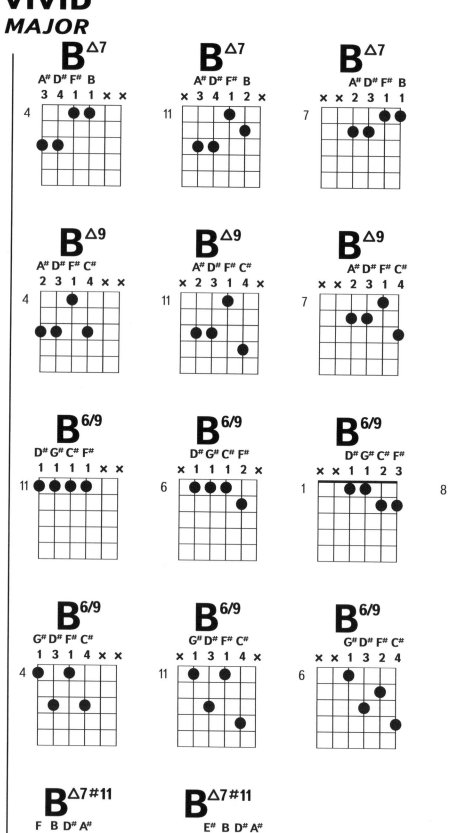

B^{△7#11}
B E# A# D#
1 2 3 4 × ×
7
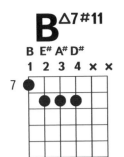

B^{△7#11}
B E# A# D#
× 1 2 3 4 ×
2
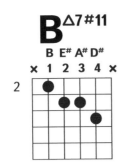

B^{△7#11}
B E# A# D#
× × 1 2 3 4
9
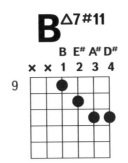

B^{△7#11}
A# D# E# B
× × 3 4 1 2
6
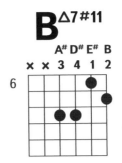

VIVID
MINOR

B^{min7}
F# A D
2 0 0 × × ×
0
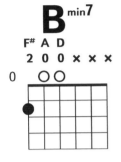

B^{min7}
F# A D
× 3 1 1 × ×
7
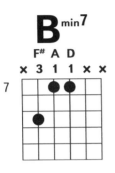

B^{min7}
F# A D
× × 3 1 2 ×
2
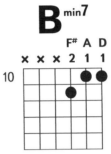

B^{min7}
F# A D
× × 2 1 1
10
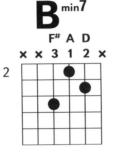

B^{min7}
A D F# B
2 3 1 1 × ×
4
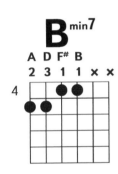

B^{min7}
A D F# B
× 2 3 1 4 ×
11
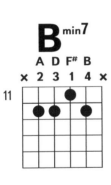

B^{min7}
A D F# B
× × 1 1 1 1
7
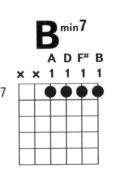

B^{min7}
F# B D A
× × 2 3 1 4
3
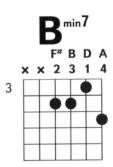

B^{min7b5}
D A B F
× 2 4 1 3 ×
4
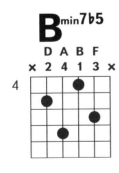

B^{min7b5}
D A B F
× × 0 2 0 1
0
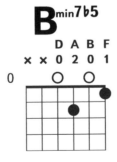

B^{min7b5}
F B D A
1 2 0 3 × ×
0
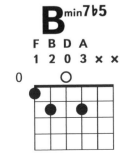

B^{min7b5}
F B D A
× 2 3 1 4 ×
7
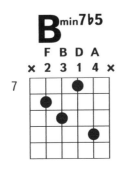

B^{min7b5}
F B D A
× × 1 2 1 4
3
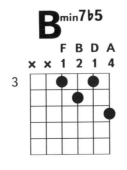

B^{min7b5}
A D F B
× 2 3 1 4 ×
10
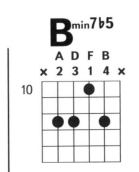

B^{min7b5}
A D F B
× × 2 3 1 4
6
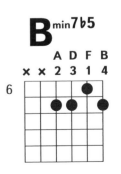

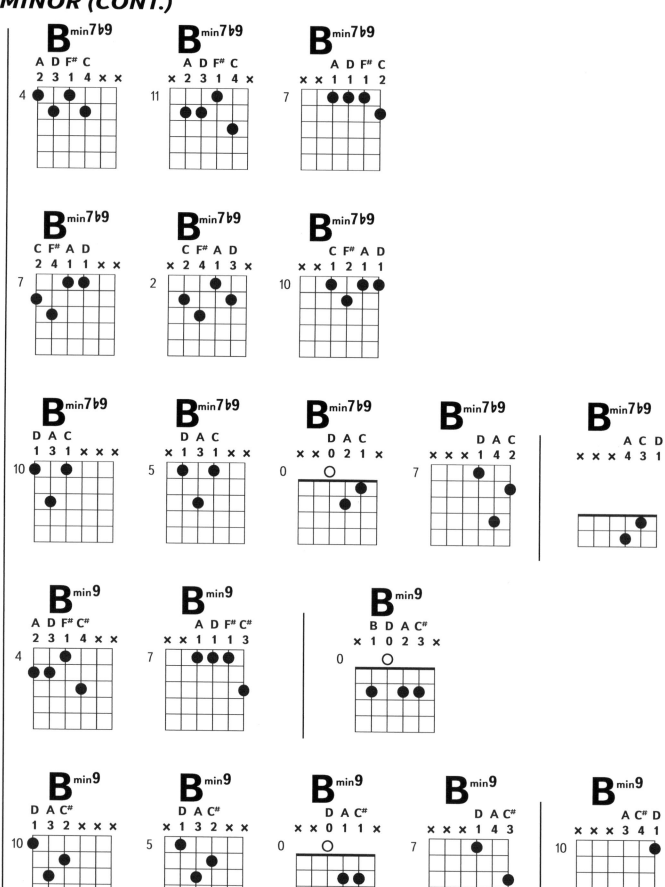

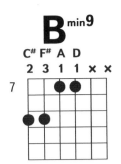

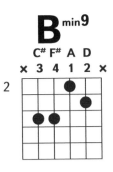

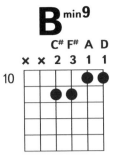

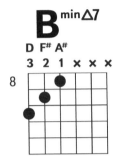

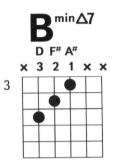

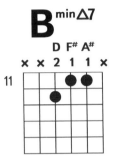

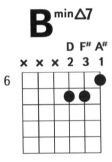

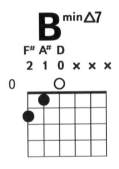

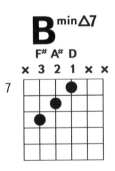

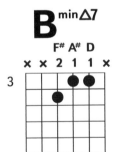

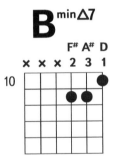

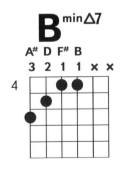

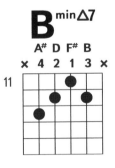

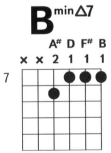

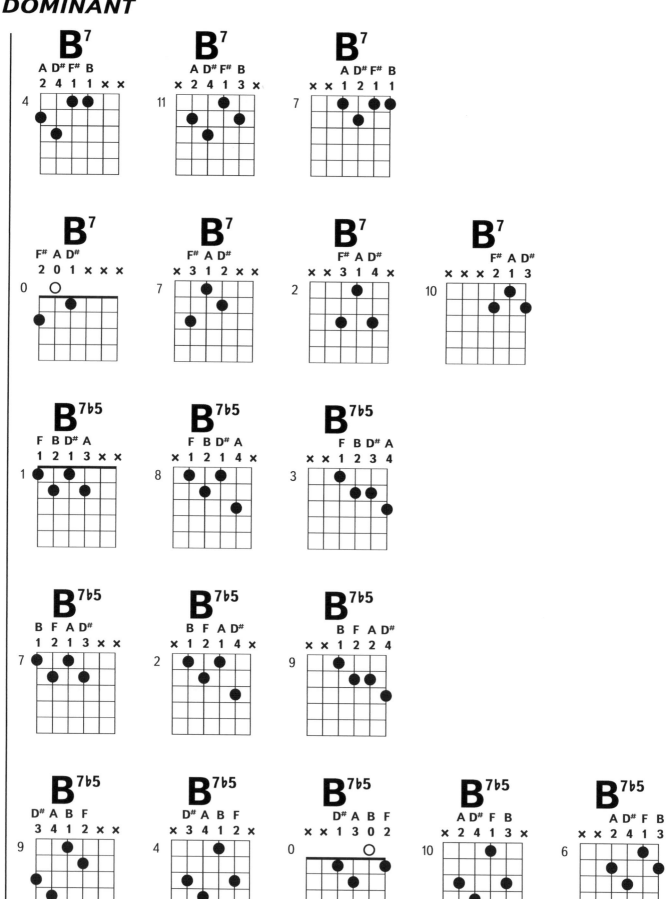

B

VIVID
DOMINANT (CONT.)

B^{7#5}

G B D# A
4 2 1 3 × ×
1

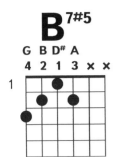

B^{7#5}

F## B D# A
× 3 2 1 4 ×
8

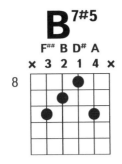

B^{7#5}

F## B D# A
× × 2 1 1 3
4

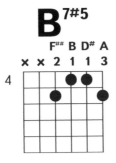

B^{7#5}

A D# F## B
2 4 3 1 × ×
4

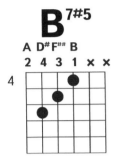

B^{7#5}

A D# F## B
× 0 1 0 0 ×
0

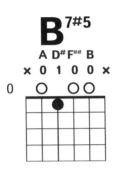

B^{7#5}

A D# F## B
× × 1 2 3 1
7

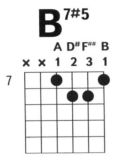

B^{7b9}

A D# F# C
2 4 1 3 × ×
4

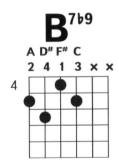

B^{7b9}

A D# F# C
× × 1 2 1 3
7

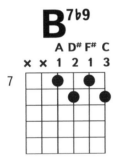

B^{7b9}

B D# A C
× 2 1 3 1 ×
1

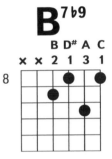

B^{7b9}

B D# A C
× × 2 1 3 1
8

B^{7b9}

C F# A D#
2 4 1 3 × ×
7

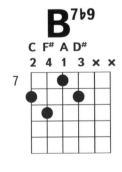

B^{7b9}

C F# A D#
× 2 3 1 4 ×
2

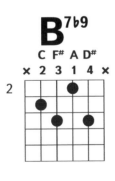

B^{7b9}

C F# A D#
× × 2 3 1 4
10

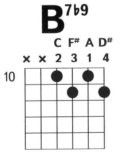

B^{7b9}

D# A C
2 3 1 × × ×
10

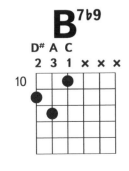

B^{7b9}

D# A C
× 2 4 1 × ×
5

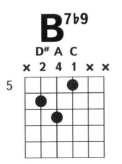

B^{7b9}

D# A C
× × × 2 4 1
8

B^{7b9}

A C D#
× × × 4 3 1
11

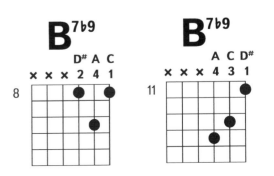

CHORDS WITH ROOT B 73

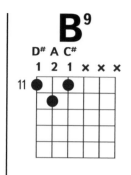
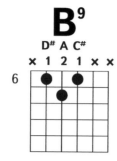
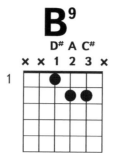
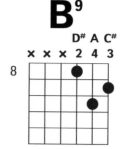
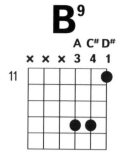

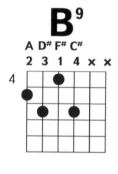
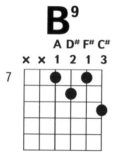

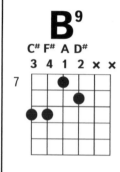
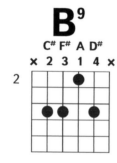
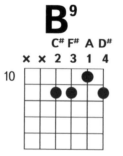

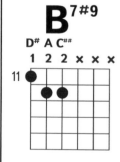
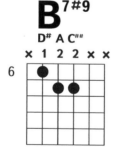
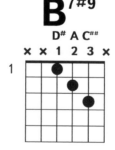
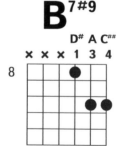

74 GUITAR CHORDS ENCYCLOPEDIA: A SEEING MUSIC METHOD BOOK

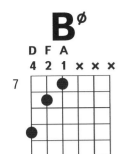

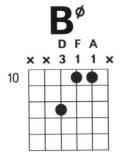

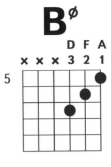

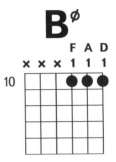

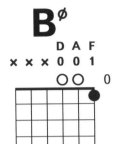

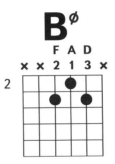

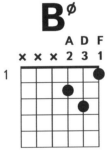

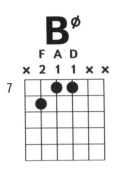

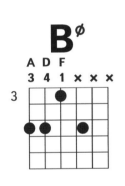

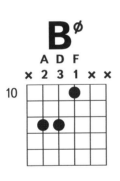

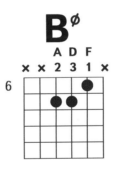

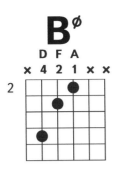

GUITAR
CHORDS
ENCYCLOPEDIA

C^{Maj}
```
C E G C E
× 3 2 0 1 0
```
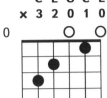

C^{Maj}
```
C E G C G
× 3 2 0 1 4
```
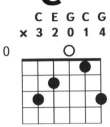

C^{Maj}
```
C G C E G C
1 3 4 2 1 1
```
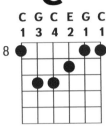

C^{Maj}
```
C G C E
× 1 3 3 3 ×
```
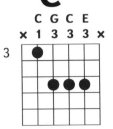

C^{△7}
```
C E G B E
× 3 2 0 0 0
```
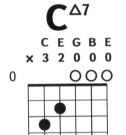

C^{△7}
```
C G B E G
× 1 3 2 4 1
```
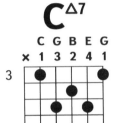

C^{△7#11}
```
C E G B F#
× 3 2 0 0 1
```
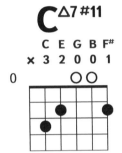

C^{△7#11}
```
C F# B E G
× 1 2 3 4 1
```
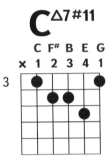

C^{△9}
```
C E B D
× 2 1 4 3 ×
```
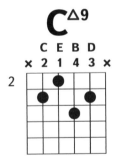

C^{△9}
```
C E B D E
× 2 1 4 3 0
```
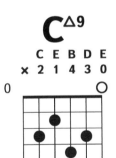

C^{6/9}
```
C     E A D
1 × × 2 4 4
```
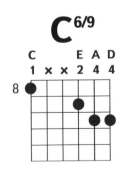

C^{6/9}
```
C E A D G
× 2 1 1 4 4
```
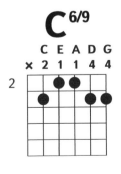

C^{6/9}
```
C E A D E
× 2 1 1 3 0
```
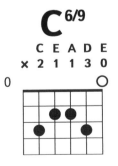

C^{add9}
```
C     E G D
1 × × 2 1 4
```
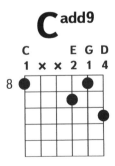

BIG
MINOR

Cmin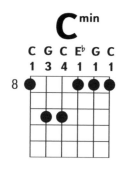

Cmin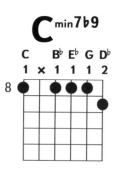

Cmin7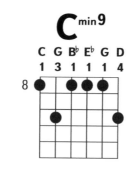

Cmin7♭5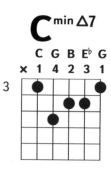

Cmin7♭9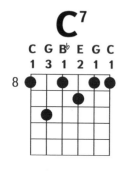

Cmin9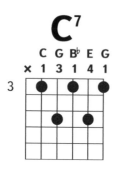

Cmin△7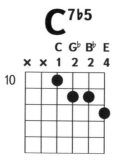

Cmin△7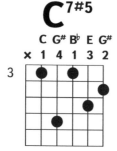

BIG
DOMINANT

C7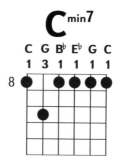

C7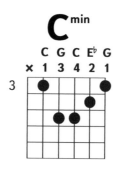

C7♭5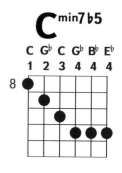

C7#5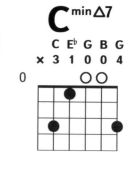

C7#5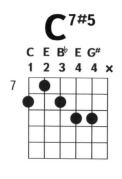

78 GUITAR CHORDS ENCYCLOPEDIA: A SEEING MUSIC METHOD BOOK

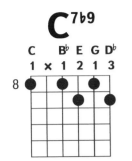

C⁷ᵇ⁹

C　Bᵇ　E　G　Dᵇ
1　×　1　2　1　3

8

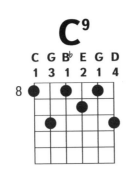

C⁹

C　G　Bᵇ　E　G　D
1　3　1　2　1　4

8

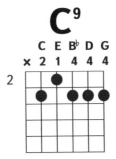

C⁹

C　E　Bᵇ　D　G
×　2　1　4　4　4

2

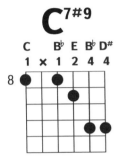

C⁷#⁹

C　Bᵇ　E　Bᵇ　D#
1　×　1　2　4　4

8

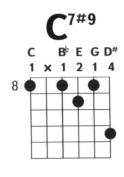

C⁷#⁹

C　Bᵇ　E　G　D#
1　×　1　2　1　4

8

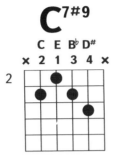

C⁷#⁹

C　E　Bᵇ　D#
×　2　1　3　4　×

2

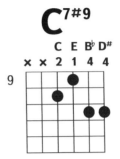

C⁷#⁹

C　E　Bᵇ　D#
×　×　2　1　4　4

9

BIG
AUGMENTED

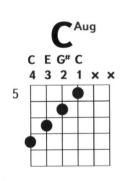

Cᴬᵘᵍ

C　E　G#　C
4　3　2　1　×　×

5

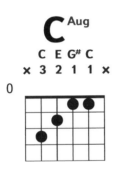

Cᴬᵘᵍ

C　E　G#　C
×　3　2　1　1　×

0

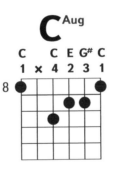

Cᴬᵘᵍ

C　C　E　G#　C
1　×　4　2　3　1

8

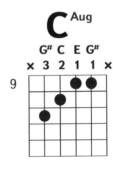

Cᴬᵘᵍ

G#　C　E　G#
×　3　2　1　1　×

9

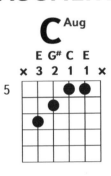

Cᴬᵘᵍ

E　G#　C　E
×　3　2　1　1　×

5

BIG
DIMINISHED

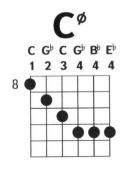

Cø

C　Gᵇ　C　Gᵇ　Bᵇ　Eᵇ
1　2　3　4　4　4

8

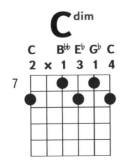

Cᵈⁱᵐ

C　Bᵇᵇ　Eᵇ　Gᵇ　C
2　×　1　3　1　4

7

BIG
STACKED 5THS

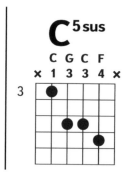

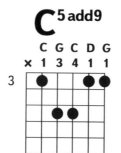

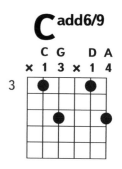

COMPACT
MAJOR

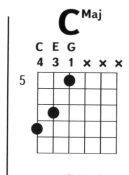

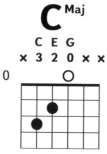

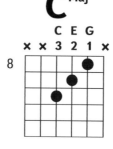

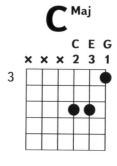

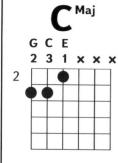

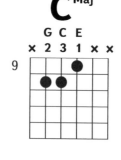

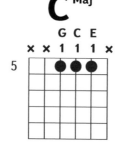

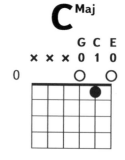

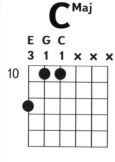

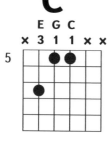

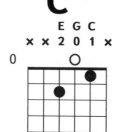

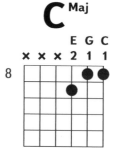

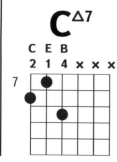

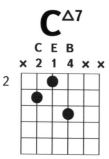

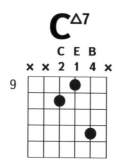

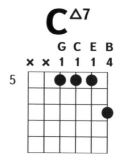

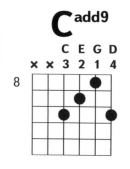

80 GUITAR CHORDS ENCYCLOPEDIA: A SEEING MUSIC METHOD BOOK

COMPACT
MINOR

Cmin   **C**min   **C**min   **C**min

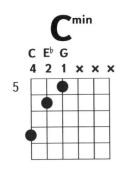
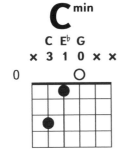
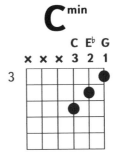
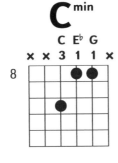

Cmin   **C**min   **C**min   **C**min

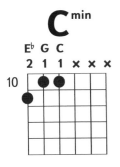
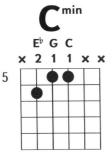
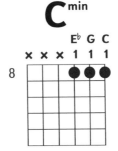
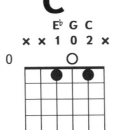

Cmin   **C**min   **C**min   **C**min

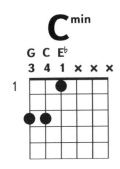
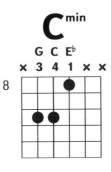
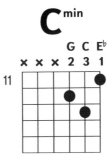
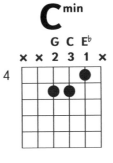

Cmin7   **C**min7   **C**min7   **C**min7

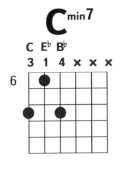
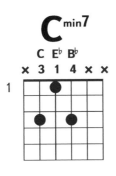
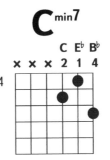
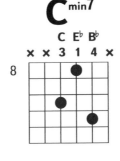

Cmin7   **C**min7   **C**min7   **C**min7   **C**min7

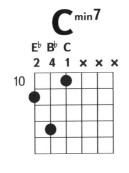
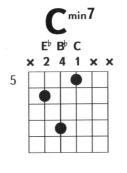
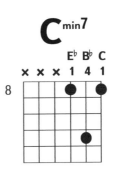
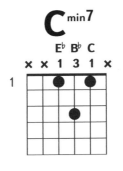
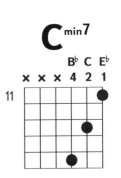

CHORDS WITH ROOT C 81

COMPACT
MINOR (CONT.)

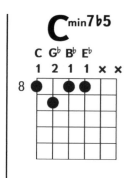

Cmin7♭5

C G♭ B♭ E♭
1 2 1 1 × ×

8

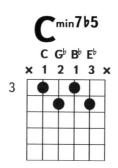

Cmin7♭5

C G♭ B♭ E♭
× 1 2 1 3 ×

3

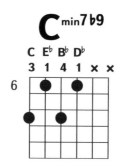

Cmin7♭9

C E♭ B♭ D♭
3 1 4 1 × ×

6

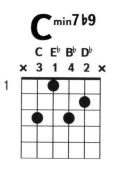

Cmin7♭9

C E♭ B♭ D♭
× 3 1 4 2 ×

1

COMPACT
DOMINANT

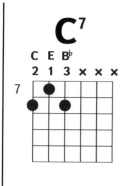

C⁷

C E B♭
2 1 3 × × ×

7

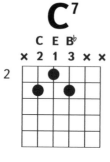

C⁷

C E B♭
× 2 1 3 × ×

2

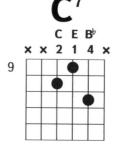

C⁷

C E B♭
× × 2 1 4 ×

9

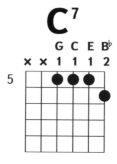

C⁷

G C E B♭
× × 1 1 1 2

5

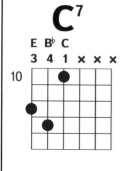

C⁷

E B♭ C
3 4 1 × × ×

10

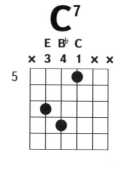

C⁷

E B♭ C
× 3 4 1 × ×

5

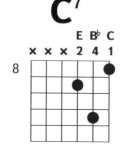

C⁷

E B♭ C
× × × 2 4 1

8

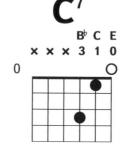

C⁷

B♭ C E
× × × 3 1 0

0

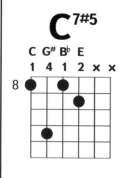

C⁷#⁵

C G# B♭ E
1 4 1 2 × ×

8

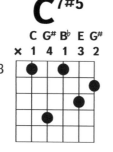

C⁷#⁵

C G# B♭ E G#
× 1 4 1 3 2

3

82 GUITAR CHORDS ENCYCLOPEDIA: A SEEING MUSIC METHOD BOOK

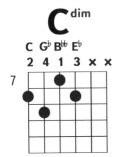

Cdim

C Gb Bbb Eb
2 4 1 3 × ×

7

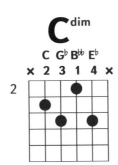

Cdim

C Gb Bbb Eb
× 2 3 1 4 ×

2

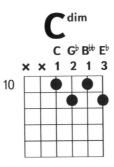

Cdim

C Gb Bbb Eb
× × 1 2 1 3

10

COMPACT
DIMINISHED

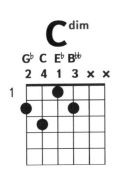

Cdim

Eb Bbb C Gb
2 4 1 3 × ×

10

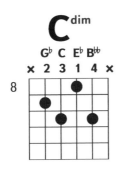

Cdim

Eb Bbb C Gb
× 2 3 1 4 ×

5

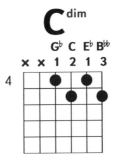

Cdim

Eb Bbb C Gb
× × 1 2 1 3

1

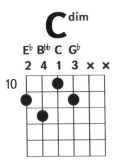

Cdim

Gb C Eb Bbb
2 4 1 3 × ×

1

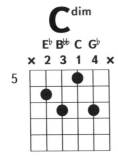

Cdim

Gb C Eb Bbb
× 2 3 1 4 ×

8

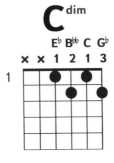

Cdim

Gb C Eb Bbb
× × 1 2 1 3

4

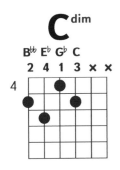

Cdim

Bbb Eb Gb C
2 4 1 3 × ×

4

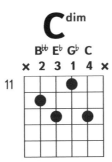

Cdim

Bbb Eb Gb C
× 2 3 1 4 ×

11

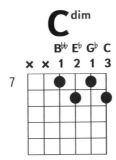

Cdim

Bbb Eb Gb C
× × 1 2 1 3

7

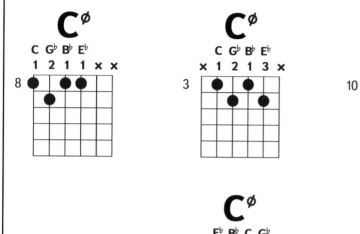

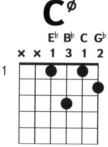

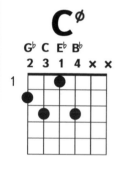

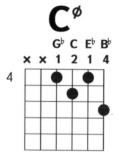

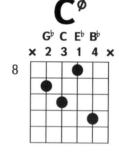

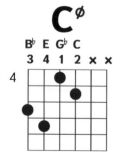

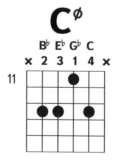

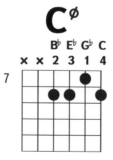

COMPACT
AUGMENTED

C^Aug
C E G#
3 2 1 × × ×
6
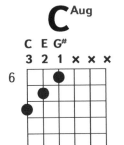

C^Aug
C E G#
× 3 2 1 × ×
0
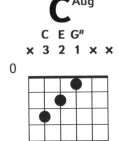

C^Aug
C E G#
× × 2 1 1 ×
9
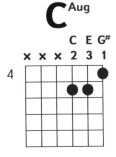

C^Aug
C E G#
× × × 2 3 1
4
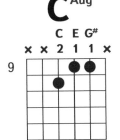

C^Aug
E G# C
3 2 1 × × ×
10
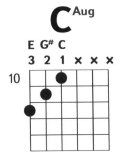

C^Aug
E G# C
× 3 2 1 × ×
5
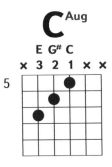

C^Aug
E G# C
× × 3 2 1 ×
1
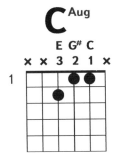

C^Aug
E G# C
× × × 2 3 1
8
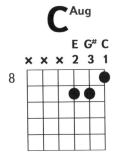

C^Aug
G# C E
3 2 1 × × ×
2
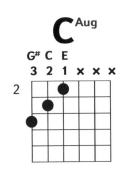

C^Aug
G# C E
× 3 2 1 × ×
9
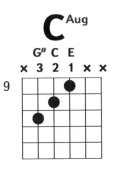

C^Aug
G# C E
× × 2 1 1 ×
5
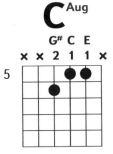

C^Aug
G# C E
× × × 1 2 0
0

CHORDS WITH ROOT C 85

COMPACT
STACKED 5THS

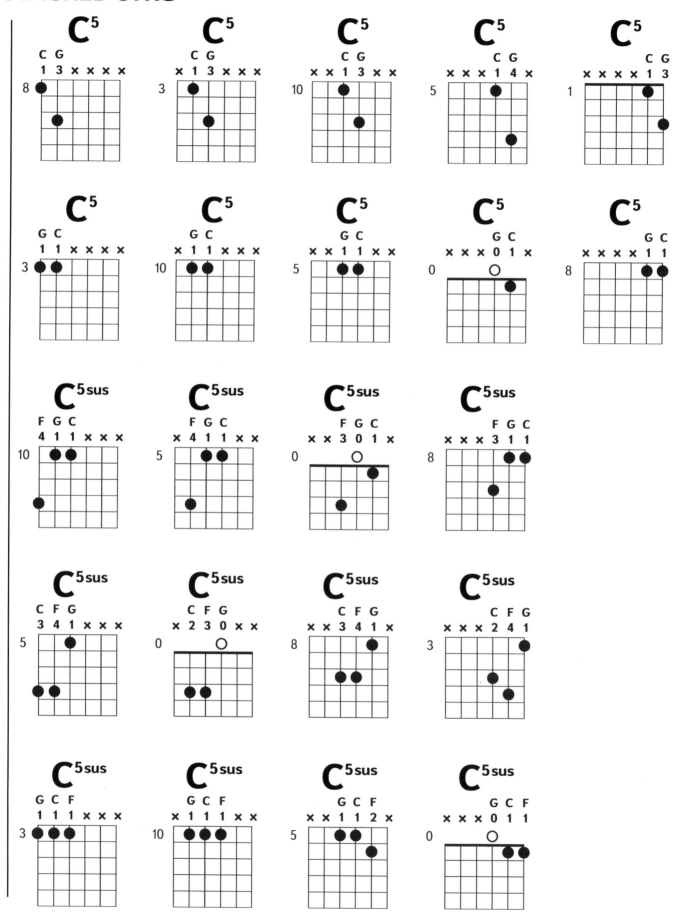

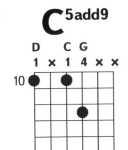 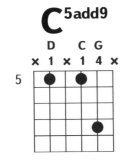 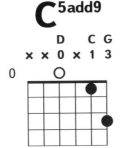

C5add9   C5add9   C5add9   C5add9

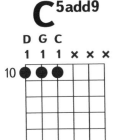 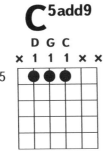 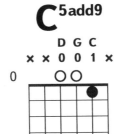 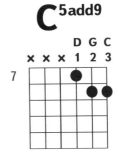

C5add9   C5add9

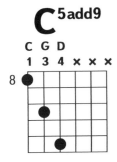 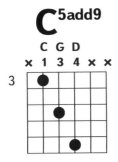

C5add6/9   C5add6/9   C5add6/9

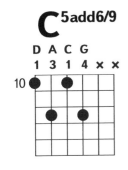 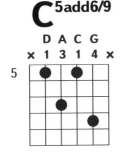 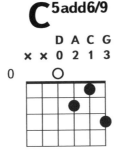

C5add6/9   C5add6/9   C5add6/9

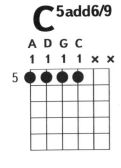 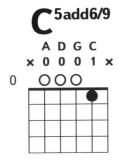 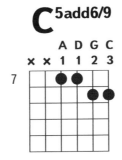

C△7
B E G C
3 4 1 1 × ×
5

C△7
B E G C
× 2 3 0 1 ×
0

C△7
B E G C
× × 2 3 1 1
8

C△9
B E G D
2 3 1 4 × ×
5

C△9
B E G D
× 1 2 0 3 ×
0

C△9
B E G D
× × 2 3 1 4
8

C6/9
E A D G
0 0 0 0 × ×
0

C6/9
E A D G
× 1 1 1 2 ×
7

C6/9
E A D G
× × 1 1 2 3
2

C6/9
E A D
× × × 1 2 2
9

C6/9
A E G D
1 3 1 4 × ×
5

C6/9
A E G D
× 0 2 0 4 ×
0

C6/9
A E G D
× × 1 3 2 4
7

C△7#11
F# C E B
1 2 1 4 × ×
2

C△7#11
F# C E B
× × 1 2 3 4
4

88 GUITAR CHORDS ENCYCLOPEDIA: A SEEING MUSIC METHOD BOOK

VIVID
MINOR

C△7#11

C F# B E
1 2 3 4 × ×
8

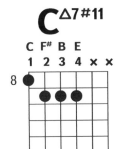

C△7#11

× 1 2 3 4 ×
3

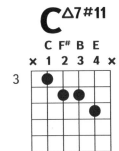

C△7#11

× × 1 2 3 4
10

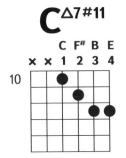

C△7#11

B E F# C
× × 3 4 1 2
7

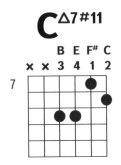

Cmin7

G B♭ E♭
3 1 1 × × ×
1

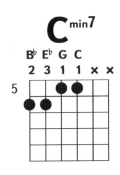

Cmin7

G B♭ E♭
× 3 1 1 × ×
8

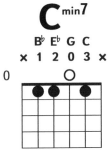

Cmin7

G B♭ E♭
× × 3 1 2 ×
3

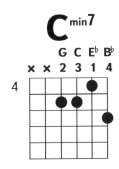

Cmin7

G B♭ E♭
× × × 2 1 1
11

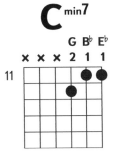

Cmin7

B♭ E♭ G C
2 3 1 1 × ×
5

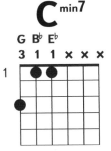

Cmin7

B♭ E♭ G C
× 1 2 0 3 ×
0

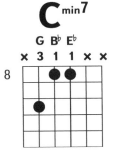

Cmin7

B♭ E♭ G C
× × 1 1 1 1
8

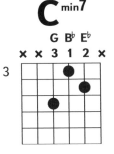

Cmin7

G C E♭ B♭
× × 2 3 1 4
4

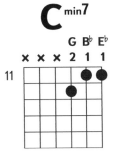

Cmin7♭5

E♭ B♭ C G♭
× 2 4 1 3 ×
5

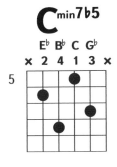

Cmin7♭5

E♭ B♭ C G♭
× × 1 4 1 2
1

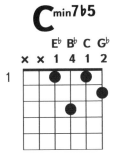

Cmin7♭5

G♭ C E♭ B♭
2 3 1 4 × ×
1

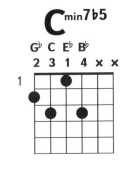

Cmin7♭5

G♭ C E♭ B♭
× 2 3 1 4 ×
8

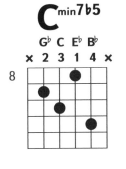

Cmin7♭5

G♭ C E♭ B♭
× × 1 2 1 4
4

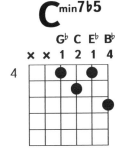

Cmin7♭5

B♭ E♭ G♭ C
× 2 3 1 4 ×
11

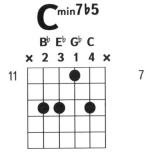

Cmin7♭5

B♭ E♭ G♭ C
× × 2 3 1 4
7

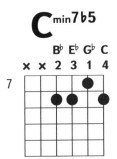

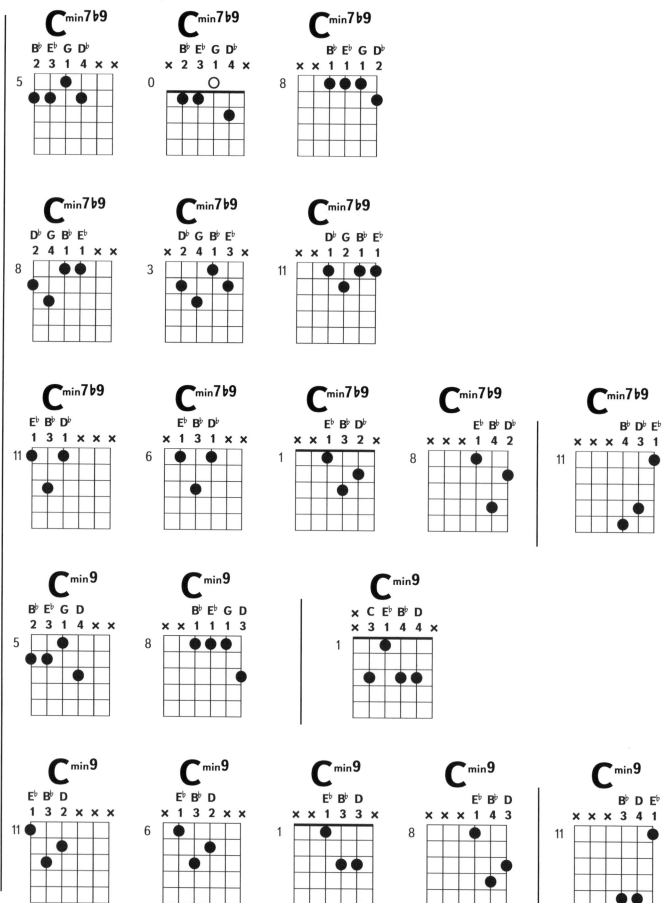

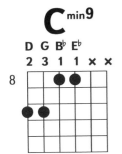

Cmin9
D G Bb Eb
2 3 1 1 × ×
8

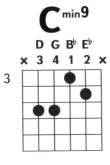

Cmin9
D G Bb Eb
× 3 4 1 2 ×
3

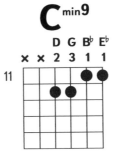

Cmin9
D G Bb Eb
× × 2 3 1 1
11

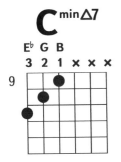

CminΔ7
Eb G B
3 2 1 × × ×
9

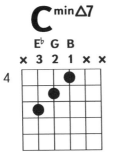

CminΔ7
Eb G B
× 3 2 1 × ×
4

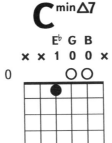

CminΔ7
Eb G B
× × 1 0 0 ×
0

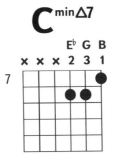

CminΔ7
Eb G B
× × × 2 3 1
7

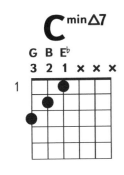

CminΔ7
G B Eb
3 2 1 × × ×
1

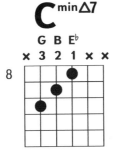

CminΔ7
G B Eb
× 3 2 1 × ×
8

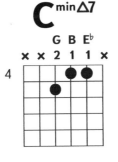

CminΔ7
G B Eb
× × 2 1 1 ×
4

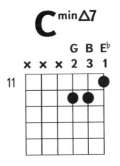

CminΔ7
G B Eb
× × × 2 3 1
11

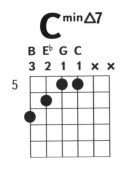

CminΔ7
B Eb G C
3 2 1 1 × ×
5

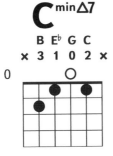

CminΔ7
B Eb G C
× 3 1 0 2 ×
0

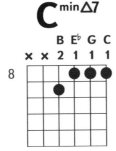

CminΔ7
B Eb G C
× × 2 1 1 1
8

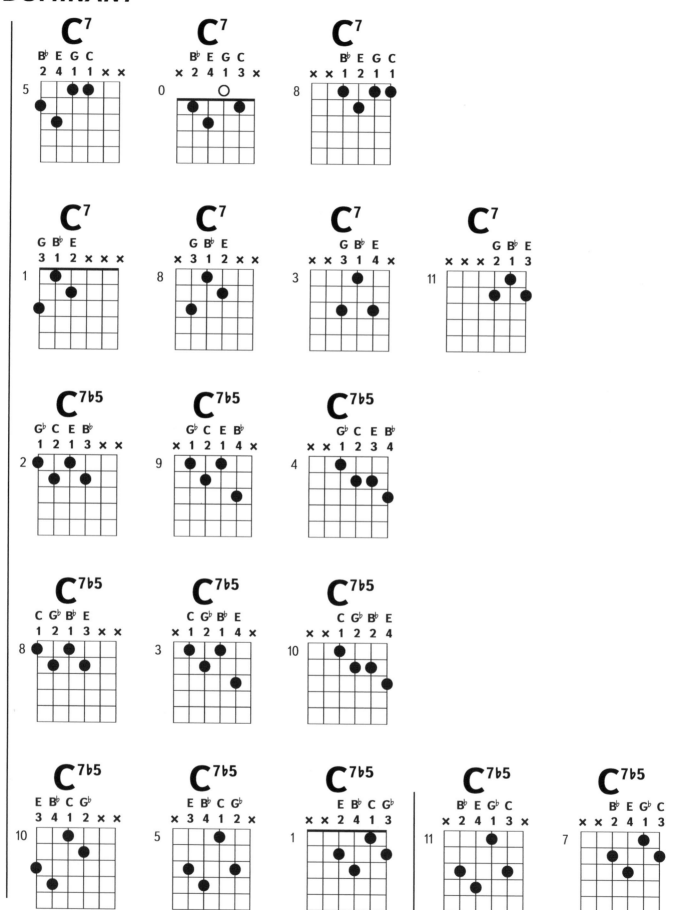

C⁷#⁵
G# C E B♭
4 2 1 3 × ×
2
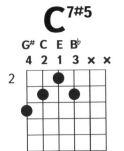

C⁷#⁵
× 3 2 1 4 ×
9
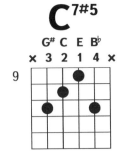

C⁷#⁵
G# C E B♭
× × 2 1 1 3
5
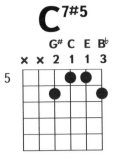

C⁷#⁵
B♭ E G# C
2 4 3 1 × ×
5
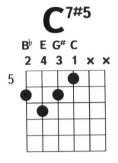

C⁷#⁵
B♭ E G# C
× 1 2 1 1 ×
1
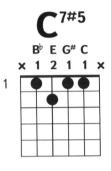

C⁷#⁵
B♭ E G# C
× × 1 2 3 1
8
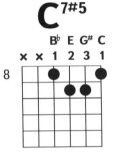

C⁷♭⁹
B♭ E G D♭
2 4 1 3 × ×
5
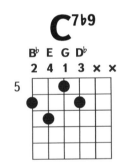

C⁷♭⁹
B♭ E G D♭
× × 1 2 1 3
8
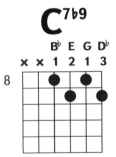

C⁷♭⁹
C E B♭ D♭
× 2 1 3 1
2
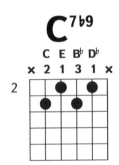

C⁷♭⁹
C E B♭ D♭
× × 2 1 3 1
9
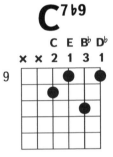

C⁷♭⁹
D♭ G B♭ E
2 4 1 3 × ×
8
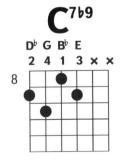

C⁷♭⁹
D♭ G B♭ E
× 2 3 1 4 ×
3
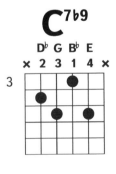

C⁷♭⁹
D♭ G B♭ E
× × 2 3 1 4
11
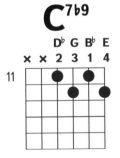

C⁷♭⁹
E B♭ D♭
2 3 1 × × ×
11
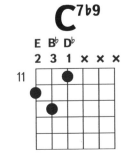

C⁷♭⁹
E B♭ D♭
× 2 4 1 × ×
6
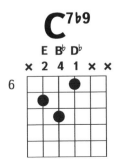

C⁷♭⁹
E B♭ D♭
× × × 2 4 1
9
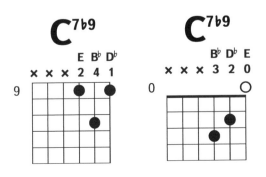

C⁷♭⁹
B♭ D♭ E
× × × 3 2 0
0

VIVID
DOMINANT

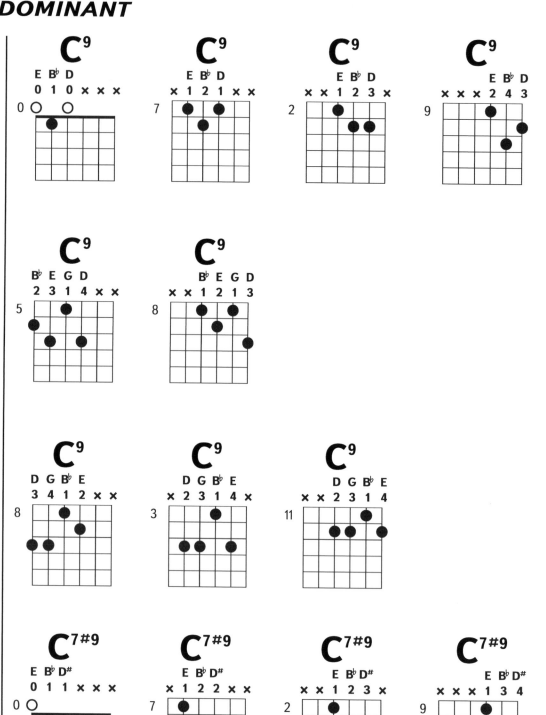

C∅
E♭ G♭ B♭
4 2 1 × × ×
8
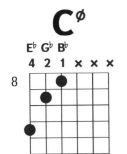

C∅
E♭ G♭ B♭
× 4 2 1 × ×
3
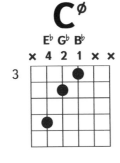

C∅
E♭ G♭ B♭
× × 3 1 1 ×
11
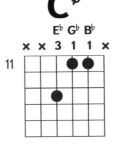

C∅
E♭ G♭ B♭
× × × 3 2 1
6
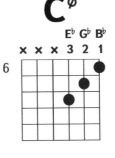

C∅
G♭ B♭ E♭
2 1 1 × × ×
1
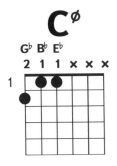

C∅
G♭ B♭ E♭
× 2 1 1 × ×
8
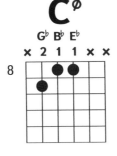

C∅
G♭ B♭ E♭
× × 2 1 3 ×
3
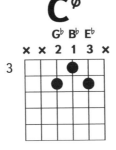

C∅
G♭ B♭ E♭
× × × 1 1 1
11
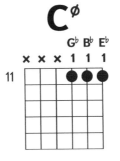

C∅
B♭ E♭ G♭
3 4 1 × × ×
4
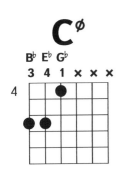

C∅
B♭ E♭ G♭
× 2 3 1 × ×
11
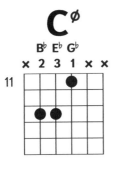

C∅
B♭ E♭ G♭
× × 2 3 1 ×
7
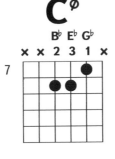

C∅
B♭ E♭ G♭
× × 2 3 1
2

SEEING MUSIC
METHOD BOOKS

96 GUITAR CHORDS ENCYCLOPEDIA: A SEEING MUSIC METHOD BOOK

BIG MAJOR

C#/Db^{Maj}

Db Ab Db F Ab Db
C# G# C# E# G# C#
1 3 4 2 1 1
9

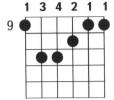

C#/Db^{Maj}

Db Ab Db F
C# G# C# F
× 1 3 3 3 ×
4

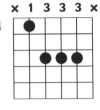

C#/Db^{△7}

Db Ab C F
C# G# B# E#
× 1 3 2 4 ×
4

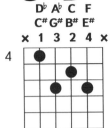

C#/Db^{△7#11}

Db G C F Ab
C# F## B# E# G#
× 1 2 3 4 1
4

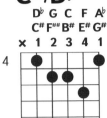

C#/Db^{6/9}

Db   F Bb Eb
C#   E# A# D#
1 × × 2 4 4
9

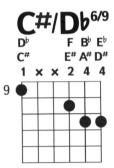

C#/Db^{6/9}

Db F Bb Eb
C# E# A# D#
× 2 1 1 3 ×
3

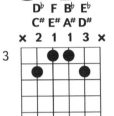

C#/Db^{add9}

Db   F Ab Eb
C#   E# G# D#
1 × × 2 1 4
9

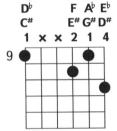

BIG MINOR

C#/Db^{min}

Db Ab Db Fb Ab Db
C# G# C# E G# C#
1 3 4 1 1 1
9

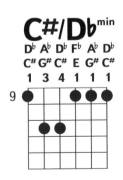

C#/Db^{min}

Db Ab Db Fb Ab
C# G# C# E G#
× 1 3 4 2 1
4

C#/Db^{min7}

Db Ab Cb Fb Ab Db
C# G# B E G# C#
1 3 1 1 1 1
9

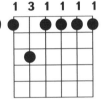

C#/Db^{min7b5}

Db Ab Db Abb Cb Fb
C# G C# G B E
1 2 3 4 4 4
9

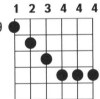

C#/Db^{min7b9}

Db   Cb Fb Ab Ebb
C#   B E G# D
1 × 1 1 1 2
9

C#/Db^{min9}

Db Ab Cb Fb Ab Eb
C# G# B E G# D#
1 3 1 1 1 4
9

C#/Db^{min△7}

Db Ab C Fb Ab
C# G# B# E G#
× 1 4 2 3 1
4

C#/Db⁷

D♭ A♭ C♭ F A♭ D♭
C# G# B E# G# C#
1 3 1 2 1 1
9

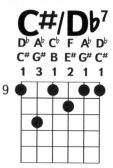

C#/Db⁷

D♭ A♭ C♭ F A♭
C# G# B E# G#
× 1 3 1 4 1
4

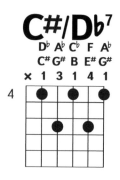

C#/Db⁷♭⁵

D♭ A♭ C♭ F
C# G B E#
× × 1 2 2 4
11

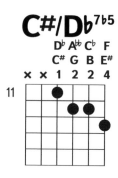

C#/Db⁷#⁵

D♭ F C♭ F A
C# E# B E# G##
1 2 3 4 4 ×
8

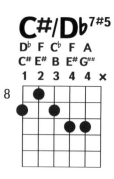

C#/Db⁷#⁵

D♭ A C♭ F A
C# G## B E# G##
× 1 4 1 3 2
4

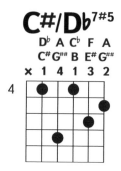

C#/Db⁷♭⁹

D♭ C♭ F A♭ E♭♭
C# B E# G# D
1 × 1 2 1 3
9

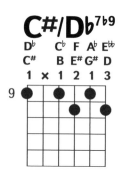

C#/Db⁹

D♭ A♭ C♭ F A♭ E♭
C# G# B E# G# D#
1 3 1 2 1 4
9

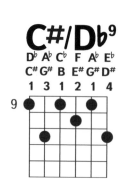

C#/Db⁹

D♭ F C♭ E♭
C# E# B D#
× 2 1 3 4 ×
3

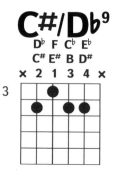

C#/Db⁷#⁹

D♭ C♭ F C♭ E
C# B E# B D##
1 × 1 2 4 4
9

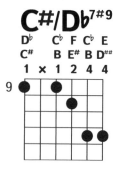

C#/Db⁷#⁹

D♭ C♭ F A♭ E
C# B E# G# D##
1 × 1 2 1 4
9

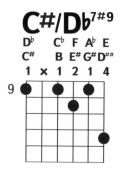

C#/Db⁷#⁹

D♭ F C♭ E
C# E# B D##
× 2 1 3 4 ×
3

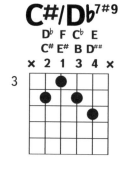

C#/Db⁷#⁹

D♭ F C♭ E
C# E# B D##
× × 2 1 4 4
10

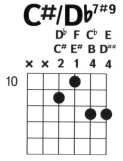

BIG
AUGMENTED

C#/Db ^{Aug}
Db F A Db
C# E# G## C#
4 3 2 1 × ×
6
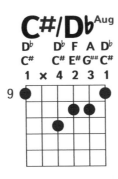

C#/Db ^{Aug}
Db F A Db
C# E# G## C#
× 3 2 1 1 ×
2
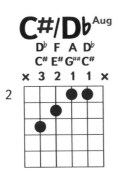

C#/Db ^{Aug}
Db Db F A Db
C# C# E# G## C#
1 × 4 2 3 1
9
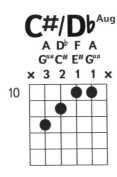

C#/Db ^{Aug}
A Db F A
G## C# E# G##
× 3 2 1 1 ×
10
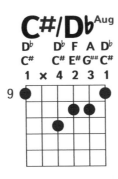

C#/Db ^{Aug}
F A Db F
E# G## C# E#
× 3 2 1 1 ×
6
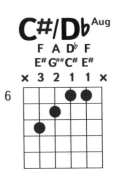

BIG
DIMINISHED

C#/Db ^ø
Db Ab Db Ab Cb Fb
C# G C# G B E
1 2 3 4 4 4
9
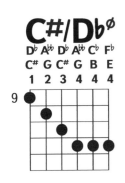

C#/Db ^{dim}
Db Cbb Fb Abb Db
C# Bb E G C#
2 × 1 3 1 4
8
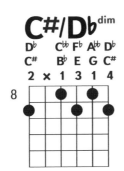

BIG
STACKED 5THS

C#/Db ^{5 sus}
Db Ab Db Gb
C# G# C# F#
× 1 3 4 1 ×
4
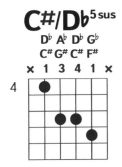

C#/Db ^{5 add9}
Db Ab Db Eb Ab
C# G# C# D# G#
× 1 3 4 1 1
4
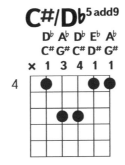

C#/Db ^{add6/9}
Db Ab Eb Bb
C# G# D# A#
× 1 3 × 1 4
4
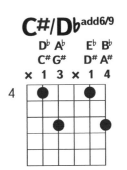

COMPACT
MAJOR

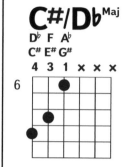
C#/Db^Maj
Db F Ab
C# E# G#
4 3 1 × × ×
6

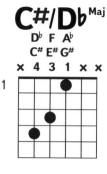
C#/Db^Maj
Db F Ab
C# E# G#
× 4 3 1 × ×
1

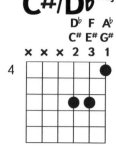
C#/Db^Maj
Db F Ab
C# E# G#
× × 3 2 1 ×
9

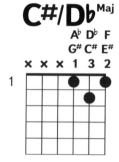
C#/Db^Maj
Db F Ab
C# E# G#
× × × 2 3 1
4

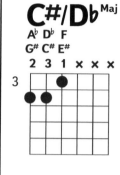
C#/Db^Maj
Ab Db F
G# C# E#
2 3 1 × × ×
3

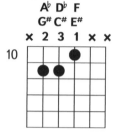
C#/Db^Maj
Ab Db F
G# C# E#
× 2 3 1 × ×
10

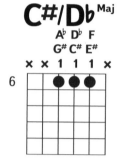
C#/Db^Maj
Ab Db F
G# C# E#
× × 1 1 1 ×
6

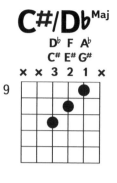
C#/Db^Maj
Ab Db F
G# C# E#
× × × 1 3 2
1

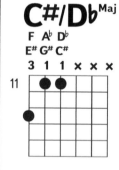
C#/Db^Maj
F Ab Db
E# G# C#
3 1 1 × × ×
11

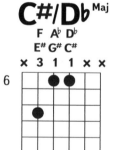
C#/Db^Maj
F Ab Db
E# G# C#
× 3 1 1 × ×
6

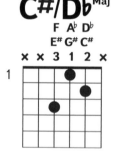
C#/Db^Maj
F Ab Db
E# G# C#
× × 3 1 2 ×
1

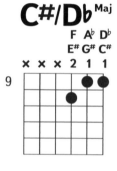
C#/Db^Maj
F Ab Db
E# G# C#
× × × 2 1 1
9

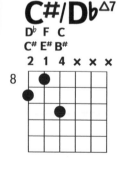
C#/Db^△7
Db F C
C# E# B#
2 1 4 × × ×
8

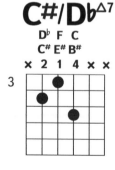
C#/Db^△7
Db F C
C# E# B#
× 2 1 4 × ×
3

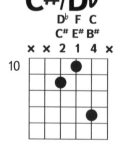
C#/Db^△7
Db F C
C# E# B#
× × 2 1 4 ×
10

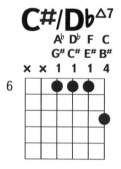
C#/Db^△7
Ab Db F C
G# C# E# B#
× × 1 1 1 4
6

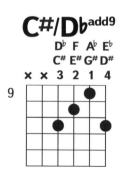
C#/Db^add9
Db F Ab Eb
C# E# G# D#
× × 3 2 1 4
9

100 GUITAR CHORDS ENCYCLOPEDIA: A SEEING MUSIC METHOD BOOK

C#/Db

COMPACT
MINOR

C#/Db min — Db Fb Ab / C# E G# — 4 2 1 × × × — fret 6
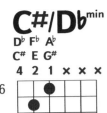

C#/Db min — Db Fb Ab / C# E G# — × 4 2 1 × × — fret 1
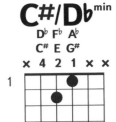

C#/Db min — Db Fb Ab / C# E G# — × × 3 1 1 × — fret 9
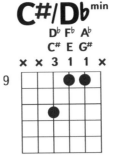

C#/Db min — Db Fb Ab / C# E G# — × × × 3 2 1 — fret 4
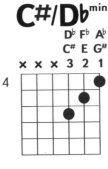

C#/Db min — Fb Ab Db / E G# C# — 2 1 1 × × × — fret 11
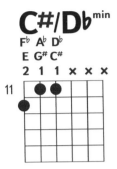

C#/Db min — Fb Ab Db / E G# C# — × 2 1 1 × × — fret 6
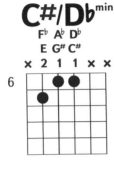

C#/Db min — Fb Ab Db / E G# C# — × × 2 1 3 × — fret 1
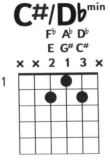

C#/Db min — Fb Ab Db / E G# C# — × × × 1 1 1 — fret 9
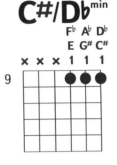

C#/Db min — Ab Db Fb / G# C# E — 3 4 1 × × × — fret 2
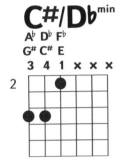

C#/Db min — Ab Db Fb / G# C# E — × 3 4 1 × × — fret 9
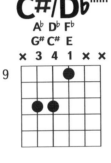

C#/Db min — Ab Db Fb / G# C# E — × × 2 3 1 × — fret 5
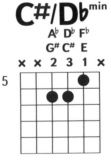

C#/Db min — Ab Db Fb / G# C# E — × × × 1 2 0 — fret 0
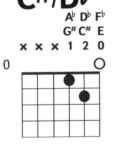

C#/Db min7 — Db Fb Cb / C# E B — 3 1 4 × × × — fret 7
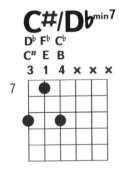

C#/Db min7 — Db Fb Cb / C# E B — × 3 1 4 × × — fret 2
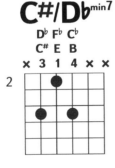

C#/Db min7 — Db Fb Cb / C# E B — × × 3 1 4 × — fret 9
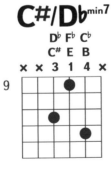

C#/Db min7 — Db Fb Cb / C# E B — × × × 2 1 4 — fret 5
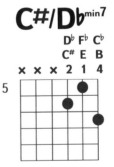

C#/Db min7 — Fb Cb Db / E B C# — 2 4 1 × × × — fret 11
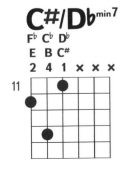

C#/Db min7 — Fb Cb Db / E B C# — × 2 4 1 × × — fret 6
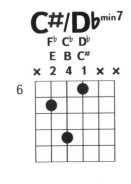

C#/Db min7 — Fb Cb Db / E B C# — × × 1 3 1 × — fret 2
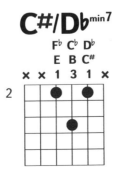

C#/Db min7 — Fb Cb Db / E B C# — × × × 1 4 1 — fret 9
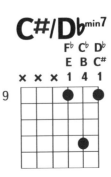

C#/Db min7 — Cb Db Fb / B C# E — × × × 3 1 0 — fret 0
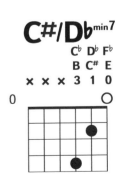

COMPACT
MINOR (CONT.)

C#/Db min7b5
D♭ A♭♭ C♭ F♭
C# G B E
1 2 1 1 × ×
9
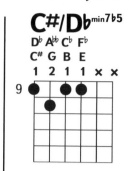

C#/Db min7b5
D♭ A♭♭ C♭ F♭
C# G B E
× 1 2 1 3 ×
4
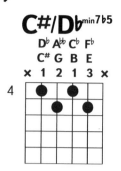

C#/Db min7b9
D♭ F♭ C♭ E♭♭
C# E B D
3 1 4 1 × ×
7
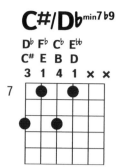

C#/Db min7b9
D♭ F♭ C♭ E♭♭
C# E B D
× 3 1 4 2 ×
2
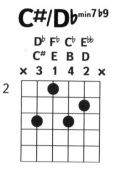

COMPACT
DOMINANT

C#/Db 7
D♭ F C♭
C# E# B
2 1 3 × × ×
8
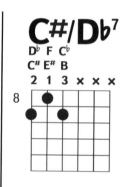

C#/Db 7
D♭ F C♭
C# E# B
× 2 1 3 × ×
3
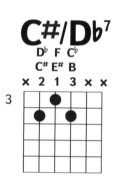

C#/Db 7
D♭ F C♭
C# E# B
× × 2 1 4 ×
10
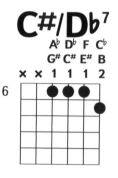

C#/Db 7
A♭ D♭ F C♭
G# C# E# B
× × 1 1 1 2
6
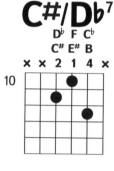

C#/Db 7
F C♭ D♭
E# B C#
3 4 1 × × ×
11
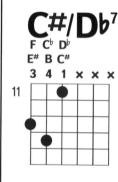

C#/Db 7
F C♭ D♭
E# B C#
× 3 4 1 × ×
6
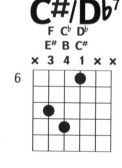

C#/Db 7
F C♭ D♭
E# B C#
× × × 2 4 1
9
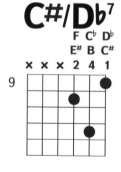

C#/Db 7
C♭ D♭ F
B C# E#
× × × 4 2 1
1
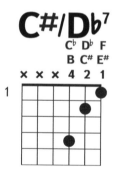

C#/Db 7#5
D♭ A C♭ F
C# G## B E#
1 4 1 2 × ×
9
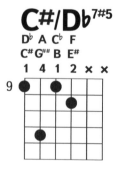

C#/Db 7#5
D♭ A C♭ F A
C# G## B E# G##
× 1 4 1 3 2
4
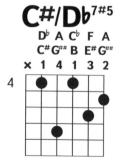

COMPACT
DIMINISHED

C#/Db^dim
D♭ A♭♭ C♭♭ F♭
C# G B♭ E
2 4 1 3 × ×
8
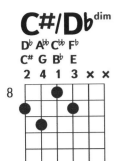

C#/Db^dim
D♭ A♭♭ C♭♭ F♭
C# G B♭ E
× 2 3 1 4 ×
3
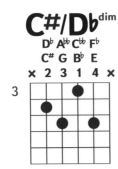

C#/Db^dim
D♭ A♭♭ C♭♭ F♭
C# G B♭ E
× × 1 2 1 3
11
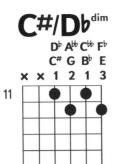

C#/Db^dim
F♭ C♭♭ D♭ A♭♭
E B♭ C# G
2 4 1 3 × ×
11
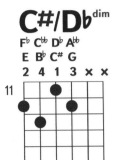

C#/Db^dim
F♭ C♭♭ D♭ A♭♭
E B♭ C# G
× 2 3 1 4 ×
6
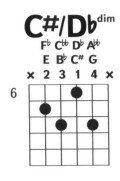

C#/Db^dim
F♭ C♭♭ D♭ A♭♭
E B♭ C# G
× × 1 2 1 3
2
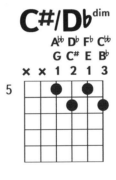

C#/Db^dim
A♭♭ D♭ F♭ C♭♭
G C# E B♭
2 4 1 3 × ×
2
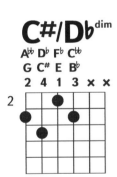

C#/Db^dim
A♭♭ D♭ F♭ C♭♭
G C# E B♭
× 2 3 1 4 ×
9
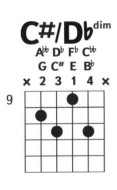

C#/Db^dim
A♭♭ D♭ F♭ C♭♭
G C# E B♭
× × 1 2 1 3
5
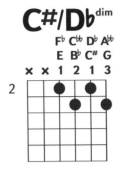

C#/Db^dim
C♭♭ F♭ A♭♭ D♭
A# E G C#
2 4 1 3 × ×
5
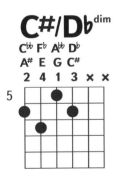

C#/Db^dim
C♭♭ F♭ A♭♭ D♭
B♭ E G C#
× 1 2 0 3 ×
0
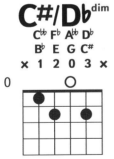

C#/Db^dim
C♭♭ F♭ A♭♭ D♭
A# E G C#
× × 1 2 1 3
8
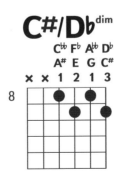

COMPACT
DIMINISHED (CONT.)

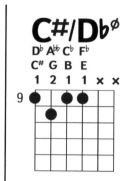

C#/Db^ø
Db Abb Cb Fb
C# G B E
1 2 1 1 x x
9

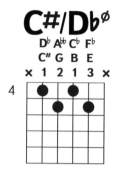

C#/Db^ø
Db Abb Cb Fb
C# G B E
x 1 2 1 3 x
4

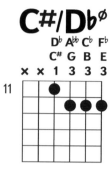

C#/Db^ø
Db Abb Cb Fb
C# G B E
x x 1 3 3 3
11

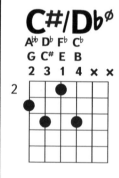

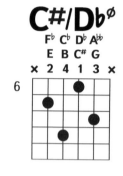

C#/Db^ø
Fb Cb Db Abb
E B C# G
x 2 4 1 3 x
6

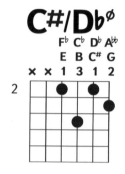

C#/Db^ø
Fb Cb Db Abb
E B C# G
x x 1 3 1 2
2

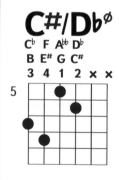

C#/Db^ø
Abb Db Fb Cb
G C# E B
2 3 1 4 x x
2

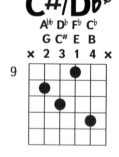

C#/Db^ø
Abb Db Fb Cb
G C# E B
x 2 3 1 4 x
9

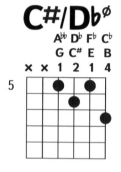

C#/Db^ø
Abb Db Fb Cb
G C# E B
x x 1 2 1 4
5

C#/Db^ø
Cb F Abb Db
B E# G C#
3 4 1 2 x x
5

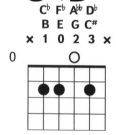

C#/Db^ø
Cb Fb Abb Db
B E G C#
x 1 0 2 3 x
0

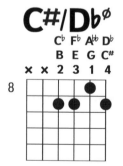

C#/Db^ø
Cb Fb Abb Db
B E G C#
x x 2 3 1 4
8

104 GUITAR CHORDS ENCYCLOPEDIA: A SEEING MUSIC METHOD BOOK

COMPACT
AUGMENTED

C#/Db Aug
Db F A
C# F G##
3 2 1 × × ×
7

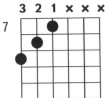

C#/Db Aug
Db F A
C# E# G##
× 3 2 1 × ×
2

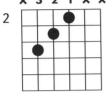

C#/Db Aug
Db F A
C# E# G##
× × 2 1 1 ×
10

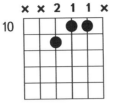

C#/Db Aug
Db F A
C# E# G##
× × × 2 3 1
5

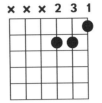

C#/Db Aug
F A Db
E# G## C#
3 2 1 × × ×
11

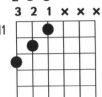

C#/Db Aug
F A Db
E# G## C#
× 3 2 1 × ×
6

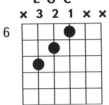

C#/Db Aug
F A Db
E# G## C#
× × 3 2 1 ×
2

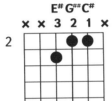

C#/Db Aug
F A Db
E# G## C#
× × × 2 3 1
9

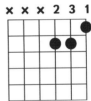

C#/Db Aug
A Db F
G## C# E#
3 2 1 × × ×
3

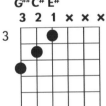

C#/Db Aug
A Db F
G## C# F
× 3 2 1 × ×
10

C#/Db Aug
A Db F
G## C# E#
× × 2 1 1 ×
6

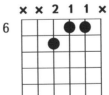

C#/Db Aug
A Db F
G## C# E#
× × × 2 3 1
1

COMPACT
STACKED 5THS

C#/Db⁵
Db Ab
C# G#
1 3 x x x x
9
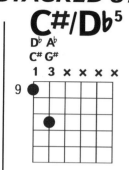

C#/Db⁵
Db Ab
C# G#
x 1 3 x x x
4
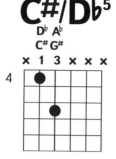

C#/Db⁵
Db Ab
C# G#
x x 1 3 x x
11
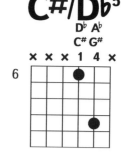

C#/Db⁵
Db Ab
C# G#
x x x 1 4 x
6
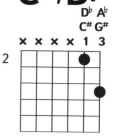

C#/Db⁵
Db Ab
C# G#
x x x x 1 3
2
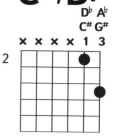

C#/Db⁵
Ab Db
G# C#
1 1 x x x x
4
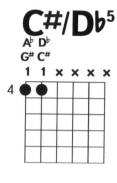

C#/Db⁵
Ab Db
G# C#
x 1 1 x x x
11
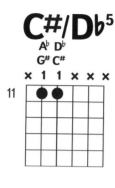

C#/Db⁵
Ab Db
G# C#
x x 1 1 x x
6
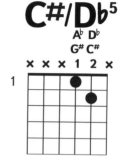

C#/Db⁵
Ab Db
G# C#
x x x 1 2 x
1
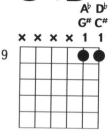

C#/Db⁵
Ab Db
G# C#
x x x x 1 1
9
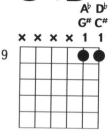

C#/Db⁵ˢᵘˢ
Gb Ab Db
F# G# C#
4 1 1 x x x
11
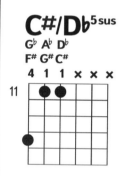

C#/Db⁵ˢᵘˢ
Db Gb Ab
C# F# G#
x x x 2 4 1
4
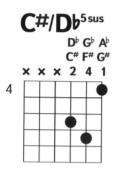

C#/Db⁵ˢᵘˢ
Gb Ab Db
F# G# C#
x x 4 1 2 x
1
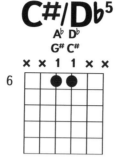

C#/Db⁵ˢᵘˢ
Gb Ab Db
F# G# C#
x x x 3 1 1
9
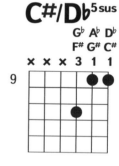

C#/Db⁵ˢᵘˢ
Db Gb Ab
C# F# G#
3 4 1 x x x
6
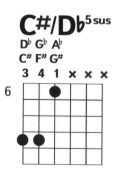

C#/Db⁵ˢᵘˢ
Db Gb Ab
C# F# G#
x 3 4 1 x x
1
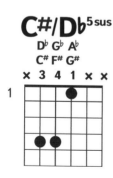

C#/Db⁵ˢᵘˢ
Db Gb Ab
C# F# G#
x x 3 4 1 x
9
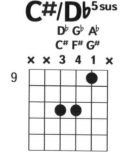

C#/Db⁵ˢᵘˢ
Db Gb Ab
C# F# G#
x x x 2 4 1
4
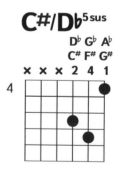

C#/Db⁵ˢᵘˢ
Ab Db Gb
G# C# F#
1 1 1 x x x
4
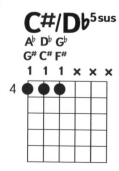

C#/Db⁵ˢᵘˢ
Ab Db Gb
G# C# F#
x 1 1 1 x x
11
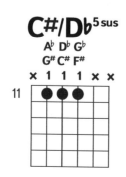

C#/Db⁵ˢᵘˢ
Ab Db Gb
G# C# F#
x x 1 1 2 x
6
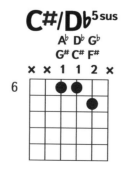

C#/Db⁵ˢᵘˢ
Ab Db Gb
G# C# F#
x x x 1 2 2
1
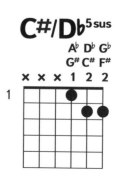

106 GUITAR CHORDS ENCYCLOPEDIA: A SEEING MUSIC METHOD BOOK

C#/Db⁵ᵃᵈᵈ⁹

E♭　　D♭ A♭
D#　　C# G#
1　×　1　4　×　×
11

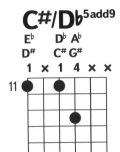

C#/Db⁵ᵃᵈᵈ⁹

E♭　　D♭ A♭
D#　　C# G#
×　1　×　1　4　×
6

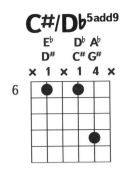

C#/Db⁵ᵃᵈᵈ⁹

E♭　　D♭ A♭
D#　　C# G#
×　×　1　×　2　4
1

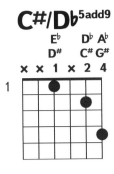

C#/Db⁵ᵃᵈᵈ⁹

E♭ A♭ D♭
D# G# C#
1　1　1　×　×　×
11

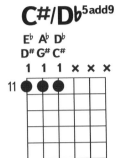

C#/Db⁵ᵃᵈᵈ⁹

E♭ A♭ D♭
D# G# C#
×　1　1　1　×　×
6

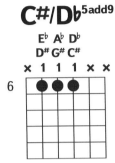

C#/Db⁵ᵃᵈᵈ⁹

E♭ A♭ D♭
D# G# C#
×　×　1　1　2　×
1

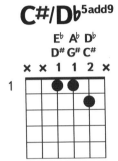

C#/Db⁵ᵃᵈᵈ⁹

E♭ A♭ D♭
D# G# C#
×　×　×　1　2　3
8

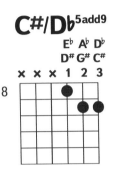

C#/Db⁵ᵃᵈᵈ⁹

D♭ A♭ E♭
C# G# D#
1　3　4　×　×　×
9

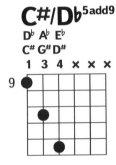

C#/Dbᵃᵈᵈ⁹

D♭ A♭ E♭
C# G# D#
×　1　3　4　×　×
4

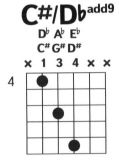

C#/Db⁵ᵃᵈᵈ⁶ᐟ⁹

E♭ B♭ D♭ A♭
D# A# C# G#
1　3　1　4　×　×
11

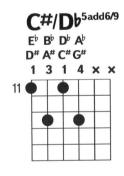

C#/Db⁵ᵃᵈᵈ⁶ᐟ⁹

E♭ B♭ D♭ A♭
D# A# C# G#
×　1　3　1　4　×
6

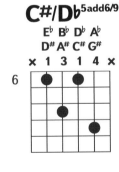

C#/Db⁵ᵃᵈᵈ⁶ᐟ⁹

E♭ B♭ D♭ A♭
D# A# C# G#
×　×　1　3　2　4
1

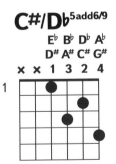

C#/Db⁵ᵃᵈᵈ⁶ᐟ⁹

B♭ E♭ A♭ D♭
A# D# G# C#
1　1　1　1　×　×
6

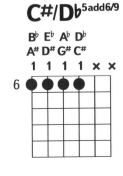

C#/Db⁵ᵃᵈᵈ⁶ᐟ⁹

B♭ E♭ A♭ D♭
A# D# G# C#
×　1　1　1　2　×
1

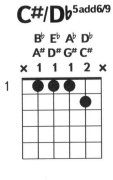

C#/Db⁵ᵃᵈᵈ⁶ᐟ⁹

B♭ E♭ A♭ D♭
A# D# G# C#
×　×　1　1　2　3
8

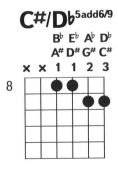

C#/Db△7
C F Ab Db
B# E# G# C#
3 4 1 1 × ×

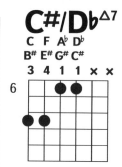

C#/Db△7
C F Ab Db
B# E# G# C#
× 3 4 1 2 ×

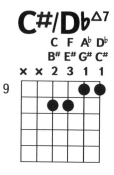

C#/Db△7
C F Ab Db
B# E# G# C#
× × 2 3 1 1

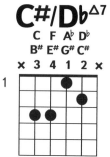

C#/Db△9
C F Ab Eb
B# E# G# D#
2 3 1 4 × ×

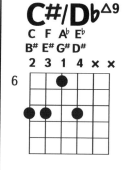

C#/Db△9
C F Ab Eb
B# E# G# D#
× 2 3 1 4 ×

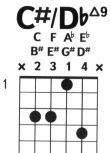

C#/Db△9
C F Ab Eb
B# E# G# D#
× × 2 3 1 4

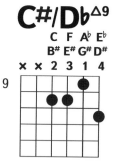

C#/Db6/9
F Bb Eb Ab
E# A# D# G#
1 1 1 1 × ×

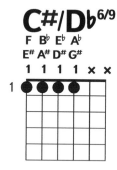

C#/Db6/9
F Bb Eb Ab
E# A# D# G#
× 1 1 1 2 ×

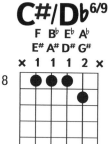

C#/Db6/9
F Bb Eb Ab
E# A# D# G#
× × 1 1 2 3

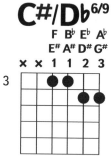

C#/Db6/9
F Bb Eb
E# A# D#
× × × 1 2 2

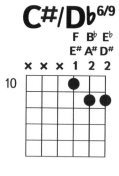

C#/Db6/9
Bb F Ab Eb
A# E# G# D#
1 3 1 4 × ×

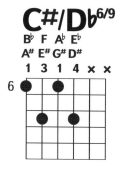

C#/Db6/9
Bb F Ab Eb
A# E# G# D#
× 1 3 1 4 ×

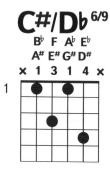

C#/Db6/9
Bb F Ab Eb
A# E# G# D#
× × 1 3 2 4

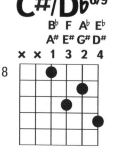

C#/Db△7#11
G Db F C
F## C# E# B#
1 2 1 4 × ×

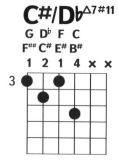

C#/Db△7#11
G Db F C
F## C# F B#
× × 1 2 3 4

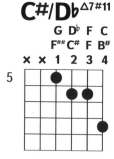

C#/Db△7#11
D♭ G C F
C# F## B# E#
1 2 3 4 × ×
9
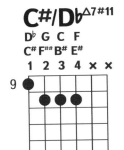

C#/Db△7#11
D♭ G C F
C# F## B# E#
× 1 2 3 4 ×
4
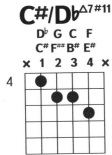

C#/Db△7#11
D♭ G C F
C# F## B# E#
× × 1 2 3 4
11
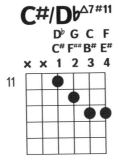

C#/Db△7#11
C F G D♭
B# E# F## C#
× × 3 4 1 2
8
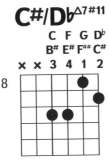

VIVID
MAJOR (CONT.)

VIVID
MINOR

C#/Db min7
A♭ C♭ F♭
G# B E
3 1 1 × × ×
2
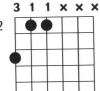

C#/Db min7
A♭ C♭ F♭
G# B E
× 3 1 1 × ×
9

C#/Db min7
A♭ C♭ F♭
G# B E
× × 3 1 2 ×
4
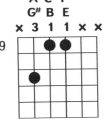

C#/Db min7
A♭ C♭ F♭
G# B E
× × × 1 0 0
0
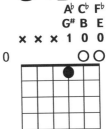

C#/Db min7
C♭ F♭ A♭ D♭
B E G# C#
2 3 1 1 × ×
6
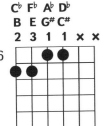

C#/Db min7
C♭ F♭ A♭ D♭
× 2 3 1 4 ×
1

C#/Db min7
C♭ F♭ A♭ D♭
B E G# C#
× × 1 1 1 1
9
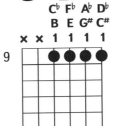

C#/Db min7
A♭ D♭ F♭ C♭
G# C# E B
× × 2 3 1 4
5
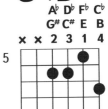

C#/Db min7b5
F♭ C♭ D♭ A♭♭
E B C# G
× 2 4 1 3 ×
6
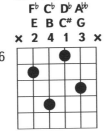

C#/Db min7b5
F♭ C♭ D♭ A♭♭
E B C# G
× × 1 4 1 2
2
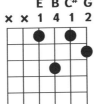

C#/Db min7b5
A♭♭ D♭ F♭ C♭
G C# E B
2 3 1 4 × ×
2
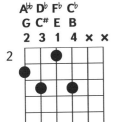

C#/Db min7b5
A♭♭ D♭ F♭ C♭
G C# E B
× 2 3 1 4 ×
9
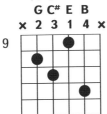

C#/Db min7b5
A♭♭ D♭ F♭ C♭
G C# E B
× × 1 2 1 4
5
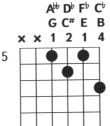

C#/Db min7b5
C♭ F♭ A♭♭ D♭
B E G C#
× 1 0 2 3 ×
0
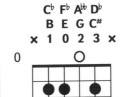

C#/Db min7b5
C♭ F♭ A♭♭ D♭
B E G C#
× × 2 3 1 4
8
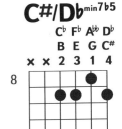

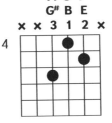
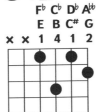

VIVID
MINOR (CONT.)

C#/D♭^{min7♭9}

C♭ F♭ A♭ E♭♭
B E G# D
2 3 1 4 × ×
6
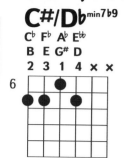

C#/D♭^{min7♭9}

C♭ F♭ A♭ E♭♭
B E G# D
× 2 3 1 4 ×
1
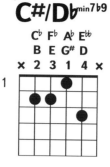

C#/D♭^{min7♭9}

C♭ F♭ A♭ E♭♭
B E G# D
× × 1 1 1 2
9
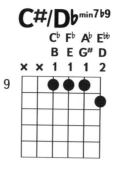

C#/D♭^{min7♭9}

E♭♭ A♭ C♭ F♭
D G# B E
2 4 1 1 × ×
9
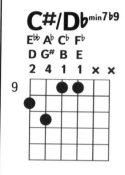

C#/D♭^{min7♭9}

E♭♭ A♭ C♭ F♭
D G# B E
× 2 4 1 3 ×
4
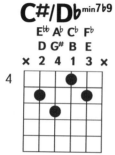

C#/D♭^{min7♭9}

E♭♭ A♭ C♭ F♭
D G# B E
× × 0 1 0 0
0
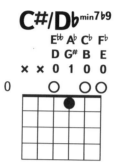

C#/D♭^{min7♭9}

F♭ C♭ E♭♭
E B D
0 2 0 × × ×
0
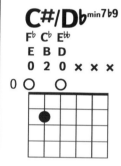

C#/D♭^{min7♭9}

F♭ C♭ E♭♭
E B D
× 1 3 1 × ×
7
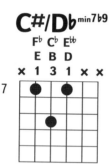

C#/D♭^{min7♭9}

F♭ C♭ E♭♭
E B D
× × 1 3 2 ×
2
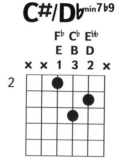

C#/D♭^{min7♭9}

F♭ C♭ E♭♭
E B D
× × × 1 4 2
9
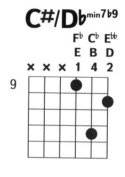

C#/D♭^{min7♭9}

C♭ E♭♭ F♭
B D E
× × × 2 1 0
0
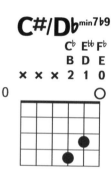

C#/D♭^{min9}

C♭ F♭ A♭ E♭
B E G# D#
2 3 1 4 × ×
6
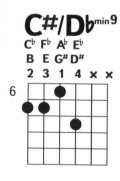

C#/D♭^{min9}

C♭ F♭ A♭ E♭
B E G# D#
× × 1 1 1 3
9
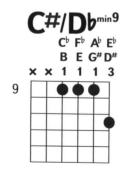

C#/D♭^{min9}

D♭ F♭ C♭ E♭
C# E B D#
× 3 1 4 4 ×
2
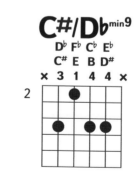

C#/D♭^{min9}

F♭ C♭ E♭
E B D#
1 3 2 × × ×
0
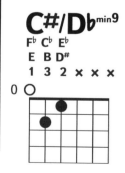

C#/D♭^{min9}

F♭ C♭ E♭
E B D#
× 1 3 2 × ×
7
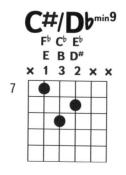

C#/D♭^{min9}

F♭ C♭ E♭
E B D#
× × 1 3 3 ×
2
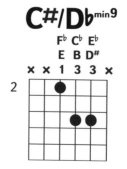

C#/D♭^{min9}

F♭ C♭ E♭
E B D#
× × × 1 4 3
9
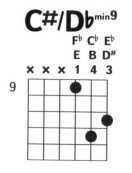

C#/D♭^{min9}

C♭ E♭♭ F♭
B D# E
× × × 1 2 0
0
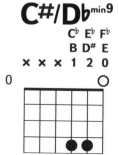

110 GUITAR CHORDS ENCYCLOPEDIA: A SEEING MUSIC METHOD BOOK

VIVID
MINOR (CONT.)

C#/Db min9
Eb Ab Cb Fb
D# G# B E
2 3 1 1 × ×
9
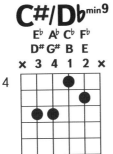

C#/Db min9
Eb Ab Cb Fb
D# G# B E
× 3 4 1 2 ×
4
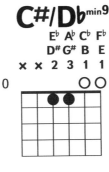

C#/Db min9
Eb Ab Cb Fb
D# G# B E
× × 2 3 1 1
0
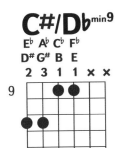

C#/Db min△7
Fb Ab C
E G# B#
3 2 1 × × ×
10
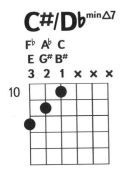

C#/Db min△7
Fb Ab C
E G# B#
× 3 2 1 × ×
5
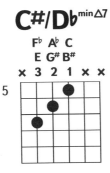

C#/Db min△7
Fb Ab C
E G# B#
× × 2 1 1 ×
1
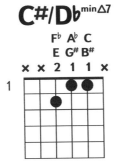

C#/Db min△7
Fb Ab C
E G# B#
× × × 2 3 1
8
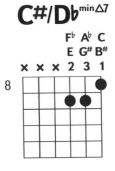

C#/Db min△7
Ab C Fb
G# B# E
3 2 1 × × ×
2
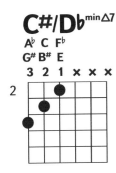

C#/Db min△7
Ab C Fb
G# B# E
× 3 2 1 × ×
9
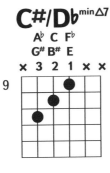

C#/Db min△7
Ab C Fb
G# B# E
× × 2 1 1 ×
5
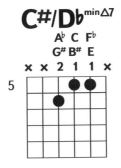

C#/Db min△7
Ab C Fb
G# B# E
× × × 2 3 1
0
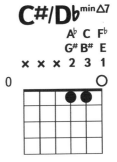

C#/Db min△7
C Fb Ab Db
B# E G# C#
3 2 1 1 × ×
6
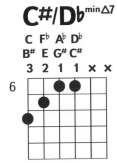

C#/Db min△7
C Fb Ab Db
B# E G# C#
× 4 2 1 3 ×
1
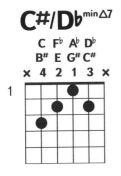

C#/Db min△7
C Fb Ab Db
B# E G# C#
× × 2 1 1 1
9

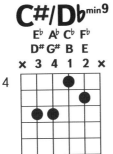

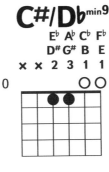

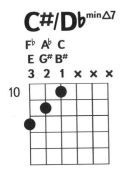

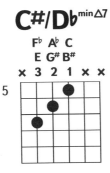

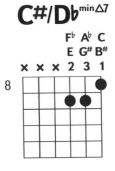

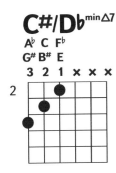

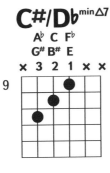

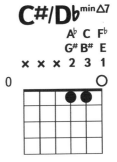

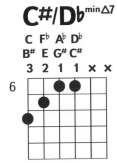

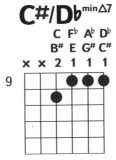

C#/Db⁷
Cb F Ab Db
B E# G# C#
2 4 1 1 x x
6
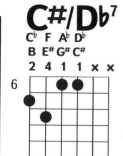

C#/Db⁷
Cb F Ab Db
B E# G# C#
x 2 4 1 3 x
1
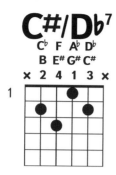

C#/Db⁷
Cb F Ab Db
B E# G# C#
x x 1 2 1 1
9
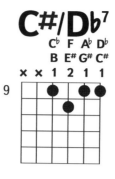

C#/Db⁷
Ab Cb F
G# B E#
3 1 2 x x x
2
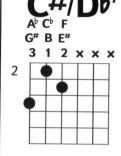

C#/Db⁷
Ab Cb F
G# B E#
x 3 1 2 x x
9
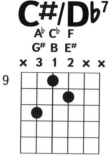

C#/Db⁷
Ab Cb F
G# B E#
x x 3 1 4 x
4
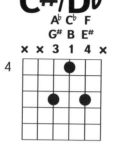

C#/Db⁷
Ab Cb F
G# B E#
x x x 1 0 2
0
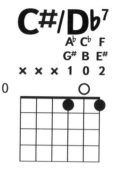

C#/Db⁷
Ab Cb F
G# B E#
3 1 2 x x x
2
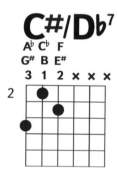

C#/Db⁷ᵇ⁵
Abb Db F Cb
G C# E# B
x 1 2 1 4 x
10
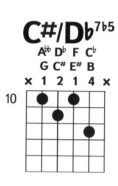

C#/Db⁷
Ab Cb F
G# B E#
x x 3 1 4 x
4
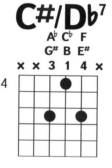

C#/Db⁷ᵇ⁵
Db Abb Cb F
C# G B E#
1 2 1 3 x x
9
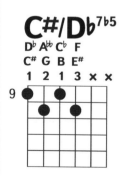

C#/Db⁷ᵇ⁵
Db Abb Cb F
C# G B F
x 1 2 1 4 x
4
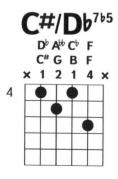

C#/Db⁷ᵇ⁵
Db Abb Cb F
C# G B E#
x x 1 2 2 4
11
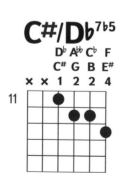

C#/Db⁷ᵇ⁵
F Cb Db Abb
E# B C# G
3 4 1 2 x x
11
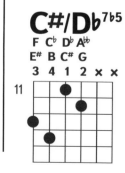

C#/Db⁷ᵇ⁵
F Cb Db Abb
E# B C# G
x 3 4 1 2 x
6
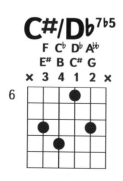

C#/Db⁷ᵇ⁵
F Cb Db Abb
E# B C# G
x x 2 4 1 3
2
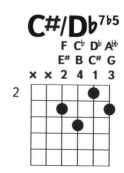

C#/Db⁷ᵇ⁵
Cb F Abb Db
B E# G C#
x 1 3 0 2 x
0
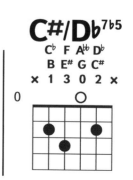

C#/Db⁷
Cb F Ab Db
B E# G# C#
x x 1 2 1 1
9
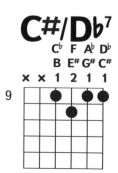

VIVID
DOMINANT (CONT.)

C#/Db⁷#⁵
A Db F Cb
G## C# E# B
4 2 1 3 × ×
3
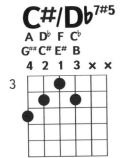

C#/Db⁷#⁵
A Db F Cb
G## C# E# B
× 3 2 1 4 ×
10
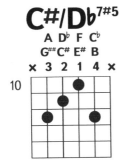

C#/Db⁷#⁵
A Db F Cb
G## C# E# B
× × 2 1 1 3
6
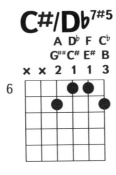

C#/Db⁷#⁵
Cb F A Db
B E# G## C#
2 4 3 1 × ×
6
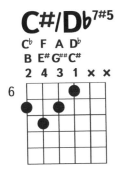

C#/Db⁷#⁵
Cb F A Db
B E# G## C#
× 1 2 1 1 ×
2
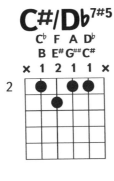

C#/Db⁷#⁵
Cb F A Db
B E# G## C#
× × 1 2 3 1
9
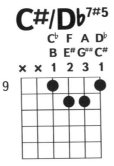

C#/Db⁷b⁹
Cb F Ab Ebb
B E# G# D
2 4 1 3 × ×
6
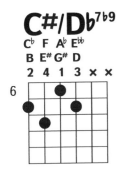

C#/Db⁷b⁹
Cb F Ab Ebb
B E# G# D
× × 1 2 1 3
9
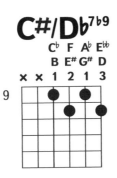

C#/Db⁷b⁹
Db F Cb Ebb
C# E# B D
× 2 1 3 1 ×
3
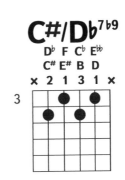

C#/Db⁷b⁹
Db F Cb Ebb
C# E# B D
× × 2 1 3 1
10
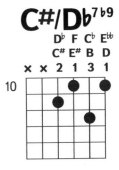

C#/Db⁷b⁹
Ebb Ab Cb F
D G# B E#
2 4 1 3 × ×
9
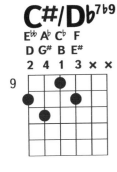

C#/Db⁷b⁹
Ebb Ab Cb F
D G# B E#
× 2 3 1 4 ×
4
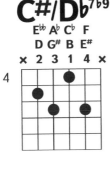

C#/Db⁷b⁹
Ebb Ab Cb F
D G# B E#
× × 0 1 0 2
0
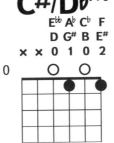

C#/Db⁷b⁹
F Cb Ebb
E# B D
1 2 0 × × ×
0
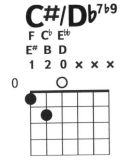

C#/Db⁷b⁹
F Cb Ebb
E# B D
× 2 4 1 × ×
7
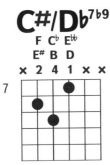

C#/Db⁷b⁹
F Cb Ebb
E# B D
× × × 2 4 1
10
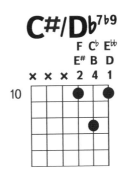

C#/Db⁷b⁹
Cb Ebb F
B D E#
× × × 4 3 1
1
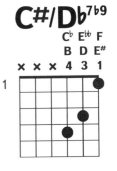

CHORDS WITH ROOT C SHARP - D FLAT 113

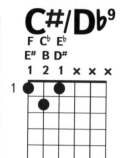

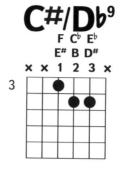

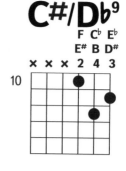

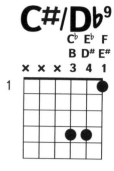

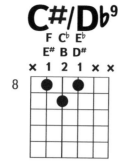

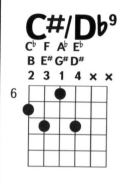

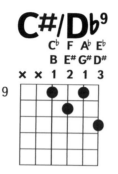

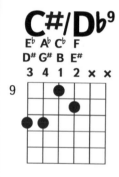

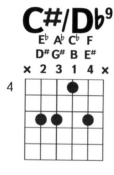

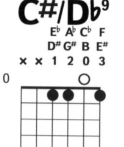

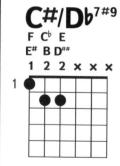

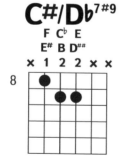

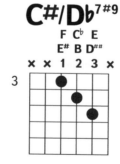

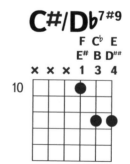

C#/Db

VIVID
DIMINISHED

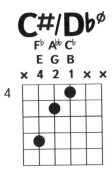

C#/Db⌀
F♭ A♭♭ C♭
E G B
4 2 1 × × ×
9

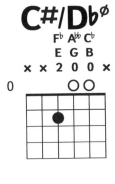

C#/Db⌀
F♭ A♭♭ C♭
E G B
× 4 2 1 × ×
4

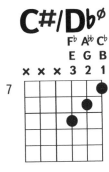

C#/Db⌀
F♭ A♭♭ C♭
E G B
× × 2 0 0 ×
0

C#/Db⌀
F♭ A♭♭ C♭
E G B
× × × 3 2 1
7

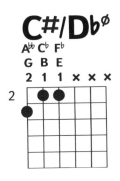

C#/Db⌀
A♭♭ C♭ F♭
G B E
2 1 1 × × ×
2

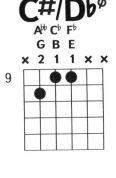

C#/Db⌀
A♭♭ C♭ F♭
G B E
× 2 1 1 × ×
9

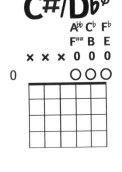

C#/Db⌀
A♭♭ C♭ F♭
G B E
× × 2 1 3 ×
4

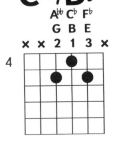

C#/Db⌀
A♭♭ C♭ F♭
F♯♯ B E
× × × 0 0 0
0

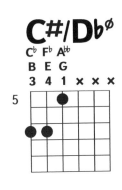

C#/Db⌀
C♭ F♭ A♭♭
B E G
3 4 1 × × ×
5

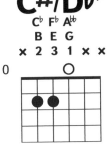

C#/Db⌀
C♭ F♭ A♭♭
B E G
× 2 3 1 × ×
0

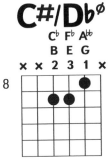

C#/Db⌀
C♭ F♭ A♭♭
B E G
× × 2 3 1 ×
8

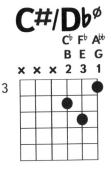

C#/Db⌀
C♭ F♭ A♭♭
B E G
× × × 2 3 1
3

SEEING MUSIC
METHOD BOOKS

116 GUITAR CHORDS ENCYCLOPEDIA: A SEEING MUSIC METHOD BOOK

D^{Maj}

D A D F#
× × 0 1 3 2

0
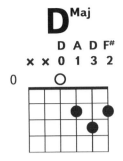

D^{Maj}

D A D F# A D
1 3 4 2 1 1

10
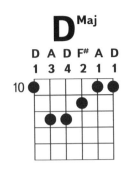

D^{Maj}

D A D F#
× 1 3 3 3 ×

5
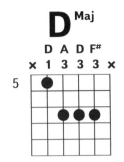

D^{△7}

D A C# F#
× × 0 1 1 1

0
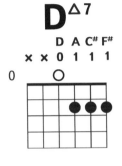

D^{△7}

D A C# F#
× 1 3 2 4 ×

5
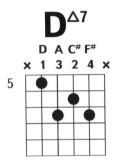

D^{△7#11}

D G# C# F# A
× 1 2 3 4 1

5
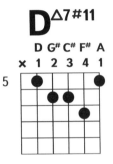

D^{△9}

D F# C# E
× 2 1 4 3 ×

4
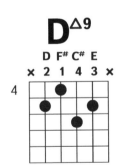

D^{6/9}

D   F# B E
1 × × 2 4 4

10
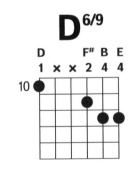

D^{6/9}

D F# B E
× 2 1 1 3 ×

4
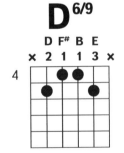

D^{add9}

D   F# A E
1 × × 2 1 4

10
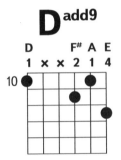

BIG
MINOR

D^{min}
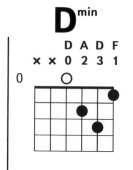

D^{min}
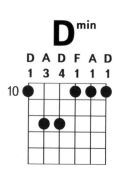

D^{min}
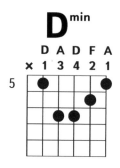

D^{min7}
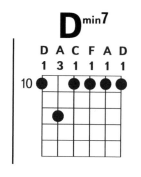

D^{min7}
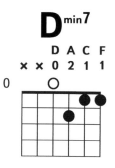

D^{min7b5}
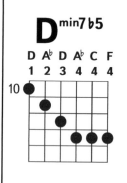

D^{min7b9}
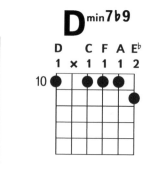

D^{min9}

D^{min△7}

BIG
DOMINANT

D⁷
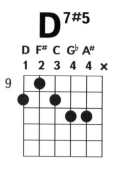

D⁷
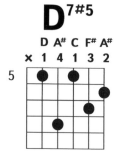

D^{7b5}
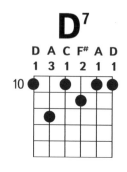

D^{7#5}
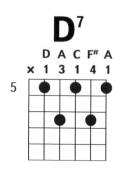

D^{7#5}
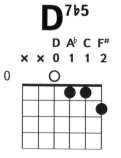

118 GUITAR CHORDS ENCYCLOPEDIA: A SEEING MUSIC METHOD BOOK

D⁷♭⁹
D C G♭ A E♭
1 × 1 2 1 3
10
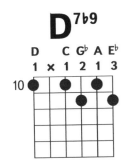

D⁹
D A C F# A E
1 3 1 2 1 4
10
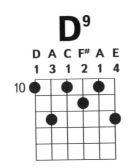

D⁹
D F F# C E
× 2 1 3 4 ×
4
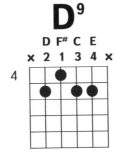

D⁷#⁹
D C F# C E#
1 × 1 2 4 4
10
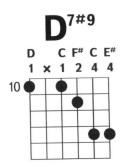

D⁷#⁹
D C F# A E#
1 × 1 2 1 4
10
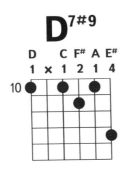

D⁷#⁹
D F# C E#
× 2 1 3 4 ×
4
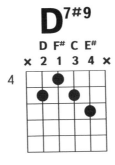

D⁷#⁹
D F# C F
× × 2 1 4 4
11
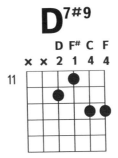

BIG
AUGMENTED

D^Aug
D F# A# D
4 3 2 1 × ×
7
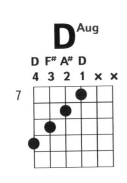

D^Aug
D F# A# D
× 3 2 1 1 ×
0
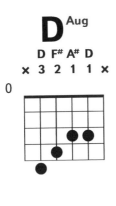

D^Aug
D D F# A# D
1 × 4 2 3 1
10
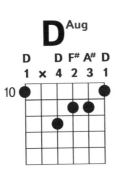

D^Aug
A# D F# A#
× 3 2 1 1 ×
11
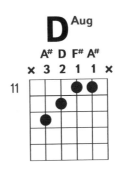

D^Aug
F# A# D F#
× 3 2 1 1 ×
7
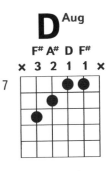

BIG
DIMINISHED

D^ø
D A♭ D A♭ C F
1 2 3 4 4 4
10
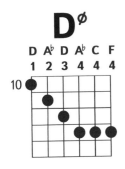

D^dim
D C♭ F A♭ D
2 × 1 3 1 4
9
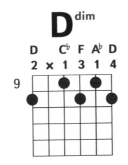

BIG
STACKED 5THS

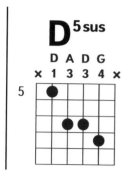

D^{5sus}

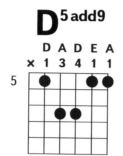

D^{5add9}

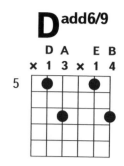

D^{add6/9}

COMPACT
MAJOR

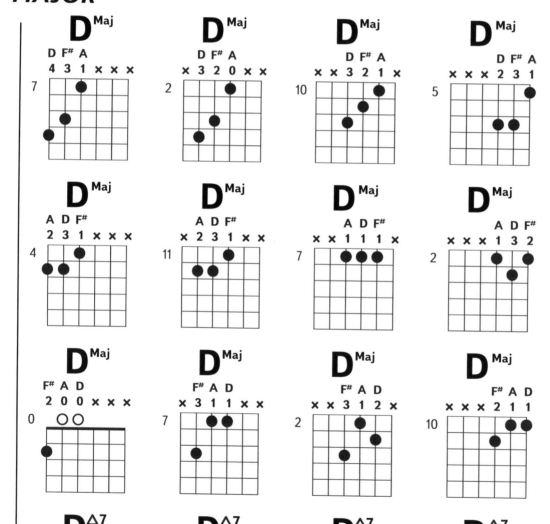

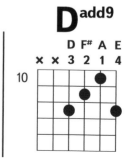

120 GUITAR CHORDS ENCYCLOPEDIA: A SEEING MUSIC METHOD BOOK

COMPACT *MINOR*

D^{min}

Dmin

D F A
4 2 1 × × ×
7
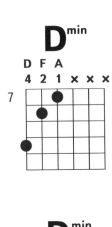

Dmin

D F A
× 3 1 0 × ×
2
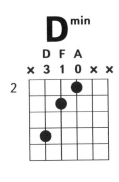

Dmin

D F A
× × 3 1 1 ×
10
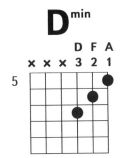

Dmin

D F A
× × × 3 2 1
5
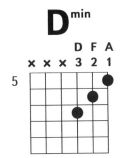

Dmin

F A D
1 0 0 × × ×
0
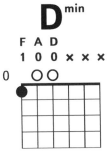

Dmin

F A D
× 2 1 1 × ×
7
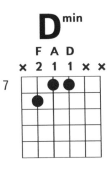

Dmin

F A D
× × 2 1 3 ×
2
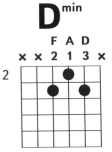

Dmin

F A D
× × × 1 1 1
10
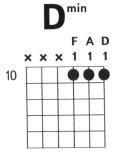

Dmin

A D F
3 4 1 × × ×
3
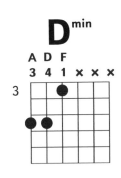

Dmin

A D F
× 3 4 1 × ×
10
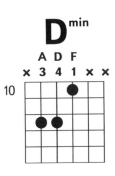

Dmin

A D F
× × 2 3 1 ×
6
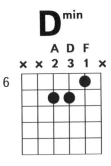

Dmin

A D F
× × × 2 3 1
1
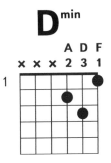

Dmin7

D F C
3 1 4 × × ×
8
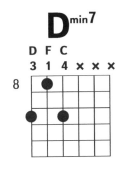

Dmin7

D F C
× 3 1 4 × ×
3
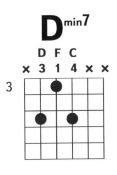

Dmin7

D F C
× × 3 1 4 ×
10
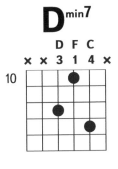

Dmin7

D F C
× × × 2 1 4
6
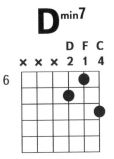

Dmin7

F C D
2 4 1 × × ×
0
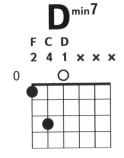

Dmin7

F C D
× 2 4 1 × ×
7
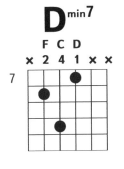

Dmin7

F C D
× × 1 3 1 ×
3
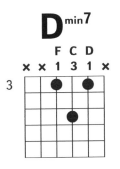

Dmin7

F C D
× × × 1 4 1
10
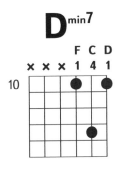

Dmin7

C D F
× × × 4 2 1
1
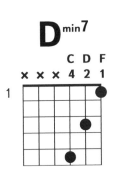

CHORDS WITH ROOT D 121

COMPACT
MINOR (CONT.)

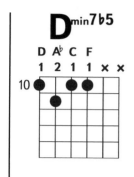

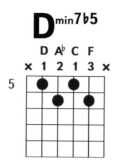

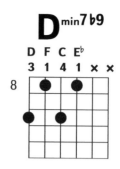

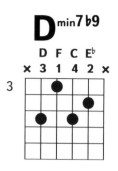

COMPACT
DOMINANT

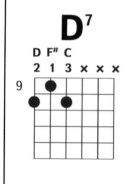

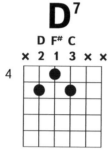

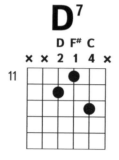

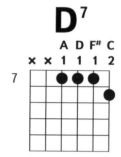

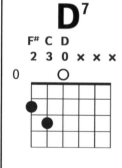

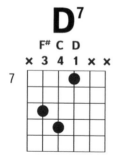

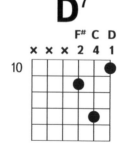

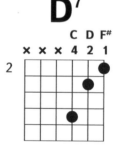

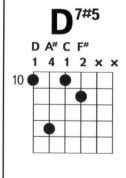

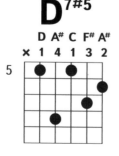

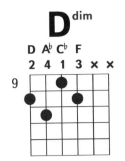

D^{dim}

D A♭ C♭ F
2 4 1 3 × ×

9

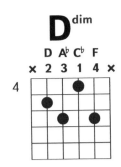

D^{dim}

D A♭ C♭ F
× 2 3 1 4 ×

4

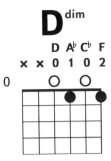

D^{dim}

D A♭ C♭ F
× × 0 1 0 2

0

COMPACT
DIMINISHED

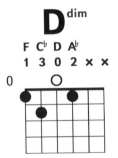

D^{dim}

F C♭ D A♭
1 3 0 2 × ×

0

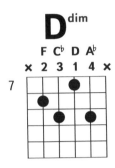

D^{dim}

F C♭ D A♭
× 2 3 1 4 ×

7

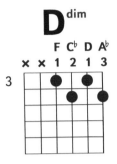

D^{dim}

F C♭ D A♭
× × 1 2 1 3

3

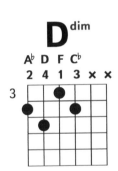

D^{dim}

A♭ D F C♭
2 4 1 3 × ×

3

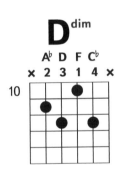

D^{dim}

A♭ D F C♭
× 2 3 1 4 ×

10

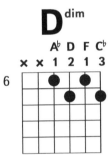

D^{dim}

A♭ D F C♭
× × 1 2 1 3

6

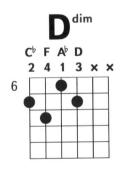

D^{dim}

C♭ F A♭ D
2 4 1 3 × ×

6

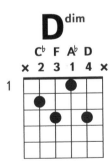

D^{dim}

C♭ F A♭ D
× 2 3 1 4 ×

1

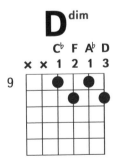

D^{dim}

C♭ F A♭ D
× × 1 2 1 3

9

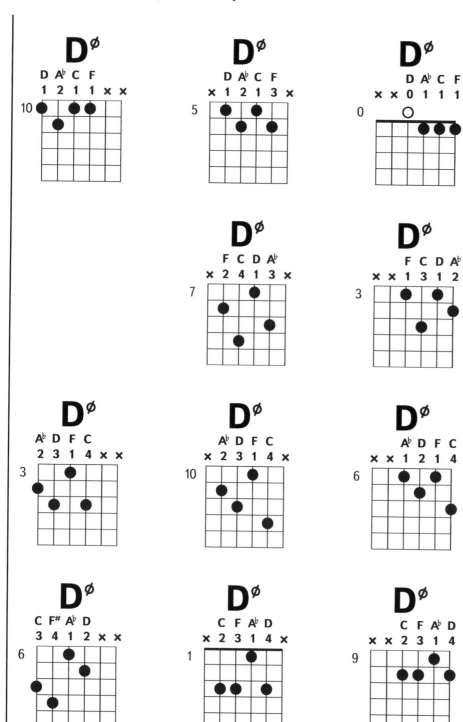

D^{Aug}

D F# A#
3 2 1 × × ×
8
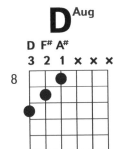

D^{Aug}

D F# A#
× 3 2 1 × ×
3
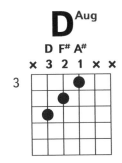

D^{Aug}

D F# A#
× × 2 1 1 ×
9
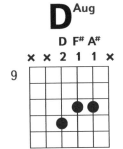

D^{Aug}

D F# A#
× × × 2 3 1
6
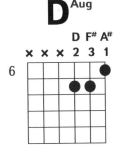

COMPACT
AUGMENTED

D^{Aug}

F# A# D
3 2 1 × × ×
0
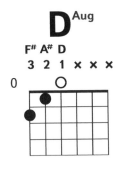

D^{Aug}

F# A# D
× 3 2 1 × ×
7
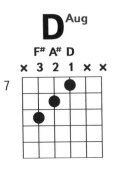

D^{Aug}

F# A# D
× × 3 2 1 ×
3
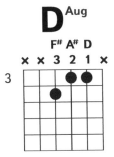

D^{Aug}

F# A# D
× × × 2 3 1
10
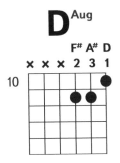

D^{Aug}

A# D F#
3 2 1 × × ×
4
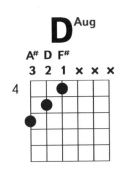

D^{Aug}

A# D F#
× 3 2 1 × ×
11
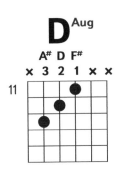

D^{Aug}

A# D F#
× × 2 1 1 ×
7
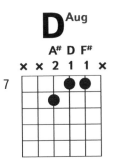

D^{Aug}

A# D F#
× × × 2 3 1
2
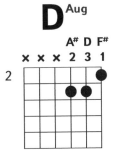

COMPACT
STACKED 5THS

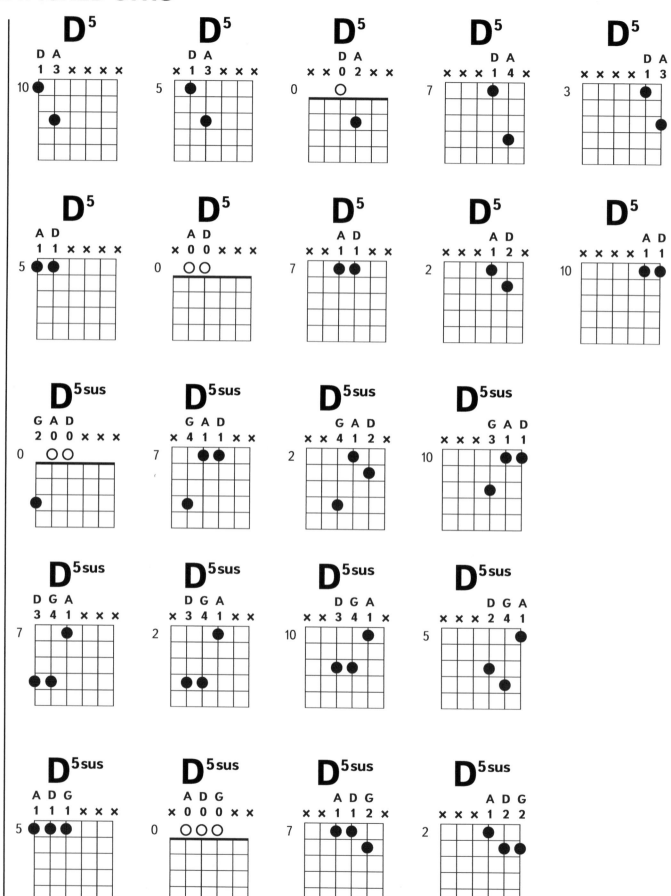

D^{5add9}

E   D A
0 × 0 2 × ×
0
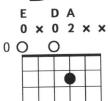

D^{5add9}

E   D A
× 1 × 1 4 ×
7
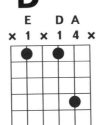

D^{5add9}

E D A
× × 1 × 2 4
2
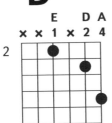

D^{5add9}

E A D
0 0 0 × × ×
0
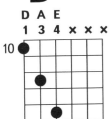

D^{5add9}

E A D
× 1 1 1 × ×
7
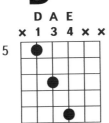

D^{5add9}

E A D
× × 1 1 2 ×
2
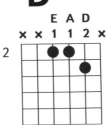

D^{5add9}

E A D
× × × 1 2 3
9
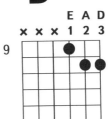

D^{5add9}

D A E
1 3 4 × × ×
10
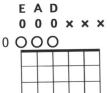

D^{5add9}

D A E
× 1 3 4 × ×
5
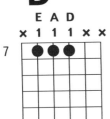

D^{5add6/9}

E B D A
0 2 0 3 × ×
0
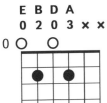

D^{5add6/9}

E B D A
× 1 3 1 4 ×
7
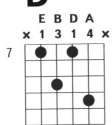

D^{5add6/9}

E B D A
× × 1 3 2 4
2
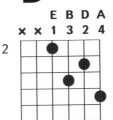

D^{5add6/9}

B E A D
1 1 1 1 × ×
7
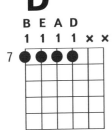

D^{5add6/9}

B E A D
× 1 1 1 2 ×
2
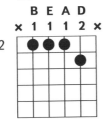

D^{5add6/9}

B E A D
× × 1 1 2 3
9
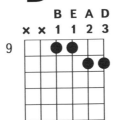

$D^{\Delta 7}$

C# F# A D
3 4 1 1 × ×

7
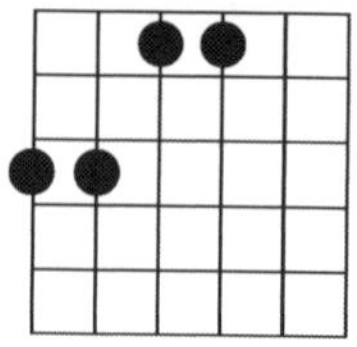

$D^{\Delta 7}$

C# F# A D
× 3 4 1 2 ×

2
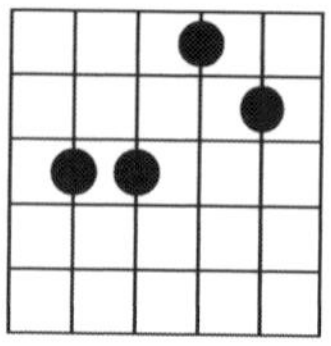

$D^{\Delta 7}$

C# F# A D
× × 2 3 1 1

10
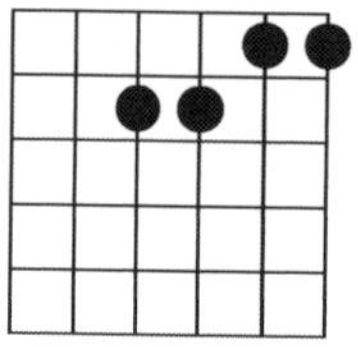

$D^{\Delta 9}$

C# F# A E
2 3 1 4 × ×

7
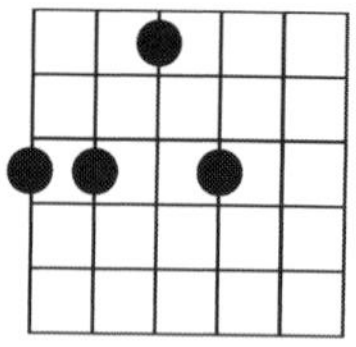

$D^{\Delta 9}$

C# F# A E
× 2 3 1 4 ×

2
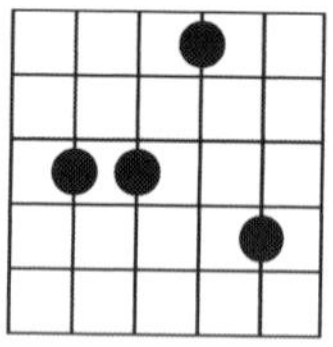

$D^{\Delta 9}$

C# F# A E
× × 2 3 1 4

10
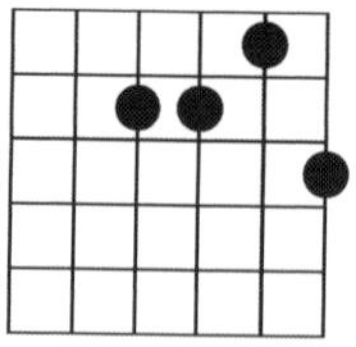

$D^{6/9}$

F# B E A
1 1 1 1 × ×

2
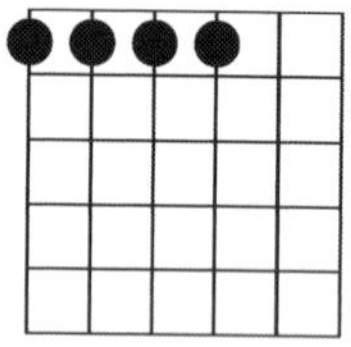

$D^{6/9}$

F# B E A
× 1 1 1 2 ×

9
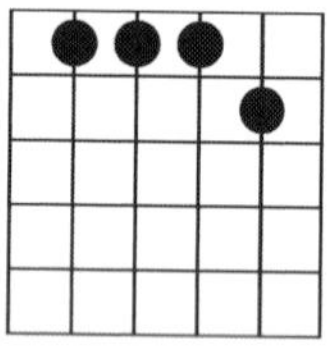

$D^{6/9}$

F# B E A
× × 1 1 2 3

4
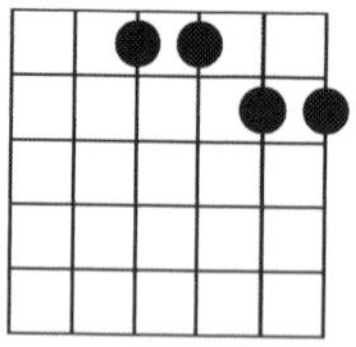

$D^{6/9}$

F# B E
× × × 1 2 2

11
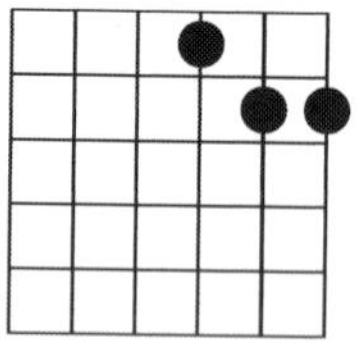

$D^{6/9}$

B F# A E
1 3 1 4 × ×

7
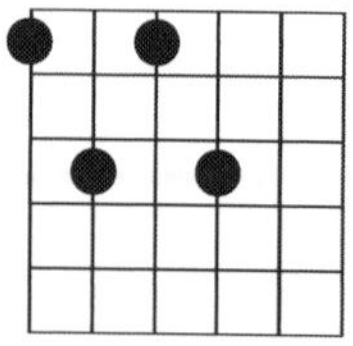

$D^{6/9}$

B F# A E
× 1 3 1 4 ×

2
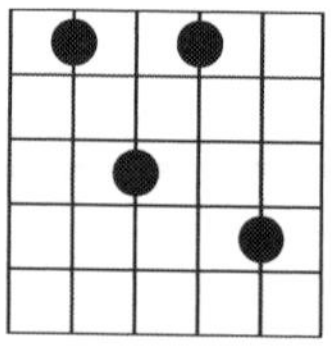

$D^{6/9}$

B F# A E
× × 1 3 2 4

9
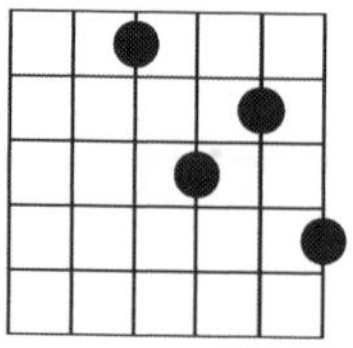

$D^{\Delta 7\#11}$

G# D F# C#
1 2 1 4 × ×

4
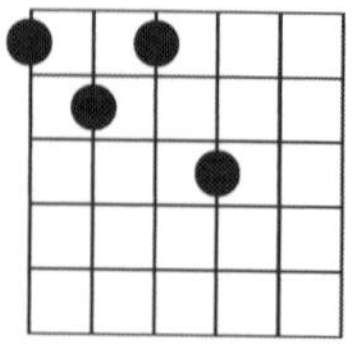

$D^{\Delta 7\#11}$

G# D F# C#
× × 1 2 3 4

6
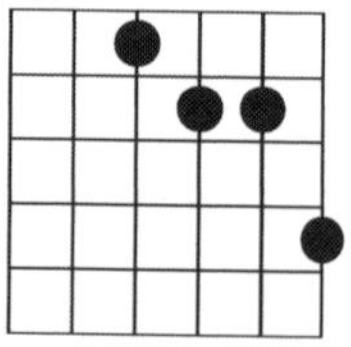

VIVID
MAJOR (CONT.)

VIVID
MINOR

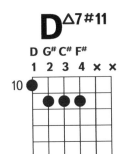
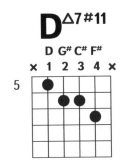
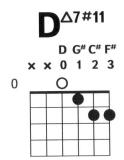
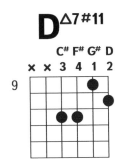

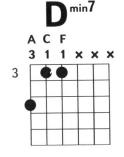
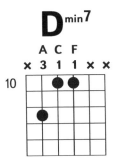

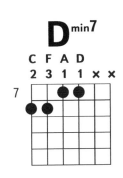
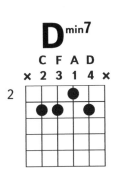
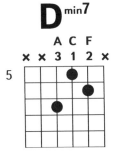

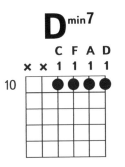
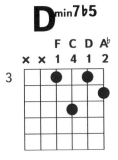

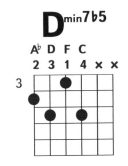
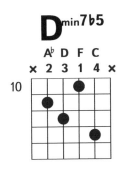
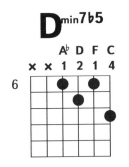
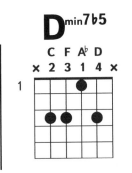
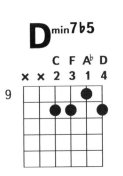

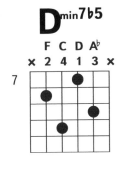

CHORDS WITH ROOT D 129

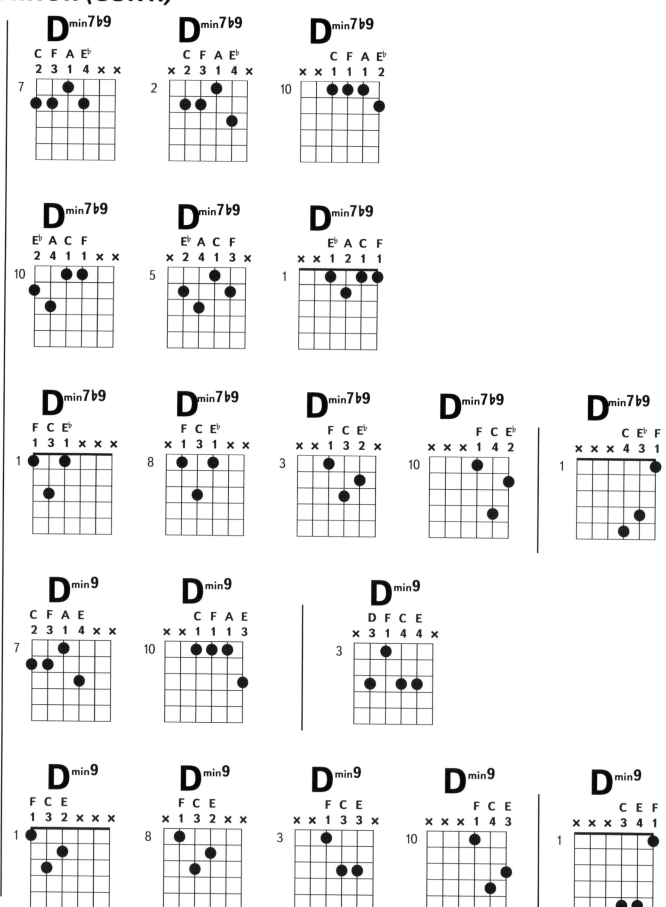

D^{min}9

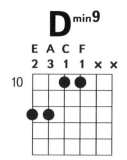

E A C F
2 3 1 1 × ×
10

D^{min}9

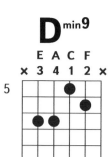

E A C F
× 3 4 1 2 ×
5

D^{min}9

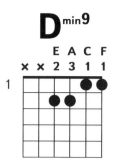

E A C F
× × 2 3 1 1
1

VIVID
MINOR (CONT.)

D^{min△7}

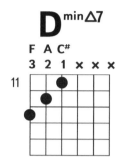

F A C#
3 2 1 × × ×
11

D^{min△7}

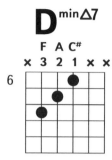

F A C#
× 3 2 1 × ×
6

D^{min△7}

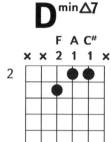

F A C#
× × 2 1 1 ×
2

D^{min△7}

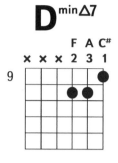

F A C#
× × × 2 3 1
9

D^{min△7}

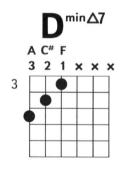

A C# F
3 2 1 × × ×
3

D^{min△7}

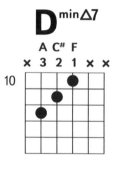

A C# F
× 3 2 1 × ×
10

D^{min△7}

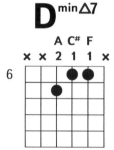

A C# F
× × 2 1 1 ×
6

D^{min△7}

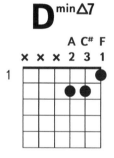

A C# F
× × × 2 3 1
1

D^{min△7}

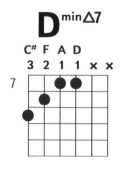

C# F A D
3 2 1 1 × ×
7

D^{min△7}

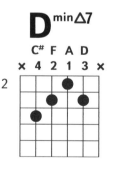

C# F A D
× 4 2 1 3 ×
2

D^{min△7}

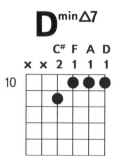

C# F A D
× × 2 1 1 1
10

CHORDS WITH ROOT D 131

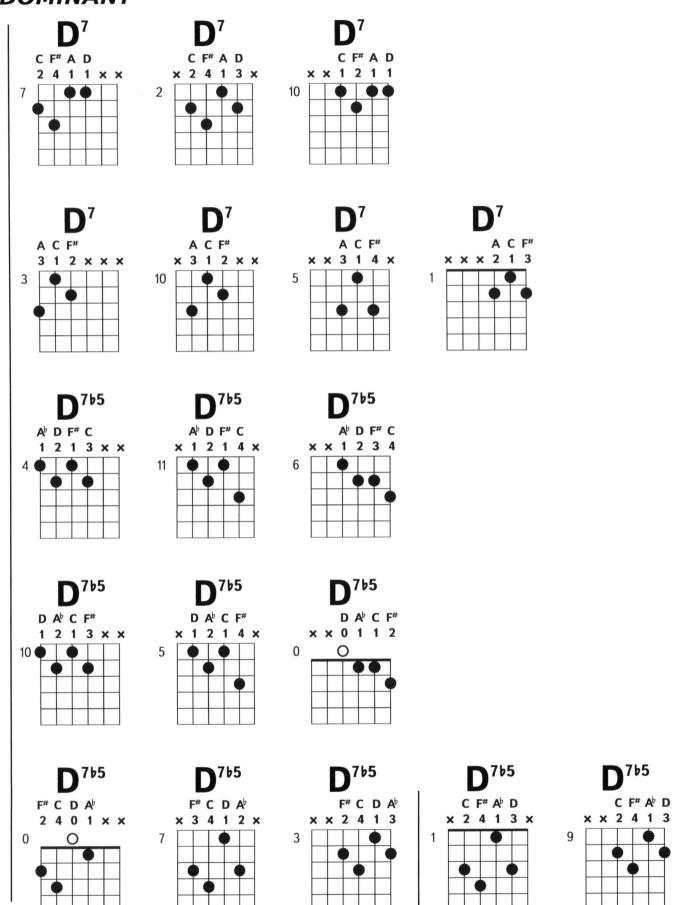

132 GUITAR CHORDS ENCYCLOPEDIA: A SEEING MUSIC METHOD BOOK

VIVID
DOMINANT (CONT.)

D$^{7\#5}$

A# D F# C
4 2 1 3 × ×
4
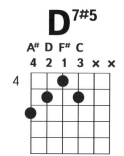

D$^{7\#5}$

A# D F# C
× 3 2 1 4 ×
11
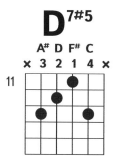

D$^{7\#5}$

A# D F# C
× × 2 1 1 3
7
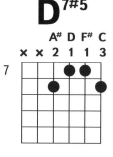

D$^{7\#5}$

C F# A# D
2 4 3 1 × ×
7
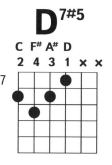

D$^{7\#5}$

C F# A# D
× 1 2 1 1 ×
3
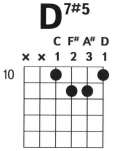

D$^{7\#5}$

C F# A# D
× × 1 2 3 1
10
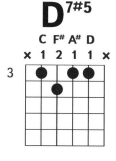

D^{7b9}

C F# A Eb
2 4 1 3 × ×
7
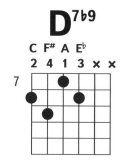

D^{7b9}

C F# A Eb
× × 1 2 1 3
10
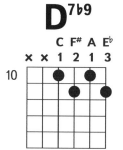

D^{7b9}

D F# C Eb
× 2 1 3 1 ×
4
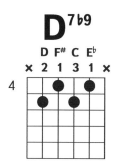

D^{7b9}

D F# C Eb
× × 2 1 3 1
11
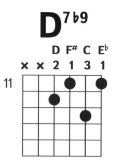

D^{7b9}

Eb A C F#
2 4 1 3 × ×
10
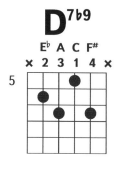

D^{7b9}

Eb A C F#
× 2 3 1 4 ×
5
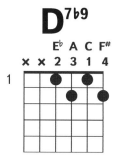

D^{7b9}

Eb A C F#
× × 2 3 1 4
1

D^{7b9}

F# C Eb
2 3 1 × × ×
1
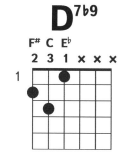

D^{7b9}

F# C Eb
× 2 4 1 × ×
8
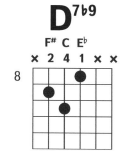

D^{7b9}

F# C Eb
× × × 2 4 1
11

D^{7b9}

C Eb F#
× × × 4 3 1
2

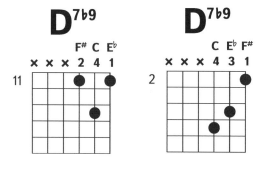

VIVID
DOMINANT

D⁹
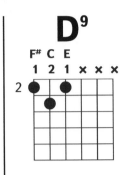

D⁹
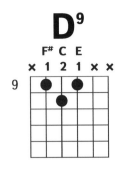

D⁹
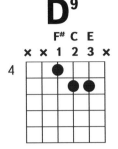

D⁹
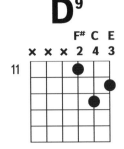

D⁹
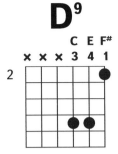

D⁹
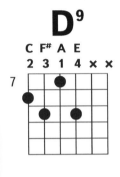

D⁹
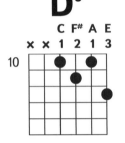

D⁹
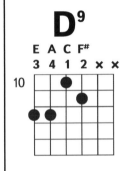

D⁹
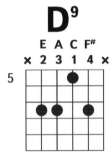

D⁹

D⁷#⁹
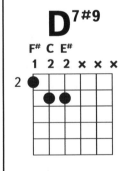

D⁷#⁹
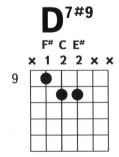

D⁷#⁹
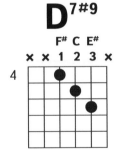

D⁷#⁹
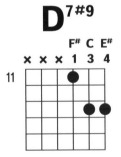

VIVID
DIMINISHED

D^ø

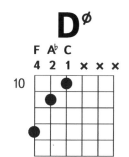

D^ø

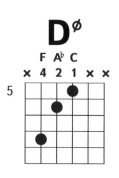

D^ø

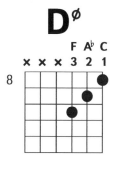

D^ø

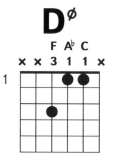

D^ø

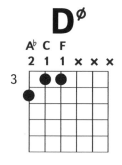

D^ø

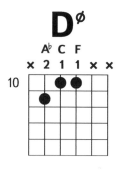

D^ø

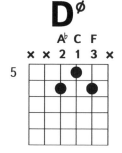

D^ø

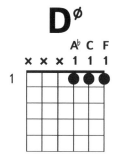

D^ø

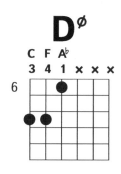

D^ø

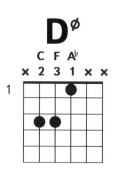

D^ø

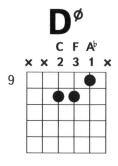

D^ø

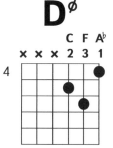

GUITAR
CHORDS
ENCYCLOPEDIA

BIG
MAJOR

D#/Eb Maj
Eb Bb Eb G Bb Eb
D# A# D# F## A# D#
1 3 4 2 1 1
11
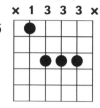

D#/Eb Maj
Eb Bb Eb G
D# A# D# F##
× 1 3 3 3 ×
6
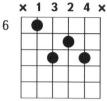

D#/Eb △7
Eb Bb D G
D# A# C## F##
× 1 3 2 4 ×
6
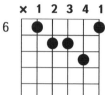

D#/Eb △7#11
Eb A D G Bb
D# G## C## F## A#
× 1 2 3 4 1
6
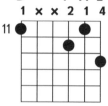

D#/Eb 6/9
Eb G C F
D# F## B# E#
1 × × 2 4 4
11
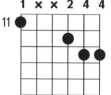

D#/Eb 6/9
Eb G C F
D# F## B# E#
× 2 1 1 3 ×
5

D#/Eb add9
Eb G Bb F
D# F## A# E#
1 × × 2 1 4
11
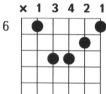

BIG
MINOR

D#/Eb min
Eb Bb Eb Gb Bb Eb
D# A# D# F# A# D#
1 3 4 1 1 1
11

D#/Eb min
Eb Bb Eb Gb Bb
D# A# D# F# A#
× 1 3 4 2 1
6
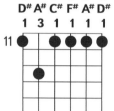

D#/Eb min7
Eb Bb Db Gb Bb Eb
D# A# C# F# A# D#
1 3 1 1 1 1
11
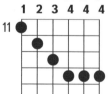

D#/Eb min7b5
Eb Bbb Eb Bbb Db Gb
D# A D# A C# F#
1 2 3 4 4 4
11

D#/Eb min7b9
Eb Db Gb Bb Fb
D# C# F# A# E
1 × 1 1 1 2
11
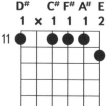

D#/Eb min9
Eb Bb Db Gb Bb F
D# A# C# F# A# E#
1 3 1 1 1 4
11

D#/Eb min △7
Eb Bb D Gb Bb
D# A# C## F# A#
× 1 4 2 3 1
6

D#/E♭⁷
E♭ B♭ D♭ G B♭ E♭
D# A# C# F## A# D#
1 3 1 2 1 1
11

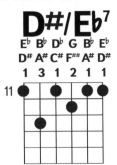

D#/E♭⁷
E♭ B♭ D♭ G B♭
D# A# C# F## A#
× 1 3 1 4 1
6

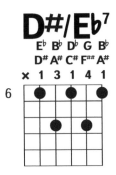

D#/E♭⁷♭5
E♭ B♭♭ D♭ G
D# A C# F##
× × 1 2 2 4
1

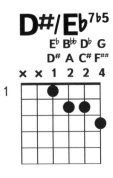

D#/E♭⁷#5
E♭ G D♭ G B
D# F## C# F## A##
1 2 3 4 4 ×
10

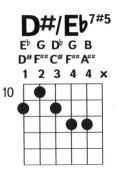

D#/E♭⁷#5
E♭ B D♭ G B
D# A## C# F## A##
× 1 4 1 3 2
6

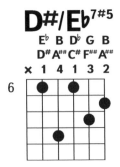

D#/E♭⁷♭9
E♭ D♭ G B♭ F♭
D# C# F## A# E
1 × 1 2 1 3
11

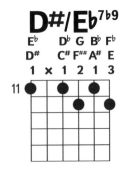

D#/E♭⁹
E♭ B♭ D♭ G B♭ F
D# A# C# F## A# E#
1 3 1 2 1 4
11

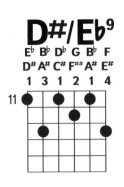

D#/E♭⁹
E♭ G D♭ F
D# F## C# E#
× 2 1 3 4 ×
5

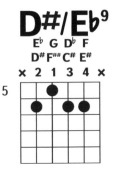

D#/E♭⁷#9
E♭ D♭ G D♭ F#
D# C# F## C# E##
1 × 1 2 4 4
11

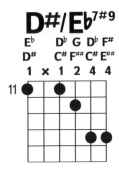

D#/E♭⁷#9
E♭ D♭ G B♭ F#
D# C# F## A# E##
1 × 1 2 1 4
11

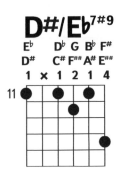

D#/E♭⁷#9
E♭ G D♭ F#
D# F## C# E##
× 2 1 3 4 ×
5

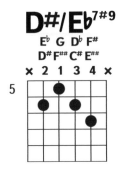

D#/E♭⁷#9
E♭ G D♭ F#
D# F## C# E##
× × 1 0 2 3
0

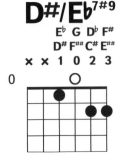

BIG
AUGMENTED

D#/E♭^{Aug}
E♭ G B E♭
D# F## A## D#
4 3 2 1 × ×
8
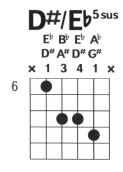

D#/E♭^{Aug}
E♭ G B E♭
D# F## A## D#
× 3 2 1 1 ×
4

D#/E♭^{Aug}
E♭ E♭ G B E♭
D# D# F## A## D#
1 × 4 2 3 1
11
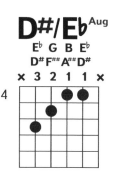

D#/E♭^{Aug}
B E♭ G B
A## D# F## A##
× 3 2 1 1 ×
0
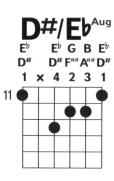

D#/E♭^{Aug}
G B E♭ G
F## A## D# F##
× 3 2 1 1 ×
8
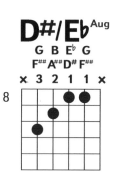

BIG
DIMINISHED

D#/E♭^ø
E♭ B♭♭ E♭ B♭♭ D♭ G♭
D# A D# A C# F#
1 2 3 4 4 4
11
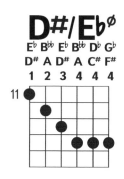

D#/E♭^{dim}
E♭ D♭ G♭ B♭♭ E♭
D# C F# A D#
2 × 1 3 1 4
10
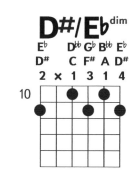

BIG
STACKED 5THS

D#/E♭^{5sus}
E♭ B♭ E♭ A♭
D# A# D# G#
× 1 3 4 1 ×
6
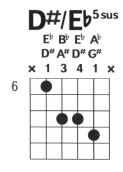

D#/E♭^{5add9}
E♭ B♭ E♭ F B♭
D# A# D# E# A#
× 1 3 4 1 1
6
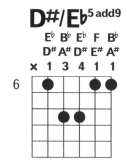

D#/E♭^{add6/9}
E♭ B♭ F C
D# A# E# B#
× 1 3 × 1 4
6
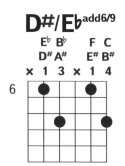

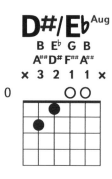

CHORDS WITH ROOT D SHARP - E FLAT 139

COMPACT
MAJOR

D#/Eb^Maj
Eb G Bb
D# F## A#
4 3 1 × × ×
8
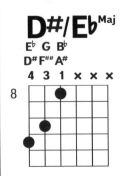

D#/Eb^Maj
Eb G Bb
D# F## A#
× 4 3 1 × ×
3
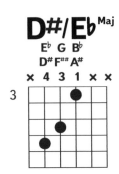

D#/Eb^Maj
Eb G Bb
D# F## A#
× × 3 2 1 ×
11
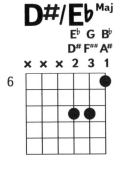

D#/Eb^Maj
Eb G Bb
D# F## A#
× × × 2 3 1
6
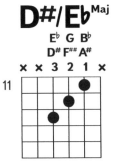

D#/Eb^Maj
Bb Eb G
A# D# F##
2 3 1 × × ×
5
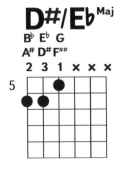

D#/Eb^Maj
Bb Eb G
A# D# F##
× 1 2 0 × ×
0
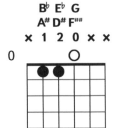

D#/Eb^Maj
Bb Eb G
A# D# F##
× × 1 1 1 ×
8
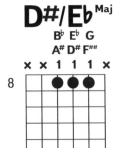

D#/Eb^Maj
Bb Eb G
A# D# F##
× × × 1 3 2
3
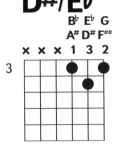

D#/Eb^Maj
G Bb Eb
F## A# D#
3 1 1 × × ×
1
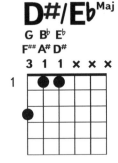

D#/Eb^Maj
G Bb Eb
F## A# D#
× 3 1 1 × ×
8
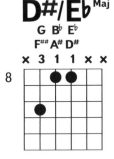

D#/Eb^Maj
G Bb Eb
F## A# D#
× × 3 1 2 ×
3
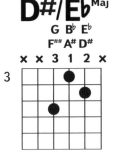

D#/Eb^Maj
G Bb Eb
F## A# D#
× × × 2 1 1
11
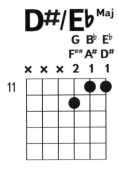

D#/Eb^Δ7
Eb G D
D# F## C##
2 1 4 × × ×
10
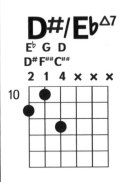

D#/Eb^Δ7
Eb G D
D# F## C##
× 2 1 4 × ×
5
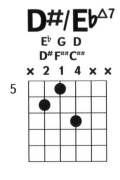

D#/Eb^Δ7
Eb G D
D# F## C##
× × 1 0 3 ×
0
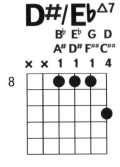

D#/Eb^Δ7
Bb Eb G D
A# D# F## C##
× × 1 1 1 4
8
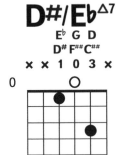

D#/Eb^add9
Eb G Bb F
D# F## A# E#
× × 3 2 1 4
11
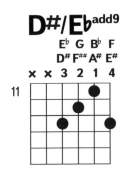

D#/Eb

COMPACT
MINOR

D#/Eb^{min}
Eb Gb Bb
D# F# A#
4 2 1 × × ×
8
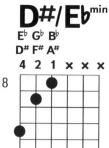

D#/Eb^{min}
Eb Gb Bb
D# F# A#
× 4 2 1 × ×
3
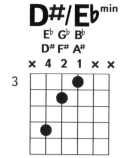

D#/Eb^{min}
Eb Gb Bb
D# F# A#
× × 3 1 1 ×
11
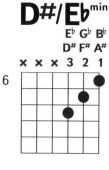

D#/Eb^{min}
Eb Gb Bb
D# F# A#
× × × 3 2 1
6
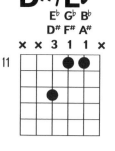

D#/Eb^{min}
Gb Bb Eb
F# A# D#
2 1 1 × × ×
1
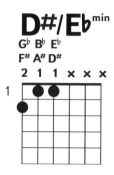

D#/Eb^{min}
Gb Bb Eb
F# A# D#
× 2 1 1 × ×
8
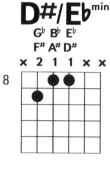

D#/Eb^{min}
Gb Bb Eb
F# A# D#
× × 2 1 3 ×
3
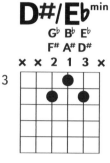

D#/Eb^{min}
Gb Bb Eb
F# A# D#
× × × 1 1 1
11
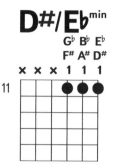

D#/Eb^{min}
Bb Eb Gb
A# D# F#
3 4 1 × × ×
4
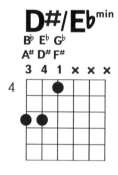

D#/Eb^{min}
Bb Eb Gb
A# D# F#
× 3 4 1 × ×
11
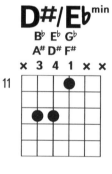

D#/Eb^{min}
Bb Eb Gb
A# D# F#
× × 2 3 1 ×
7
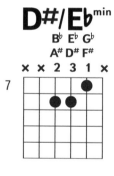

D#/Eb^{min}
Bb Eb Gb
A# D# F#
× × × 2 3 1
2
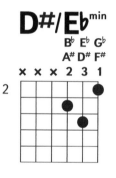

D#/Eb^{min7}
Eb Gb Db
D# F# C#
3 1 4 × × ×
9
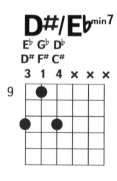

D#/Eb^{min7}
Eb Gb Db
D# F# C#
× 3 1 4 × ×
4
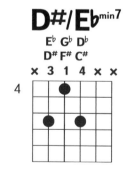

D#/Eb^{min7}
Eb Gb Db
D# F# C#
× × 3 1 4 ×
11
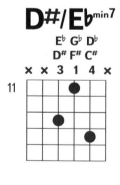

D#/Eb^{min7}
Eb Gb Db
D# F# C#
× × × 2 1 4
7
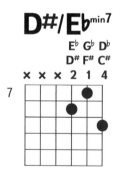

D#/Eb^{min7}
Gb Db Eb
F# C# D#
2 4 1 × × ×
1
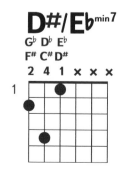

D#/Eb^{min7}
Gb Db Eb
F# C# D#
× 2 4 1 × ×
8
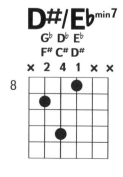

D#/Eb^{min7}
Gb Db Eb
F# C# D#
× × 1 3 1 ×
4
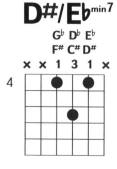

D#/Eb^{min7}
Gb Db Eb
F# C# D#
× × × 1 4 1
11
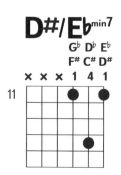

D#/Eb^{min7}
Db Eb Gb
C# D# F#
× × × 4 2 1
2
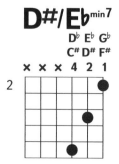

CHORDS WITH ROOT D SHARP - E FLAT 141

COMPACT
MINOR (CONT.)

D#/E♭min7♭5
E♭ B♭♭ D♭ G♭
D# A C# F#
1 2 1 1 × ×
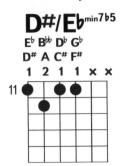
11

D#/E♭min7♭5
E♭ B♭♭ D♭ G♭
D# A C# E##
× 1 2 1 3 ×
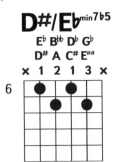
6

D#/E♭min7♭9
E♭ G♭ D♭ F♭
D# F# C# E
3 1 4 1 × ×
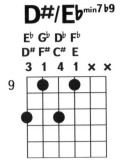
9

D#/E♭min7♭9
E♭ G♭ D♭ F♭
D# F# C# E
× 3 1 4 2 ×
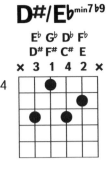
4

COMPACT
DOMINANT

D#/E♭7
E♭ G D♭
D# F## C#
2 1 3 × × ×
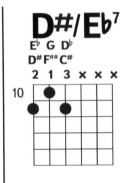
10

D#/E♭7
E♭ G D♭
D# F## C#
× 2 1 3 × ×
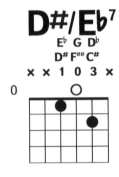
5

D#/E♭7
E♭ G D♭
D# F## C#
× × 1 0 3 ×
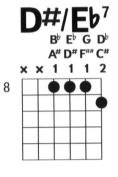
0

D#/E♭7
B♭ E♭ G D♭
A# D# F## C#
× × 1 1 1 2
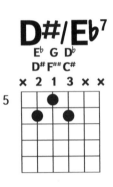
8

D#/E♭7
G D♭ E♭
F## C# D#
3 4 1 × × ×
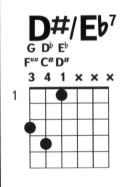
1

D#/E♭7
G D♭ E♭
F## C# D#
× 3 4 1 × ×
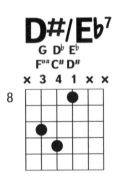
8

D#/E♭7
G D♭ E♭
F## C# D#
× × × 2 4 1
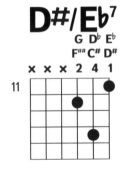
11

D#/E♭7
D♭ E♭ G
C# D# F##
× × × 4 2 1
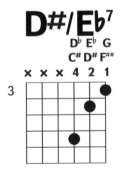
3

D#/E♭7#5
E♭ B D♭ G
D# A## C# F##
1 4 1 2 × ×
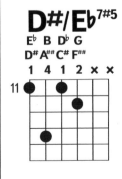
11

D#/E♭7#5
E♭ B D♭ G B
D# A## C# F## A##
× 1 4 1 3 2
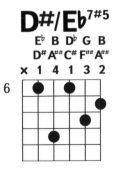
6

142 GUITAR CHORDS ENCYCLOPEDIA: A SEEING MUSIC METHOD BOOK

COMPACT
DIMINISHED

D#/Ebdim
Eb Bbb Dbb Gb
D# A C F#
2 4 1 3 × ×
10
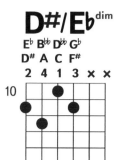

D#/Ebdim
Eb Bbb Dbb Gb
D# A C F#
× 2 3 1 4 ×
5
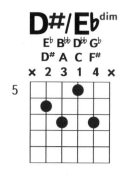

D#/Ebdim
Eb Bbb Dbb Gb
D# A C F#
× × 1 2 1 3
1

D#/Ebdim
Gb Dbb Eb Bbb
F# C D# A
2 4 1 3 × ×
1
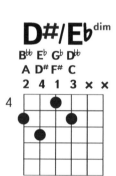

D#/Ebdim
Gb Dbb Eb Bbb
F# C D# A
× 2 3 1 4 ×
8
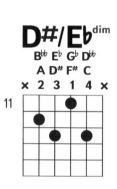

D#/Ebdim
Gb Dbb Eb Bbb
F# C D# A
× × 1 2 1 3
4
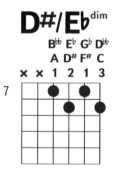

D#/Ebdim
Bbb Eb Gb Dbb
A D# F# C
2 4 1 3 × ×
4
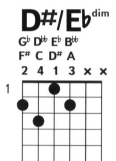

D#/Ebdim
Bbb Eb Gb Dbb
A D# F# C
× 2 3 1 4 ×
11
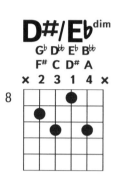

D#/Ebdim
Bbb Eb Gb Dbb
A D# F# C
× × 1 2 1 3
7
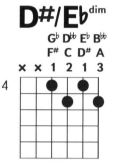

D#/Ebdim
Dbb Gb Bbb Eb
B# F# A D#
2 4 1 3 × ×
7
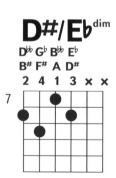

D#/Ebdim
Dbb Gb Bbb Eb
C F# A D#
× 2 3 1 4 ×
2
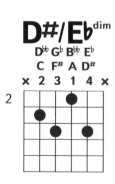

D#/Ebdim
Dbb Gb Bbb Eb
B# F# A D#
× × 1 2 1 3
10
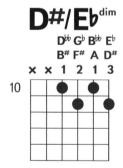

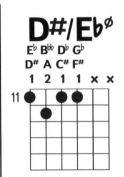

D#/Ebø
Eb Bbb Db Gb
D# A C# F#
1 2 1 1 × ×
11

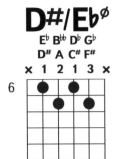

D#/Ebø
Eb Bbb Db Gb
D# A C# F#
× 1 2 1 3 ×
6

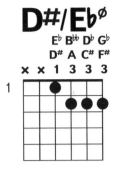

D#/Ebø
Eb Bbb Db Gb
D# A C# F#
× × 1 3 3 3
1

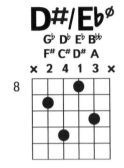

D#/Ebø
Gb Db Eb Bbb
F# C# D# A
× 2 4 1 3 ×
8

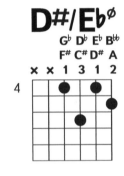

D#/Ebø
Gb Db Eb Bbb
F# C# D# A
× × 1 3 1 2
4

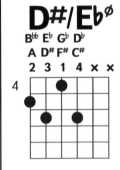

D#/Ebø
Bbb Eb Gb Db
A D# F# C#
2 3 1 4 × ×
4

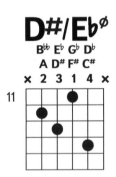

D#/Ebø
Bbb Eb Gb Db
A D# F# C#
× 2 3 1 4 ×
11

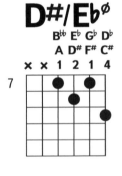

D#/Ebø
Bbb Eb Gb Db
A D# F# C#
× × 1 2 1 4
7

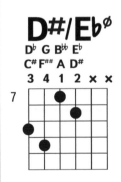

D#/Ebø
Db G Bbb Eb
C# F## A D#
3 4 1 2 × ×
7

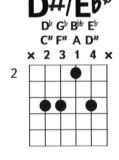

D#/Ebø
Db Gb Bbb Eb
C# F# A D#
× 2 3 1 4 ×
2

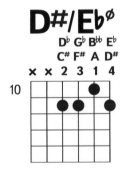

D#/Ebø
Db Gb Bbb Eb
C# F# A D#
× × 2 3 1 4
10

COMPACT
AUGMENTED

D#/Eb^Aug
Eb G B
D# F## A##
3 2 1 × × ×
9
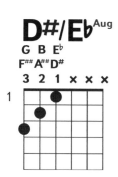

D#/Eb^Aug
Eb G B
D# F## A##
× 3 2 1 × ×
4
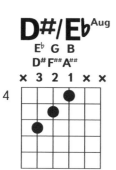

D#/Eb^Aug
Eb G B
D# F## A##
× × 1 0 0 ×
0
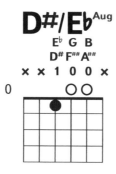

D#/Eb^Aug
Eb G B
D# F## A##
× × × 2 3 1
7
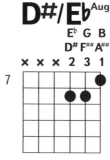

D#/Eb^Aug
G B Eb
F## A## D#
3 2 1 × × ×
1
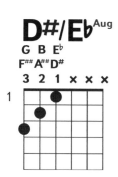

D#/Eb^Aug
G B Eb
F## A## D#
× 3 2 1 × ×
8
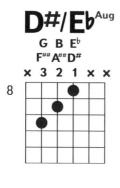

D#/Eb^Aug
G B Eb
F## A## D#
× × 3 2 1 ×
4
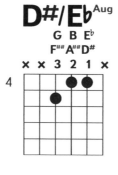

D#/Eb^Aug
G B Eb
F## A## D#
× × × 2 3 1
11
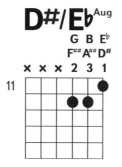

D#/Eb^Aug
B Eb G
A## D# F##
3 2 1 × × ×
5
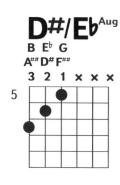

D#/Eb^Aug
B Eb G
A## D# F##
× 2 1 0 × ×
0
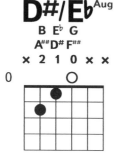

D#/Eb^Aug
B Eb G
A## D# F##
× × 2 1 1 ×
8
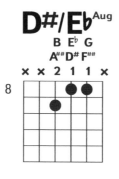

D#/Eb^Aug
B Eb G
A## D# F##
× × × 2 3 1
3
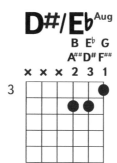

COMPACT
STACKED 5THS

D#/E♭⁵
E♭ B♭
D# A#
1 3 × × ×
11
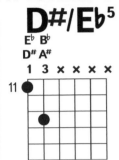

D#/E♭⁵
E♭ B♭
D# A#
× 1 3 × × ×
6
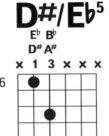

D#/E♭⁵
E♭ B♭
D# A#
× × 1 3 × ×
1
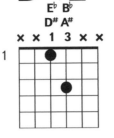

D#/E♭⁵
E♭ B♭
D# A#
× × × 1 4 ×
8
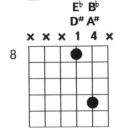

D#/E♭⁵
E♭ B♭
D# A#
× × × × 1 3
4
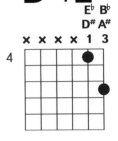

D#/E♭⁵
B♭ E♭
A# D#
1 1 × × ×
6
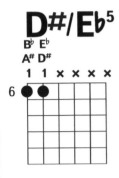

D#/E♭⁵
B♭ E♭
A# D#
× 1 1 × × ×
1
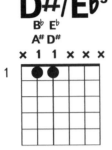

D#/E♭⁵
B♭ E♭
A# D#
× × 1 1 × ×
8
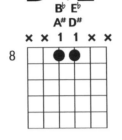

D#/E♭⁵
B♭ E♭
A# D#
× × × 1 2 ×
3
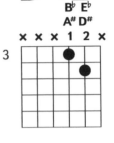

D#/E♭⁵
B♭ E♭
A# D#
× × × × 1 1
11
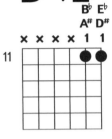

D#/E♭⁵ˢᵘˢ
A♭ B♭ E♭
G# A# D#
4 1 1 × × ×
1
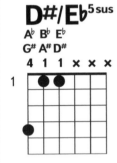

D#/E♭⁵ˢᵘˢ
E♭ A♭ B♭
D# G# A#
× × 2 4 1
6
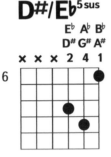

D#/E♭⁵ˢᵘˢ
A♭ B♭ E♭
G# A# D#
× × 4 1 2 ×
3
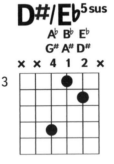

D#/E♭⁵ˢᵘˢ
A♭ B♭ E♭
G# A# D#
× × × 3 1 1
11
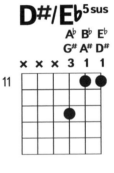

D#/E♭⁵ˢᵘˢ
E♭ A♭ B♭
D# G# A#
3 4 1 × × ×
8
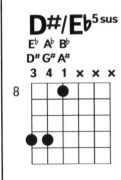

D#/E♭⁵ˢᵘˢ
E♭ A♭ B♭
D# G# A#
× 3 4 1 × ×
3
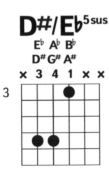

D#/E♭⁵ˢᵘˢ
E♭ A♭ B♭
D# G# A#
× × 3 4 1 ×
11
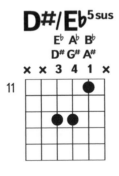

D#/E♭⁵ˢᵘˢ
E♭ A♭ B♭
D# G# A#
× × × 2 4 1
6
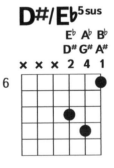

D#/E♭⁵ˢᵘˢ
B♭ E♭ A♭
A# D# G#
1 1 1 × × ×
6
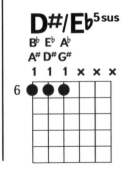

D#/E♭⁵ˢᵘˢ
B♭ E♭ A♭
A# D# G#
× 1 1 1 × ×
1
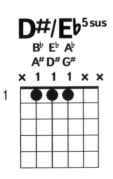

D#/E♭⁵ˢᵘˢ
B♭ E♭ A♭
A# D# G#
× × 1 1 2 ×
8
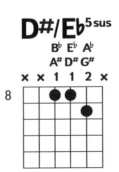

D#/E♭⁵ˢᵘˢ
B♭ E♭ A♭
A# D# G#
× × × 1 2 2
3
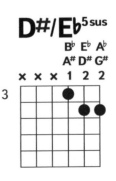

146 GUITAR CHORDS ENCYCLOPEDIA: A SEEING MUSIC METHOD BOOK

COMPACT
STACKED 5THS
(CONT.)

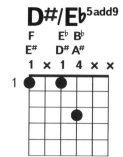

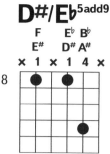

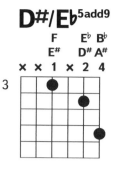

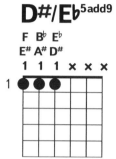

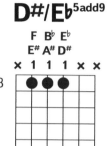

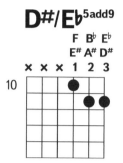

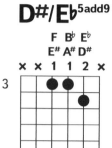

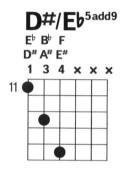

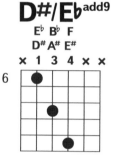

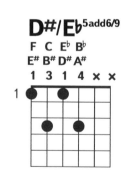

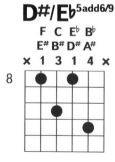

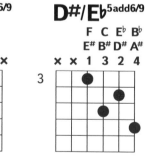

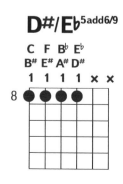

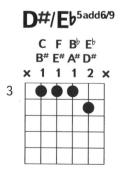

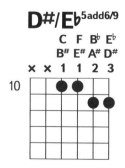

CHORDS WITH ROOT D SHARP - E FLAT 147

VIVID
MAJOR

D#/Eb$^{\triangle7}$
D G Bb Eb
C## F## A# D#
3 4 1 1 × ×
8
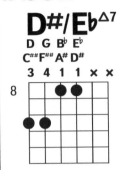

D#/Eb$^{\triangle7}$
D G Bb Eb
C## F## A# D#
× 3 4 1 2 ×
3
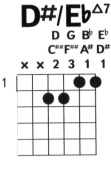

D#/Eb$^{\triangle7}$
D G Bb Eb
C## F## A# D#
× × 2 3 1 1
1
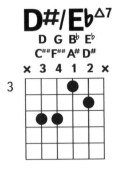

D#/Eb$^{\triangle9}$
D G Bb F
C## F## A# E#
2 3 1 4 × ×
8
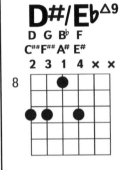

D#/Eb$^{\triangle9}$
D G Bb F
C## F## A# E#
× 2 3 1 4 ×
3
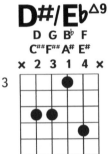

D#/Eb$^{\triangle9}$
D G Bb F
C## F## A# E#
× × 2 3 1 4
11
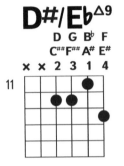

D#/Eb$^{6/9}$
G C F Bb
F## B# E# A#
1 1 1 1 × ×
3
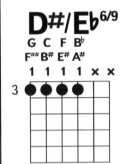

D#/Eb$^{6/9}$
G C F Bb
F## B# E# A#
× 1 1 1 2 ×
10
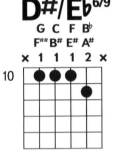

D#/Eb$^{6/9}$
G C F Bb
F## B# E# A#
× × 1 1 2 3
5
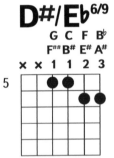

D#/Eb$^{6/9}$
G C F
F## B# E#
× × × 0 1 1
0
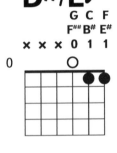

D#/Eb$^{6/9}$
C G Bb F
B# F## A# E#
1 3 1 4 × ×
8
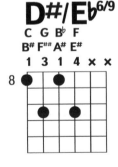

D#/Eb$^{6/9}$
C G Bb F
B# F## A# E#
× 1 3 1 4 ×
3
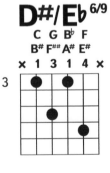

D#/Eb$^{6/9}$
C G Bb F
B# F## A# E#
× × 1 3 2 4
10
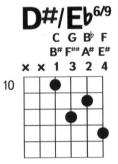

D#/Eb$^{\triangle7\#11}$
A Eb G D
G## D# F## C##
1 2 1 4 × ×
5
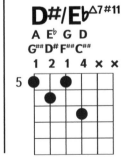

D#/Eb$^{\triangle7\#11}$
A Eb G D
G## D# F## C##
× × 1 2 3 4
7
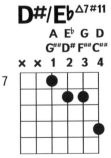

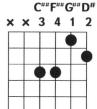

D#/Eb

VIVID
MAJOR (CONT.)

D#/Eb△7#11
Eb A D G
D# G## C## F##
1 2 3 4 × ×
11

D#/Eb△7#11
Eb A D G
D# G## C## F##
× 1 2 3 4 ×
6

D#/Eb△7#11
Eb A D G
D# G## C## F##
× × 1 2 3 4
1

D#/Eb△7#11
D G A Eb
C## F## G## D#
× × 3 4 1 2
10

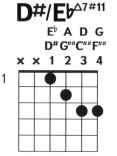
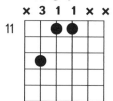
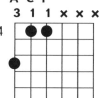

VIVID
MINOR

D#/Ebmin7
Bb Db Gb
A# C# F#
3 1 1 × × ×
4

D#/Ebmin7
Bb Db Gb
A# C# F#
× 3 1 1 × ×
11

D#/Ebmin7
Bb Db Gb
A# C# F#
× × 3 1 2
6

D#/Ebmin7
Bb Db Gb
A# C# F#
× × 2 1 1
2

D#/Ebmin7
Db Gb Bb Eb
C# F# A# D#
2 3 1 1 × ×
8

D#/Ebmin7
Db Gb Bb Eb
C# F# A# D#
× 2 3 1 4 ×
3

D#/Ebmin7
Db Gb Bb Eb
C# F# A# D#
× × 1 1 1 1
11

D#/Ebmin7
Bb Eb Gb Db
A# D# F# C#
× × 2 3 1 4
7

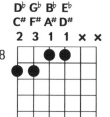
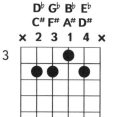
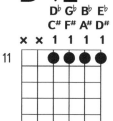
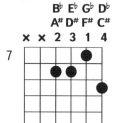
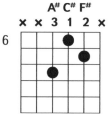
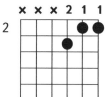

D#/Ebmin7b5
Gb Db Eb Bbb
F# C# D# A
× 2 4 1 3 ×
8

D#/Ebmin7b5
Gb Db Eb Bbb
F# C# D# A
× × 1 4 1 2
4

D#/Ebmin7b5
Bbb Eb Gb Db
A D# F# C#
2 3 1 4 × ×
4

D#/Ebmin7b5
Bbb Eb Gb Db
A D# F# C#
× 2 3 1 4 ×
11

D#/Ebmin7b5
Bbb Eb Gb Db
A D# E## C#
× × 1 2 1 4
7

D#/Ebmin7b5
Db Gb Bbb Eb
C# F# A D#
× 2 3 1 4 ×
2

D#/Ebmin7b5
Db Gb Bbb Eb
C# F# A D#
× × 2 3 1 4
10

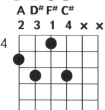
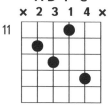
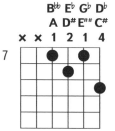

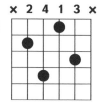
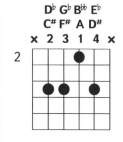
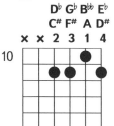

CHORDS WITH ROOT D SHARP - E FLAT 149

D#/Eb min7b9
Db Gb Bb Fb
C# F# A# E
2 3 1 4 × ×
8
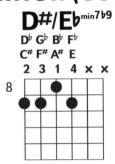

D#/Eb min7b9
Db Gb Bb Fb
C# F# A# E
× 2 3 1 4 ×
3
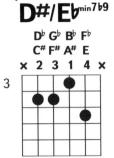

D#/Eb min7b9
Db Gb Bb Fb
C# F# A# E
× × 1 1 1 2
11
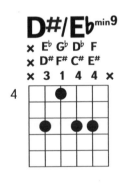

D#/Eb min7b9
Fb Bb Db Gb
E A# C# F#
2 4 1 1 × ×
11
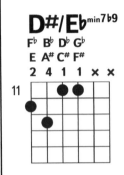

D#/Eb min7b9
Fb Bb Db Gb
E A# C# F#
× 2 4 1 3 ×
6
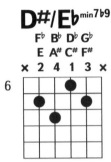

D#/Eb min7b9
Fb Bb Db Gb
E A# C# F#
× × 1 2 1 1
2
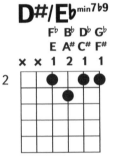

D#/Eb min7b9
Gb Db Fb
F# C# E
1 3 1 × × ×
2
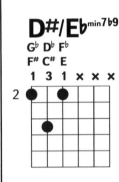

D#/Eb min7b9
Gb Db Fb
F# C# E
× 1 3 1 × ×
9
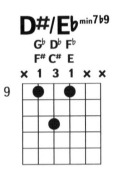

D#/Eb min7b9
Gb Db Fb
F# C# E
× × 1 3 2 ×
4
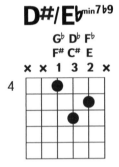

D#/Eb min7b9
Gb Db Fb
F# C# E
× × × 1 4 2
11
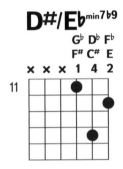

D#/Eb min7b9
Db Fb Gb
C# E F#
× × × 4 3 1
2
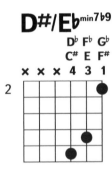

D#/Eb min9
Db Gb Bb F
C# F# A# E#
2 3 1 4 × ×
8
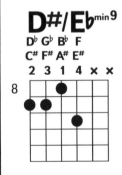

D#/Eb min9
Db Gb Bb F
C# F# A# E#
× × 1 1 1 3
11
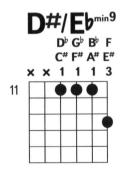

D#/Eb min9
× Eb Gb Db F
× D# F# C# E#
× 3 1 4 4 ×
4
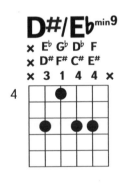

D#/Eb min9
Gb Db F
F# C# F
1 3 2 × × ×
2
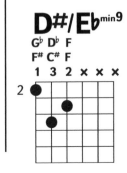

D#/Eb min9
Gb Db F
F# C# F
× 1 3 2 × ×
9
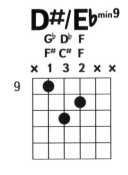

D#/Eb min9
Gb Db F
F# C# E#
× × 1 3 3 ×
4
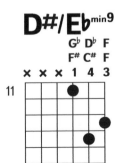

D#/Eb min9
Gb Db F
F# C# F
× × × 1 4 3
11
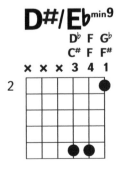

D#/Eb min9
Db F Gb
C# F F#
× × × 3 4 1
2
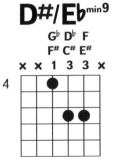

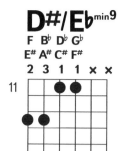

D#/Ebmin9

F Bb Db Gb
E# A# C# F#

2 3 1 1 × ×

11

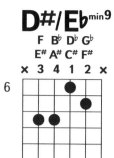

D#/Ebmin9

F Bb Db Gb
E# A# C# F#

× 3 4 1 2 ×

6

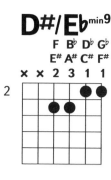

D#/Ebmin9

F Bb Db Gb
E# A# C# F#

× × 2 3 1 1

2

D#/Ebmin△7

Gb Bb D
F# A# C##

2 1 0 × × ×

0

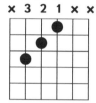

D#/Ebmin△7

Gb Bb D
F# A# C##

× 3 2 1 × ×

7

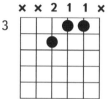

D#/Ebmin△7

Gb Bb D
F# A# C##

× × 2 1 1 ×

3

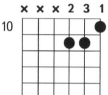

D#/Ebmin△7

Gb Bb D
F# A# C##

× × × 2 3 1

10

D#/Ebmin△7

Bb D Gb
A# C## F#

3 2 1 × × ×

4

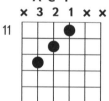

D#/Ebmin△7

Bb D Gb
A# C## F#

× 3 2 1 × ×

11

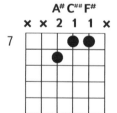

D#/Ebmin△7

Bb D Gb
A# C## F#

× × 2 1 1 ×

7

D#/Ebmin△7

Bb D Gb
A# C## F#

× × × 2 3 1

2

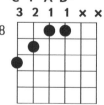

D#/Ebmin△7

D Gb Bb Eb
C## F# A# D#

3 2 1 1 × ×

8

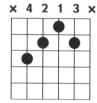

D#/Ebmin△7

D Gb Bb Eb
C## F# A# D#

× 4 2 1 3 ×

3

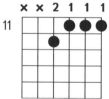

D#/Ebmin△7

D Gb Bb Eb
C## F# A# D#

× × 2 1 1 1

11

VIVID
DOMINANT

D#/Eb⁷
Db G Bb Eb
C# F## A# D#
2 4 1 1 x x
8
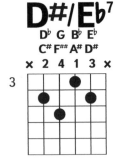

D#/Eb⁷
Db G Bb Eb
C# F## A# D#
x 2 4 1 3 x
3
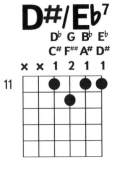

D#/Eb⁷
Db G Bb Eb
C# F## A# D#
x x 1 2 1 1
11
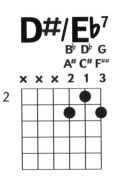

D#/Eb⁷
Bb Db G
A# C# F##
3 1 2 x x x
4
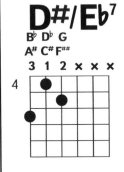

D#/Eb⁷
Bb Db G
A# C# F##
x 3 1 2 x x
11
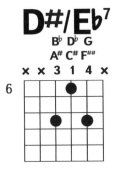

D#/Eb⁷
Bb Db G
A# C# F##
x x 3 1 4 x
6
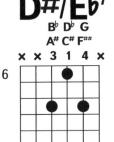

D#/Eb⁷
Bb Db G
A# C# F##
x x x 2 1 3
2
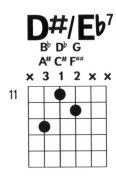

D#/Eb⁷
Bb Db G
A# C# F##
3 1 2 x x x
4
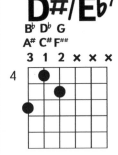

D#/Eb⁷ᵇ⁵
Bbb Eb G Db
A D# F## C#
x 0 1 0 3 x
0
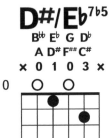

D#/Eb⁷
Bb Db G
A# C# F##
x x 3 1 4 x
6
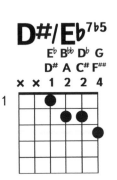

D#/Eb⁷ᵇ⁵
Eb Bbb Db G
D# A C# F##
1 2 1 3 x x
11
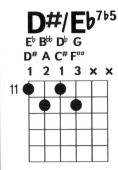

D#/Eb⁷ᵇ⁵
Eb Bbb Db G
D# A C# F##
x 1 2 1 4 x
6
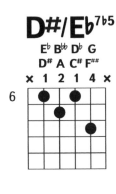

D#/Eb⁷ᵇ⁵
Eb Bbb Db G
D# A C# F##
x x 1 2 2 4
1
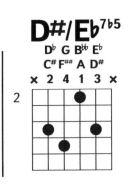

D#/Eb⁷ᵇ⁵
G Db Eb Bbb
F## C# D# A
3 4 1 2 x x
1
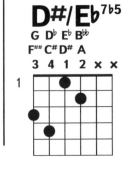

D#/Eb⁷ᵇ⁵
G Db Eb Bbb
F## C# D# A
x 3 4 1 2 x
8
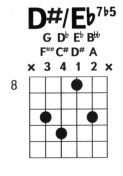

D#/Eb⁷ᵇ⁵
G Db Eb Bbb
F## C# D# A
x x 2 4 1 3
4
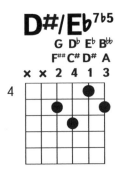

D#/Eb⁷ᵇ⁵
Db G Bbb Eb
C# F## A D#
x 2 4 1 3 x
2

D#/Eb⁷
Db G Bb Eb
C# F## A# D#
x x 1 2 1 1
11

152 GUITAR CHORDS ENCYCLOPEDIA: A SEEING MUSIC METHOD BOOK

VIVID
DOMINANT (CONT.)

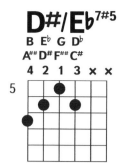

D#/Eb⁷#⁵
B Eb G Db
A## D# F## C#
4 2 1 3 × ×
5

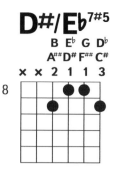

D#/Eb⁷#⁵
B Eb G Db
A## D# F## C#
× 2 1 0 3 ×
0

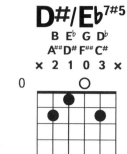

D#/Eb⁷#⁵
B Eb G Db
A## D# F## C#
× × 2 1 1 3
8

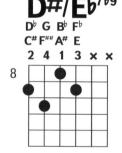

D#/Eb⁷#⁵
Db G B Eb
C# F## A## D#
2 4 3 1 × ×
8

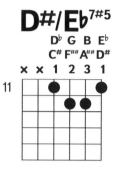

D#/Eb⁷#⁵
Db G B Eb
C# F## A## D#
× 1 2 1 1 ×
4

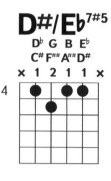

D#/Eb⁷#⁵
Db G B Eb
C# F## A## D#
× × 1 2 3 1
11

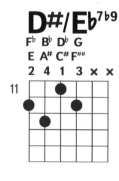

D#/Eb⁷b⁹
Db G Bb Fb
C# F## A# E
2 4 1 3 × ×
8

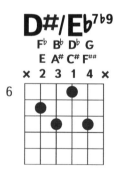

D#/Eb⁷b⁹
Db G Bb Fb
C# F## A# E
× × 1 2 1 3
11

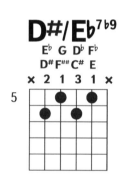

D#/Eb⁷b⁹
Eb G Db Fb
D# F## C# E
× 2 1 3 1 ×
5

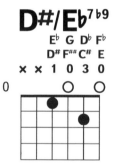

D#/Eb⁷b⁹
Eb G Db Fb
D# F## C# E
× × 1 0 3 0
0

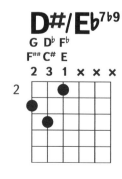

D#/Eb⁷b⁹
Fb Bb Db G
E A# C# F##
2 4 1 3 × ×
11

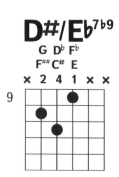

D#/Eb⁷b⁹
Fb Bb Db G
E A# C# F##
× 2 3 1 4 ×
6

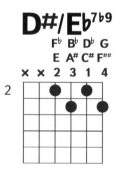

D#/Eb⁷b⁹
Fb Bb Db G
E A# C# F##
× × 2 3 1 4
2

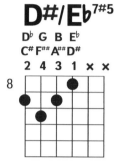

D#/Eb⁷b⁹
G Db Fb
F## C# E
2 3 1 × × ×
2

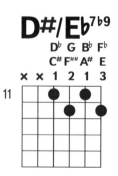

D#/Eb⁷b⁹
G Db Fb
F## C# E
× 2 4 1 × ×
9

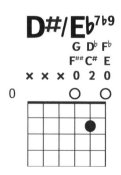

D#/Eb⁷b⁹
G Db Fb
F## C# E
× × × 0 2 0
0

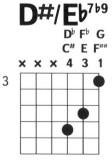

D#/Eb⁷b⁹
Db Fb G
C# E F##
× × × 4 3 1
3

CHORDS WITH ROOT D SHARP - E FLAT 153

VIVID
DOMINANT

D#/E♭⁹
G D♭ F
F## C# E#
1 2 1 × × ×
3

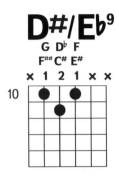

D#/E♭⁹
G D♭ F
F## C# E#
× 1 2 1 × ×
10

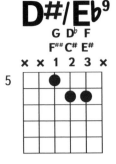

D#/E♭⁹
G D♭ F
F## C# E#
× × 1 2 3 ×
5

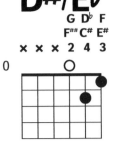

D#/E♭⁹
G D♭ F
F## C# E#
× × × 2 4 3
0

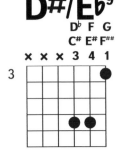

D#/E♭⁹
D♭ F G
C# E# F##
× × × 3 4 1
3

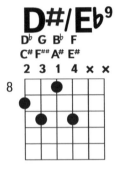

D#/E♭⁹
D♭ G B♭ F
C# F## A# E#
2 3 1 4 × ×
8

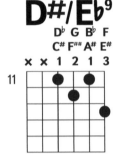

D#/E♭⁹
D♭ G B♭ F
C# F## A# E#
× × 1 2 1 3
11

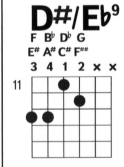

D#/E♭⁹
F B♭ D♭ G
E# A# C# F##
3 4 1 2 × ×
11

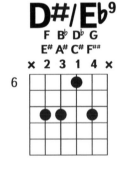

D#/E♭⁹
F B♭ D♭ G
E# A# C# F##
× 2 3 1 4 ×
6

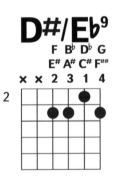

D#/E♭⁹
F B♭ D♭ G
E# A# C# F##
× × 2 3 1 4
2

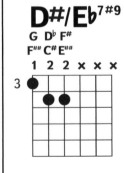

D#/E♭⁷#⁹
G D♭ F#
F## C# E##
1 2 2 × × ×
3

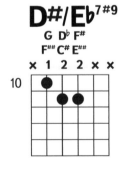

D#/E♭⁷#⁹
G D♭ F#
F## C# E##
× 1 2 2 × ×
10

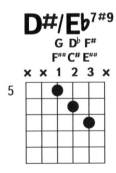

D#/E♭⁷#⁹
G D♭ F#
F## C# E##
× × 1 2 3 ×
5

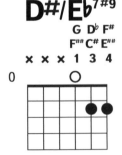

D#/E♭⁷#⁹
G D♭ F#
F## C# E##
× × × 1 3 4
0

VIVID
DIMINISHED

D#/Eb ø
G♭ B♭♭ D♭
F# A C#
4 2 1 × × ×
11
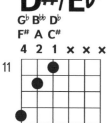

D#/Eb ø
G♭ B♭♭ D♭
F# A C#
× 4 2 1 × ×
6
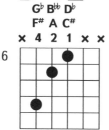

D#/Eb ø
G♭ B♭♭ D♭
F# A C#
× × 3 1 1 ×
2
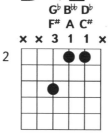

D#/Eb ø
G♭ B♭♭ D♭
F# A C#
× × × 3 2 1
9
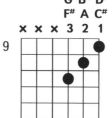

D#/Eb ø
B♭♭ D♭ G♭
A C# F#
2 1 1 × × ×
4
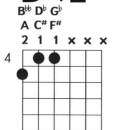

D#/Eb ø
B♭♭ D♭ G♭
A C# F#
× 2 1 1 × ×
11
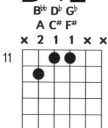

D#/Eb ø
B♭♭ D♭ G♭
A C# F#
× × 2 1 3 ×
6
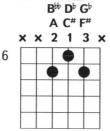

D#/Eb ø
B♭♭ D♭ G♭
G♯♯ C# F#
× × × 1 1 1
2
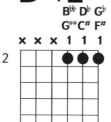

D#/Eb ø
D♭ G♭ B♭♭
C# F# A
3 4 1 × × ×
7
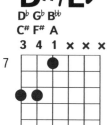

D#/Eb ø
D♭ G♭ B♭♭
C# F# A
× 2 3 1 × ×
2
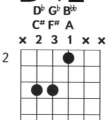

D#/Eb ø
D♭ G♭ B♭♭
C# F# A
× × 2 3 1 ×
10
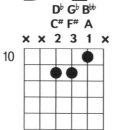

D#/Eb ø
D♭ G♭ B♭♭
C# F# A
× × × 2 3 1
5
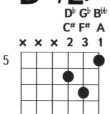

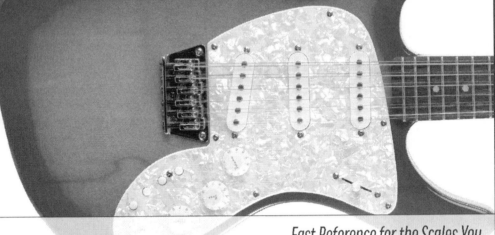
156 GUITAR CHORDS ENCYCLOPEDIA: A SEEING MUSIC METHOD BOOK

E^Maj

E B E G# B E
0 2 3 1 0 0

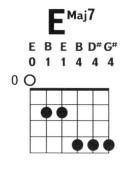

E^Maj

E B E G#
× 1 3 3 3 ×

7

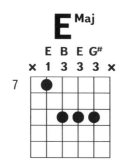

E^Maj7

E B E B D# G#
0 1 1 4 4 4

0

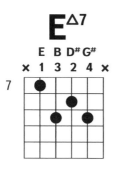

E^Δ7

E B D# G#
× 1 3 2 4 ×

7

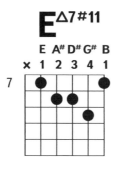

E^Δ7#11

E A# D# G# B
× 1 2 3 4 1

7

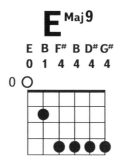

E^Maj9

E B F# B D# G#
0 1 4 4 4 4

0

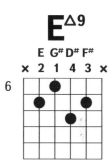

E^Δ9

E G# D# F#
× 2 1 4 3 ×

6

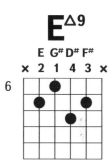

E^6/9

E G# C# F#
0 × × 1 2 3

0

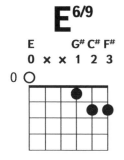

E^6/9

E G# C# F#
× 2 1 1 3 ×

6

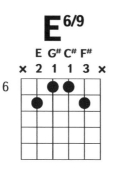

E^add9

E G# B F#
0 × × 1 0 3

0

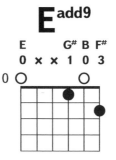

BIG
MINOR

E^{min}

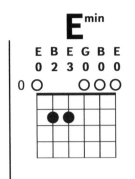

E^{min}

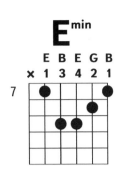

E^{min7}

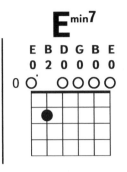

E^{min7}

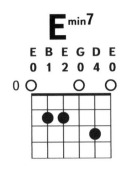

E^{min7♭5}

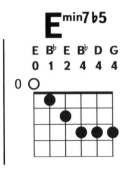

E^{min♭9}

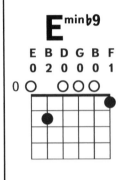

E^{min9}

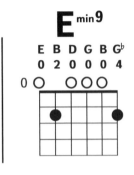

E^{min △7}

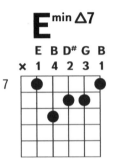

BIG
DOMINANT

E⁷

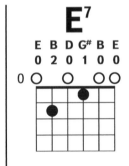

E⁷

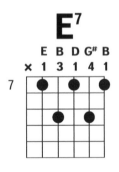

E^{7♭5}

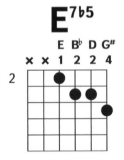

E^{7#5}

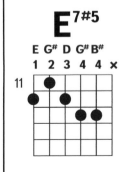

E^{7#5}

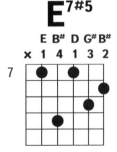

158 GUITAR CHORDS ENCYCLOPEDIA: A SEEING MUSIC METHOD BOOK

E⁷ᵇ⁹

E   D G# B F
0 × 0 1 0 2

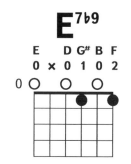

E⁹

E B D G# B F#
0 2 0 1 0 3

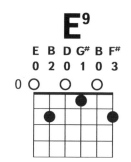

E⁹

E G# D F#
× 2 1 3 4 ×

6

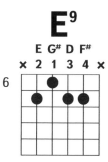

E⁷#⁹

E   D G# D G
0 × 0 1 4 4

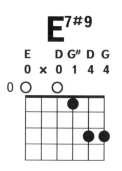

E⁷#⁹

E   D G# B F##
0 × 0 1 0 4

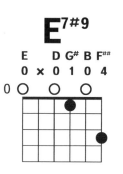

E⁷#⁹

E G# D F##
× 2 1 3 4 ×

6

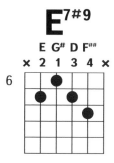

E⁷#⁹

E G# D F##
× × 2 1 4 4

1

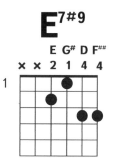

E^Aug

E G# B# E
4 3 2 1 × ×

9

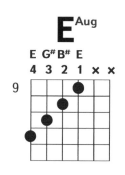

E^Aug

E G# B# E
× 3 2 1 1 ×

5

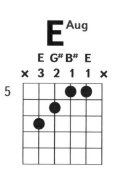

E^Aug

E   E G# B# E
0 × 3 1 2 0

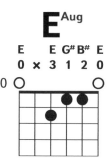

E^Aug

B# E G# B#
× 3 2 1 1 ×

1

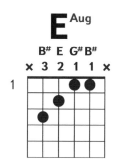

E^Aug

G# B# E G#
× 3 2 1 1 ×

9

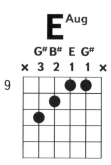

Eø

E Bb E Bb D G
1 2 3 4 4 4

0

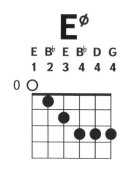

E^dim

E   Db G Bb E
2 × 1 3 1 4

11

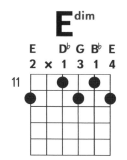

CHORDS WITH ROOT E 159

BIG
STACKED 5THS

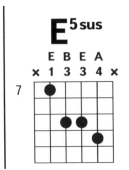
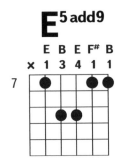
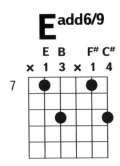

COMPACT
MAJOR

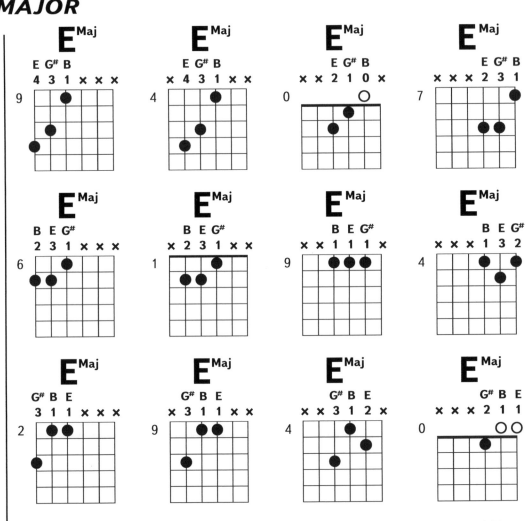

160 GUITAR CHORDS ENCYCLOPEDIA: A SEEING MUSIC METHOD BOOK

COMPACT
MINOR

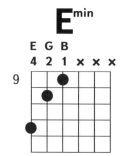

E^{min}
E G B
4 2 1 × × ×
9

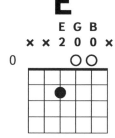

E^{min}
E G B
× 4 2 1 × ×
4

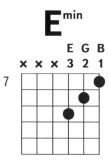

E^{min}
E G B
× × 2 0 0 ×
0

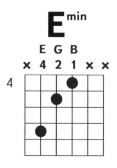

E^{min}
E G B
× × × 3 2 1
7

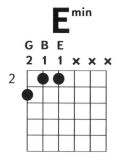

E^{min}
G B E
2 1 1 × × ×
2

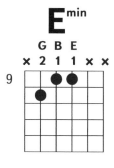

E^{min}
G B E
× 2 1 1 × ×
9

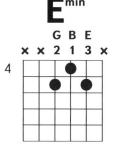

E^{min}
G B E
× × 2 1 3 ×
4

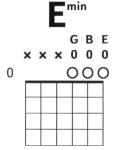

E^{min}
G B E
× × × 0 0 0
0

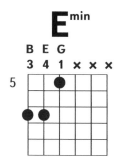

E^{min}
B E G
3 4 1 × × ×
5

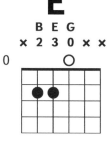

E^{min}
B E G
× 2 3 0 × ×
0

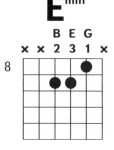

E^{min}
B E G
× × 2 3 1 ×
8

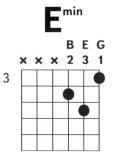

E^{min}
B E G
× × × 2 3 1
3

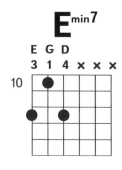

E^{min}7
E G D
3 1 4 × × ×
10

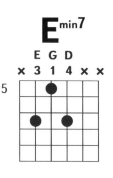

E^{min}7
E G D
× 3 1 4 × ×
5

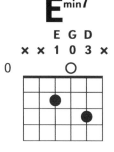

E^{min}7
E G D
× × 1 0 3 ×
0

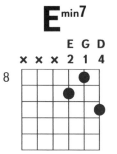

E^{min}7
E G D
× × × 2 1 4
8

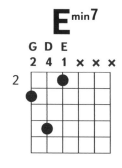

E^{min}7
G D E
2 4 1 × × ×
2

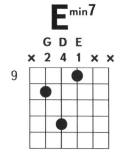

E^{min}7
G D E
× 2 4 1 × ×
9

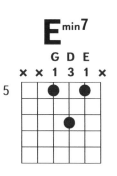

E^{min}7
G D E
× × 1 3 1 ×
5

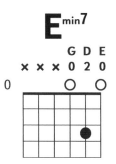

E^{min}7
G D E
× × × 0 2 0
0

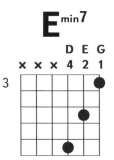

E^{min}7
D E G
× × × 4 2 1
3

COMPACT
MINOR (CONT.)

Emin7♭5
E B♭ D G
0 1 0 0 × ×
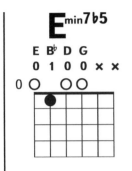

Emin7♭5
E B♭ D G
× 1 2 1 3 ×
7
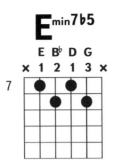

Emin7♭9
E G D F
3 1 4 1 × ×
10
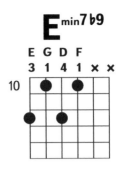

Emin7♭9
E G D F
× 3 1 4 2 ×
5
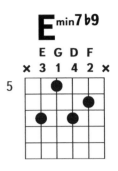

COMPACT
DOMINANT

E7
E G# D
2 1 3 × × ×
11
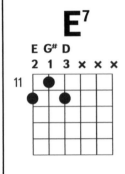

E7
E G# D
× 2 1 3 × ×
6
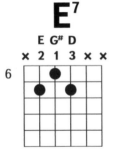

E7
E G# D
× × 2 1 4 ×
1
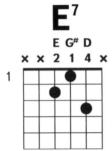

E7
B E G# D
× × 1 1 1 2
9
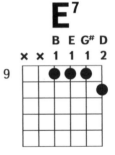

E7
G# D E
3 4 1 × × ×
2
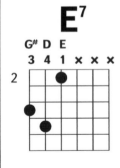

E7
G# D E
× 3 4 1 × ×
9
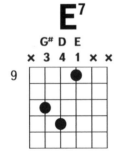

E7
G# D E
× × × 2 4 1
0
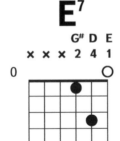

E7
D E G#
× × × 4 2 1
4
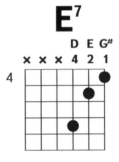

E7#5
E B# D G#
1 4 1 2 × ×
0
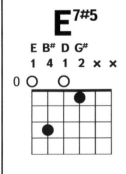

E7#5
E B# D G# B#
× 1 4 1 3 2
7
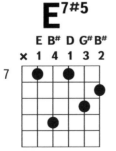

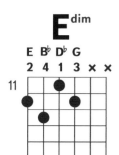

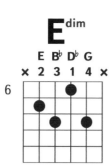

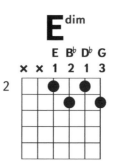

COMPACT
DIMINISHED

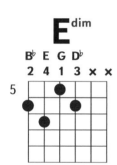

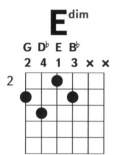

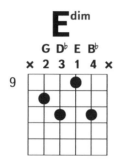

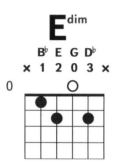

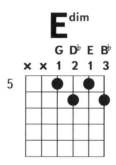

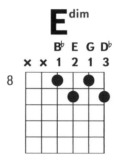

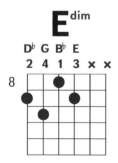

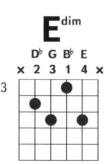

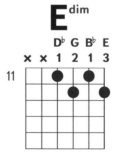

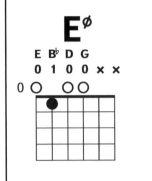

Eø

E Bb D G
0 1 0 0 x x

0

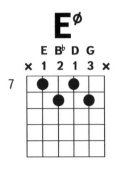

Eø

E Bb D G
x 1 2 1 3 x

7

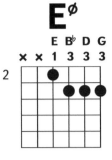

Eø

E Bb D G
x x 1 3 3 3

2

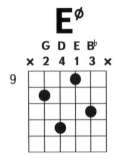

Eø

G D E Bb
x 2 4 1 3 x

9

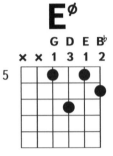

Eø

G D E Bb
x x 1 3 1 2

5

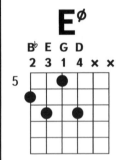

Eø

Bb E G D
2 3 1 4 x x

5

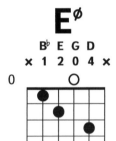

Eø

Bb E G D
x 1 2 0 4 x

0

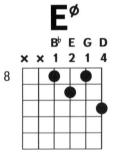

Eø

Bb E G D
x x 1 2 1 4

8

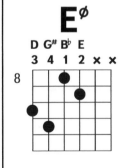

Eø

D G# Bb E
3 4 1 2 x x

8

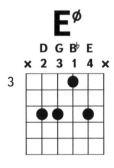

Eø

D G Bb E
x 2 3 1 4 x

3

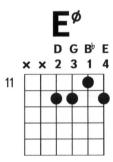

Eø

D G Bb E
x x 2 3 1 4

11

COMPACT
AUGMENTED

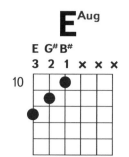
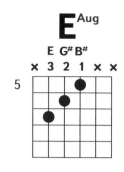
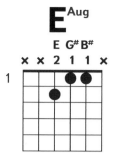
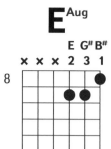

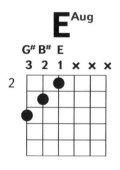
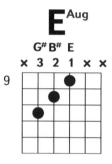
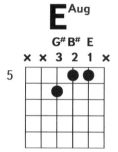
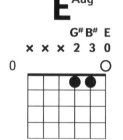

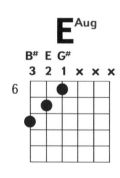
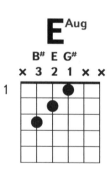
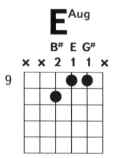
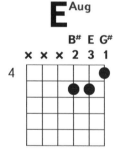

COMPACT
STACKED 5THS

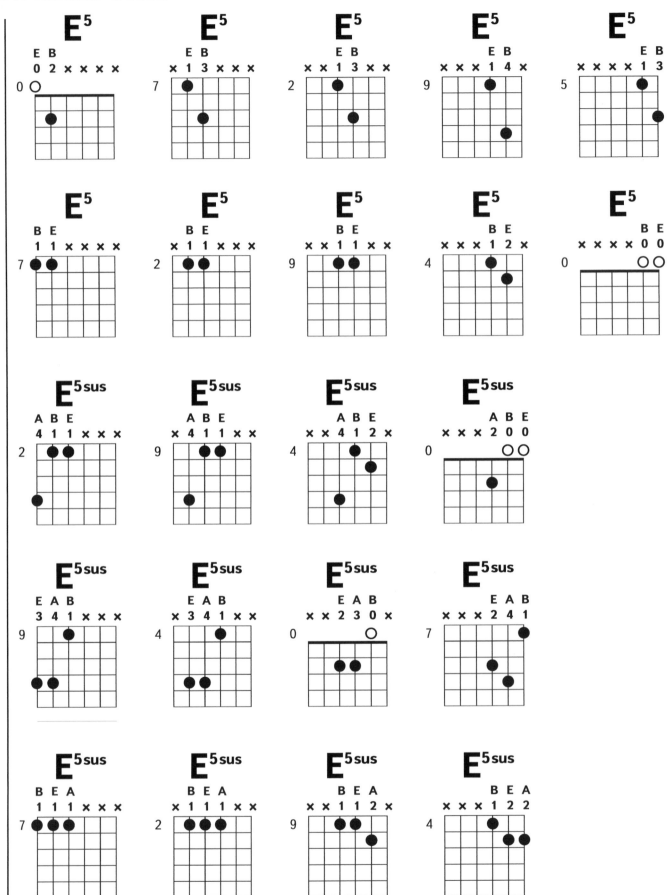

E⁵add9

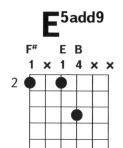

F#   E B
1 × 1 4 × ×
2

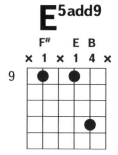

F#   E B
× 1 × 1 4 ×
9

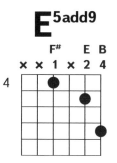

F# E B
× × 1 × 2 4
4

E⁵add9

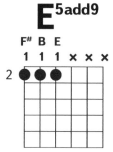

F# B E
1 1 1 × × ×
2

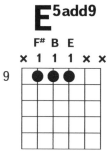

F# B E
× 1 1 1 × ×
9

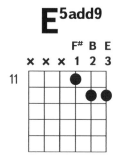

F# B E
× × 1 1 2 ×
4

E⁵add9

F# B E
× × × 1 2 3
11

E⁵add9

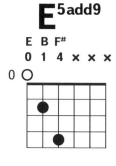

E B F#
0 1 4 × × ×
0 ○

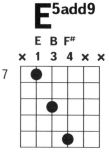

E B F#
× 1 3 4 × ×
7

E⁵add6/9

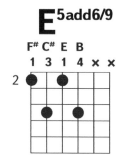

F# C# E B
1 3 1 4 × ×
2

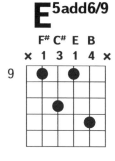

F# C# E B
× 1 3 1 4 ×
9

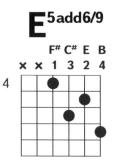

F# C# E B
× × 1 3 2 4
4

E⁵add6/9

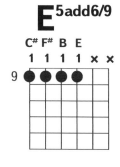

C# F# B E
1 1 1 1 × ×
9

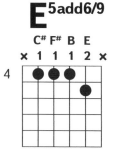

C# F# B E
× 1 1 1 2 ×
4

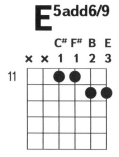

C# F# B E
× × 1 1 2 3
11

COMPACT
STACKED 5THS
(CONT.)

CHORDS WITH ROOT E 167

VIVID
MAJOR

E△7
D# G# B E
3 4 1 1 × ×
9

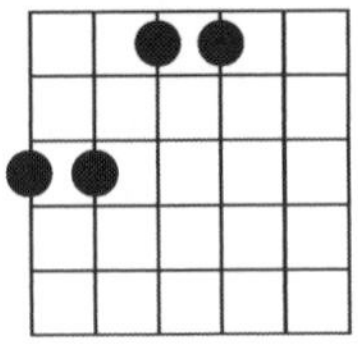

E△7
D# G# B E
× 3 4 1 2 ×
4

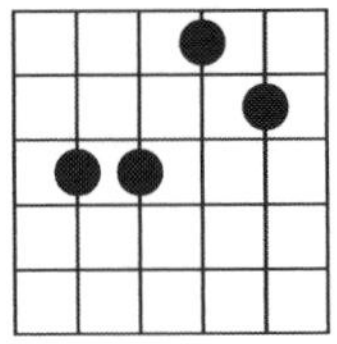

E△7
D# G# B E
× × 1 2 0 0
0

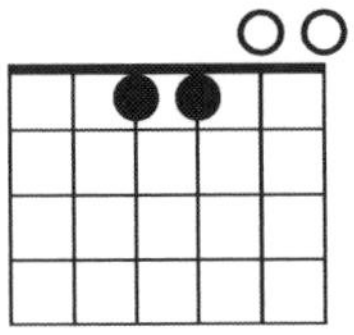

E△9
D# G# B F#
2 3 1 4 × ×
9

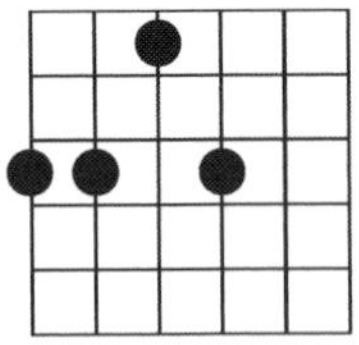

E△9
D# G# B F#
× 2 3 1 4 ×
4

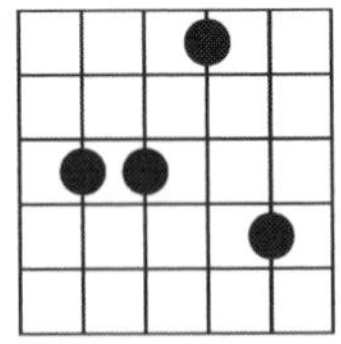

E△9
D# G# B F#
× × 1 2 0 4
0

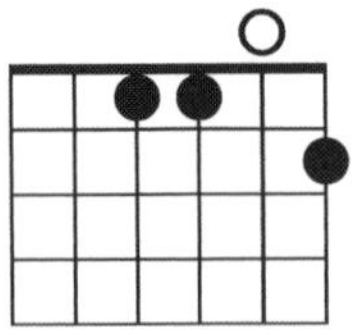

E6/9
G# C# F# B
1 1 1 1 × ×
4

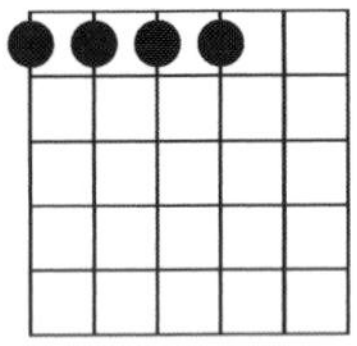

E6/9
G# C# F# B
× 1 1 1 2 ×
11

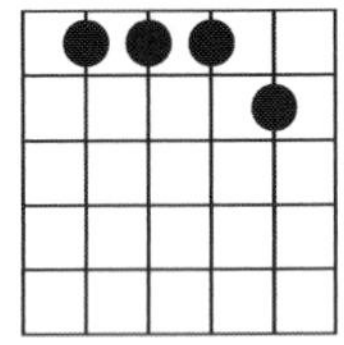

E6/9
G# C# F# B
× × 1 1 2 3
6

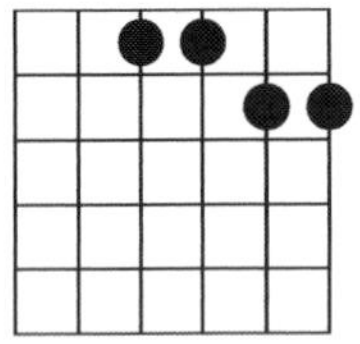

E6/9
G# C# F#
× × × 1 2 2
1

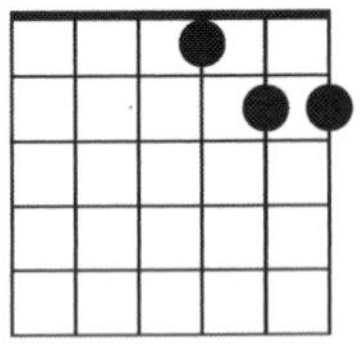

E6/9
C# G# B F#
1 3 1 4 × ×
9

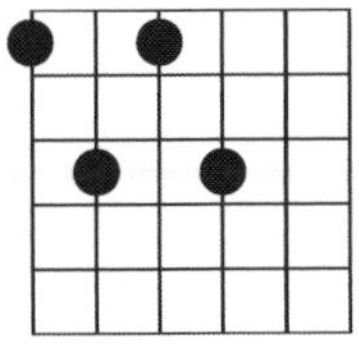

E6/9
C# G# B F#
× 1 3 1 4 ×
4

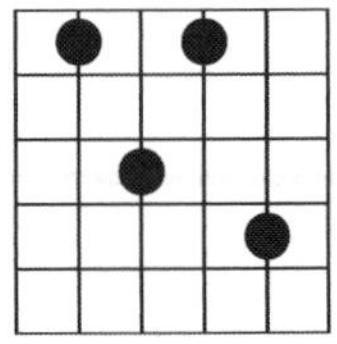

E6/9
C# G# B F#
× × 1 3 2 4
11

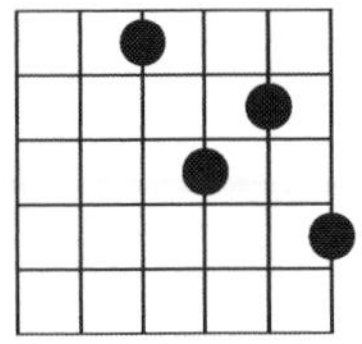

E△7#11
A# E G# D#
1 2 1 4 × ×
6

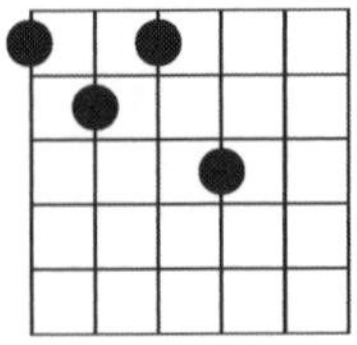

E△7#11
A# E G# D#
× × 1 2 3 4
8

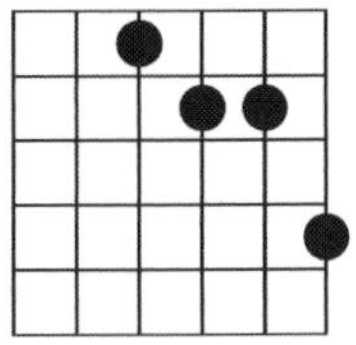

168 GUITAR CHORDS ENCYCLOPEDIA: A SEEING MUSIC METHOD BOOK

E△7#11

E A# D# G#
0 1 2 3 × ×
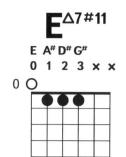

E△7#11

E A# D# G#
× 1 2 3 4 ×
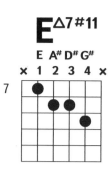
7

E△7#11

E A# D# G#
× × 1 2 3 4
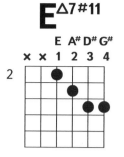
2

E△7#11

D# G# A# E
× × 3 4 1 2
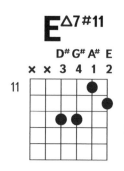
11

Emin7

B D G
3 1 1 × × ×
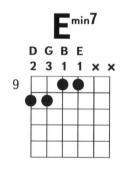
5

Emin7

B D G
× 2 0 0 × ×
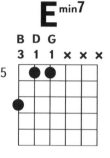
0

Emin7

B D G
× × 3 1 2 ×
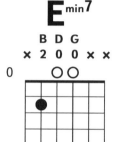
7

Emin7

B D G
× × × 2 1 1
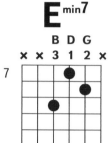
3

Emin7

D G B E
2 3 1 1 × ×
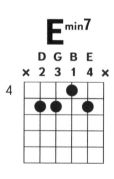
9

Emin7

D G B E
× 2 3 1 4 ×
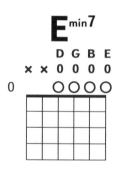
4

Emin7

D G B E
× × 0 0 0 0
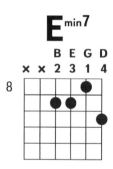
0

Emin7

B E G D
× × 2 3 1 4
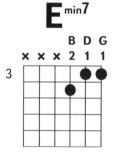
8

Emin7b5

G D E Bb
× 2 4 1 3 ×
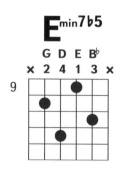
9

Emin7b5

G D E Bb
× × 1 4 1 2
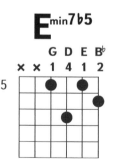
5

Emin7b5

Bb E G D
2 3 1 4 × ×
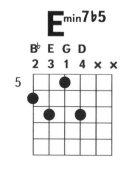
5

Emin7b5

Bb E G D
× 1 2 0 3 ×
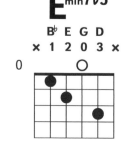
0

Emin7b5

Bb E G D
× × 1 2 1 4
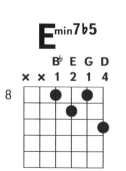
8

Emin7b5

D G Bb E
× 2 3 1 4 ×
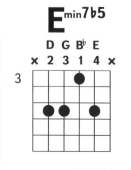
3

Emin7b5

D G Bb E
× × 2 3 1 4
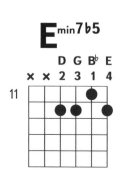
11

CHORDS WITH ROOT E 169

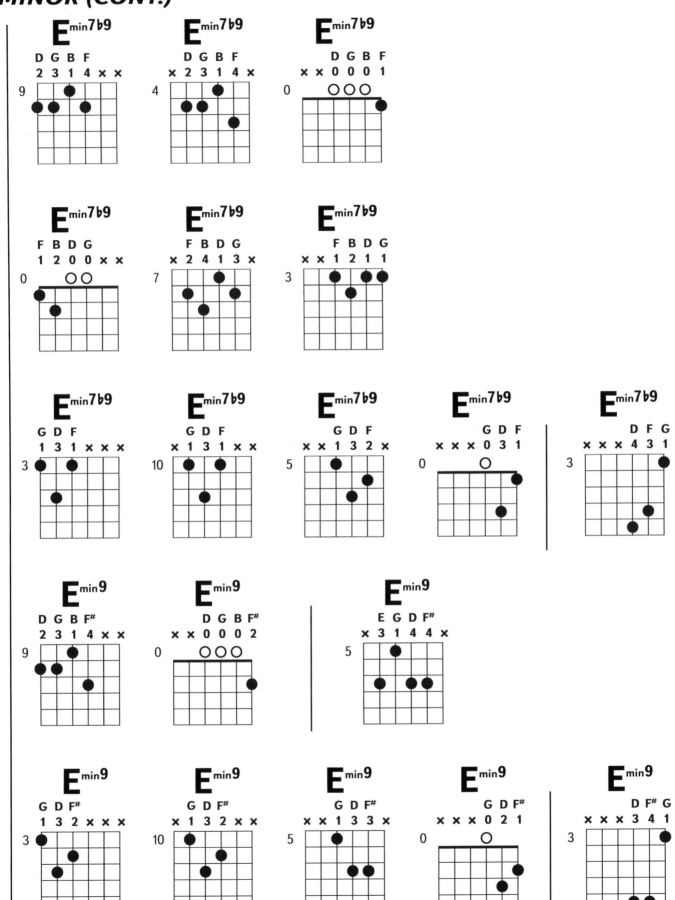

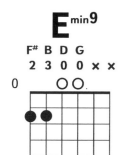

Emin9

F# B D G
2 3 0 0 × ×
0

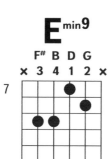

Emin9

F# B D G
× 3 4 1 2 ×
7

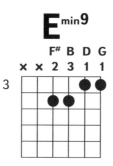

Emin9

F# B D G
× × 2 3 1 1
3

E

VIVID
MINOR (CONT.)

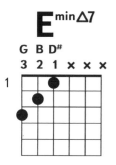

Emin△7

G B D#
3 2 1 × × ×
1

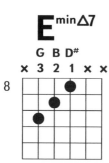

Emin△7

G B D#
× 3 2 1 × ×
8

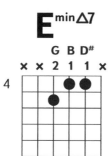

Emin△7

G B D#
× × 2 1 1 ×
4

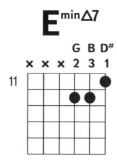

Emin△7

G B D#
× × × 2 3 1
11

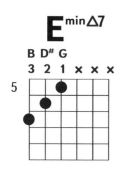

Emin△7

B D# G
3 2 1 × × ×
5

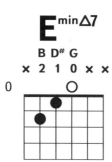

Emin△7

B D# G
× 2 1 0 × ×
0

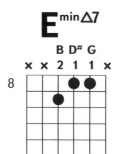

Emin△7

B D# G
× × 2 1 1 ×
8

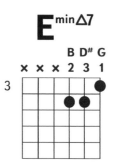

Emin△7

B D# G
× × × 2 3 1
3

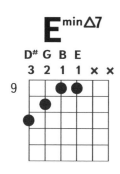

Emin△7

D# G B E
3 2 1 1 × ×
9

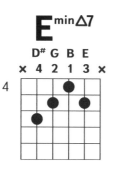

Emin△7

D# G B E
× 4 2 1 3 ×
4

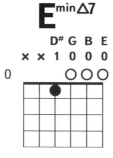

Emin△7

D# G B E
× × 1 0 0 0
0

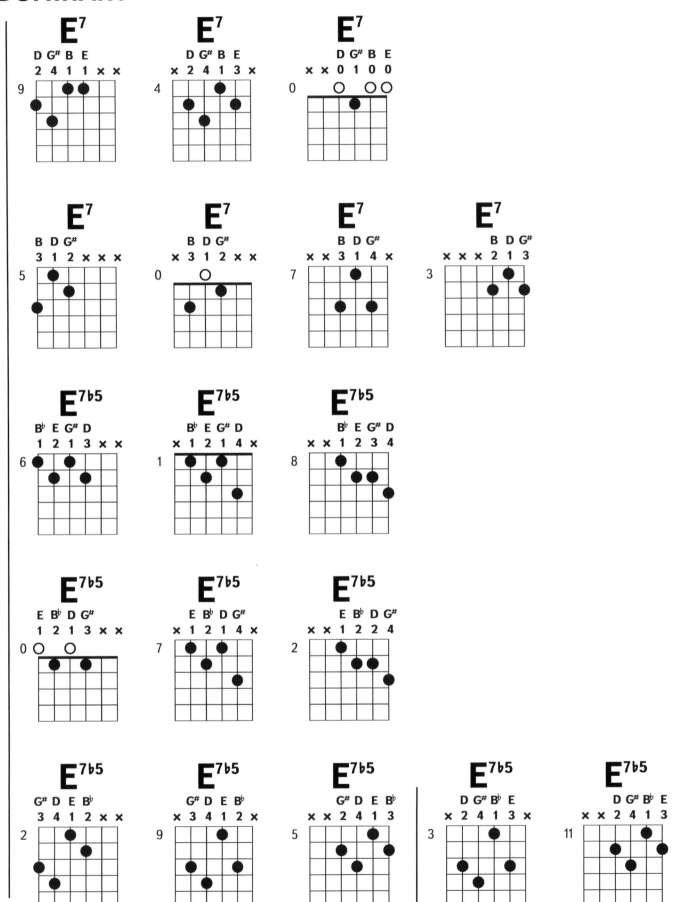

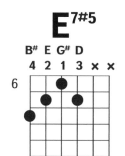

E⁷#5

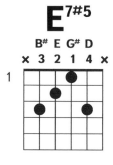

E⁷#5

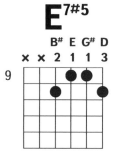

E⁷#5

VIVID
DOMINANT (CONT.)

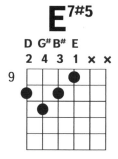

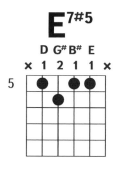

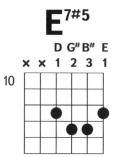

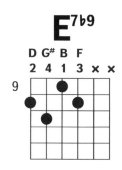

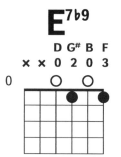

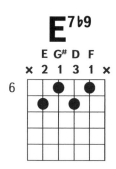

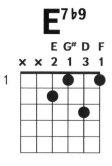

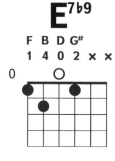

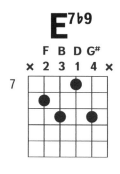

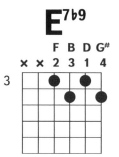

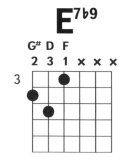

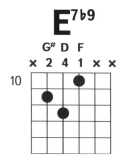

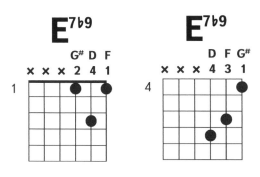

CHORDS WITH ROOT E 173

E⁹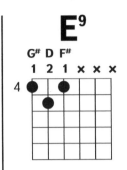
E⁹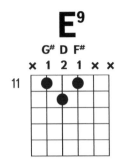
E⁹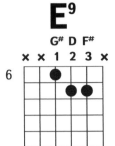
E⁹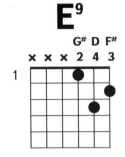
E⁹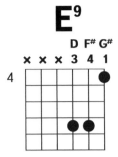

E⁹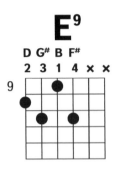
E⁹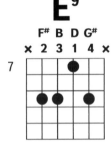

E⁹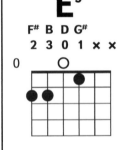
E⁹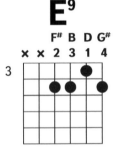
E⁹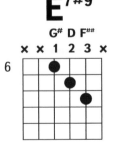

E⁷#⁹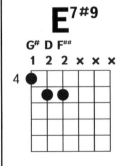
E⁷#⁹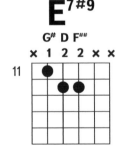
E⁷#⁹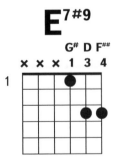
E⁷#⁹

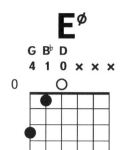

E$^\emptyset$

G B♭ D
4 1 0 × × ×
0

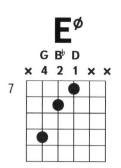

E$^\emptyset$

G B♭ D
× 4 2 1 × ×
7

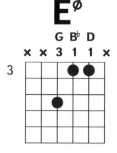

E$^\emptyset$

G B♭ D
× × 3 1 1 ×
3

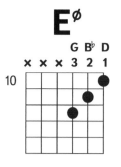

E$^\emptyset$

G B♭ D
× × × 3 2 1
10

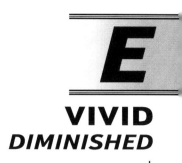

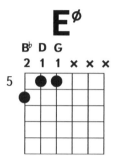

E$^\emptyset$

B♭ D G
2 1 1 × × ×
5

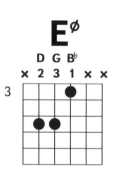

E$^\emptyset$

B♭ D G
× 1 0 0 × ×
0

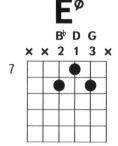

E$^\emptyset$

B♭ D G
× × 2 1 3 ×
7

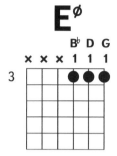

E$^\emptyset$

B♭ D G
× × × 1 1 1
3

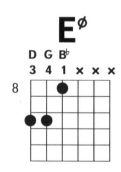

E$^\emptyset$

D G B♭
3 4 1 × × ×
8

E$^\emptyset$

D G B♭
× 2 3 1 × ×
3

E$^\emptyset$

D G B♭
× × 2 3 1 ×
11

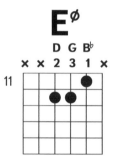

E$^\emptyset$

D G B♭
× × × 2 3 1
6

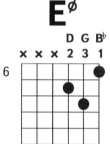

E$^\emptyset$

E$^\emptyset$

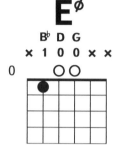

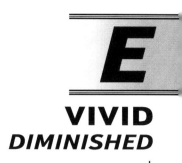

VIVID
DIMINISHED

F^{Maj}

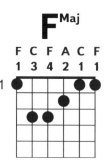

F^{Maj}

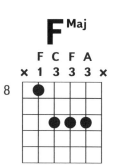

F^{△7}

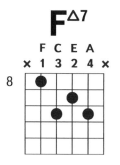

F^{△7#11}

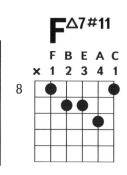

F^{△9}

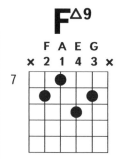

F^{6/9}

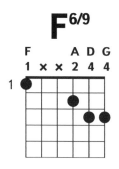

F^{6/9}

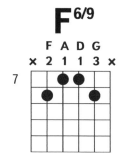

F^{add9}

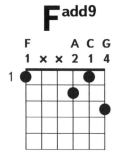

GUITAR CHORDS ENCYCLOPEDIA

BIG
MINOR

F^{min}
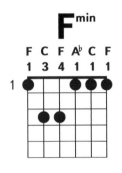

F^{min}
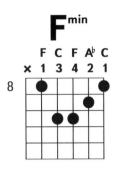

F^{min}7

F^{min}7♭5
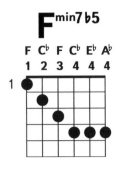

F^{min}7♭9
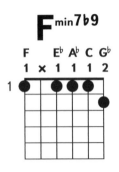

F^{min}9

F^{min}△7
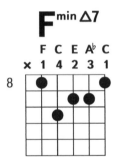

BIG
DOMINANT

F⁷
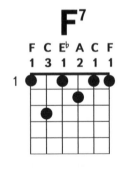

F⁷
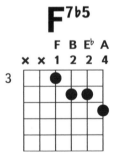

F^{7♭5}
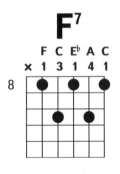

F^{7#5}
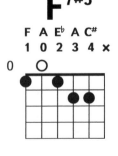

F^{7#5}
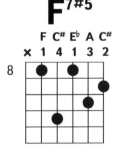

178 GUITAR CHORDS ENCYCLOPEDIA: A SEEING MUSIC METHOD BOOK

F$^{7\flat 9}$

F E$^\flat$ A C G$^\flat$
1 × 1 2 1 3

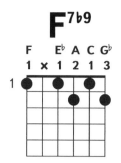

F^9

F C E$^\flat$ A C G
1 3 1 2 1 4

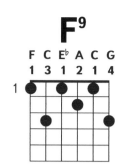

F^9

F A E$^\flat$ G
× 2 1 3 4 ×

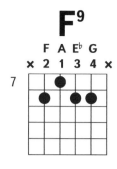

F$^{7\#9}$

F E$^\flat$ A E$^\flat$ G$^\#$
1 × 1 2 4 4

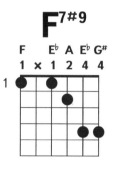

F$^{7\#9}$

F E$^\flat$ A C G$^\#$
1 × 1 2 1 4

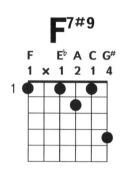

F$^{7\#9}$

F A E$^\flat$ G$^\#$
× 2 1 3 4 ×

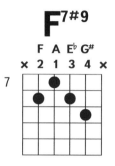

F$^{7\#9}$

F A E$^\flat$ G$^\#$
× × 2 1 4 4

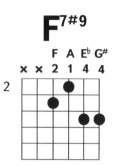

F^{Aug}

F A C$^\#$ F
4 3 2 1 × ×

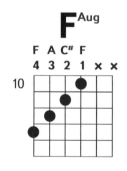

F^{Aug}

F A C$^\#$ F
× 3 2 1 1 ×

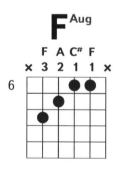

F^{Aug}

F F A C$^\#$ F
1 × 4 2 3 1

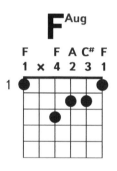

F^{Aug}

C$^\#$ F A C$^\#$
× 3 2 1 1 ×

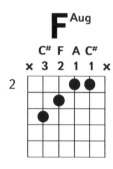

F^{Aug}

A C$^\#$ F A
× 3 2 1 1 ×

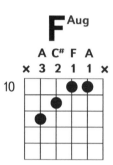

F$^{\emptyset}$

F B F B E$^\flat$ A$^\flat$
1 2 3 4 4 4

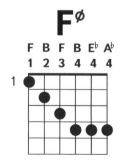

F^{dim}

F E$^{\flat\flat}$ A$^\flat$ C$^\flat$ F
1 × 0 2 0 3

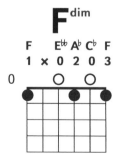

BIG
STACKED 5THS

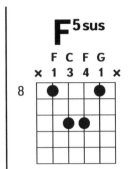

F^{5sus}

F C F G
× 1 3 4 1 ×
8

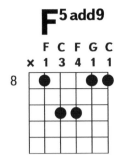

F^{5add9}

F C F G C
× 1 3 4 1 1
8

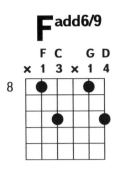

F^{add6/9}

F C G D
× 1 3 × 1 4
8

COMPACT
MAJOR

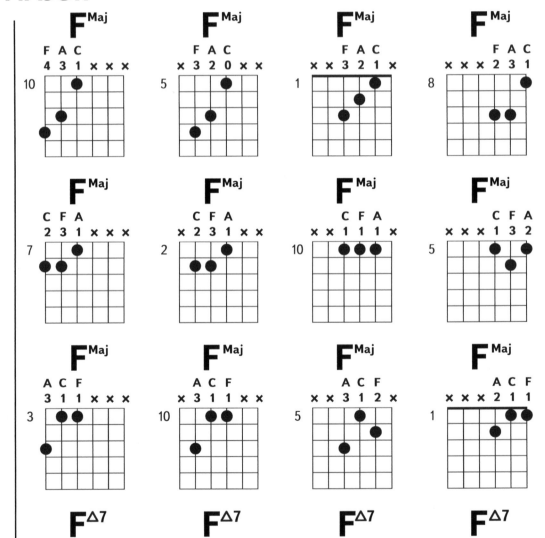

F^{Maj}

F A C
4 3 1 × × ×
10

F^{Maj}

F A C
× 3 2 0 × ×
5

F^{Maj}

F A C
× × 3 2 1 ×
1

F^{Maj}

F A C
× × × 2 3 1
8

F^{Maj}

C F A
2 3 1 × × ×
7

F^{Maj}

C F A
× 2 3 1 × ×
2

F^{Maj}

C F A
× × 1 1 1 ×
10

F^{Maj}

C F A
× × × 1 3 2
5

F^{Maj}

A C F
3 1 1 × × ×
3

F^{Maj}

A C F
× 3 1 1 × ×
10

F^{Maj}

A C F
× × 3 1 2 ×
5

F^{Maj}

A C F
× × × 2 1 1
1

F^{Δ7}

F A E
1 0 3 × × ×
0

F^{Δ7}

F A E
× 2 1 4 × ×
7

F^{Δ7}

F A E
× × 2 1 4 ×
2

F^{Δ7}

C F A E
× × 1 1 1 4
10

F^{add9}

F A C G
× × 3 2 1 4
1

180 GUITAR CHORDS ENCYCLOPEDIA: A SEEING MUSIC METHOD BOOK

COMPACT
MINOR

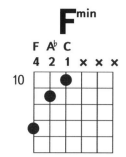

Fmin
F Ab C
4 2 1 × × ×
10

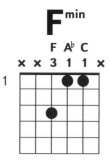

Fmin
F Ab C
× 4 2 1 × ×
5

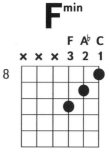

Fmin
× × 3 1 1 ×
F Ab C
1

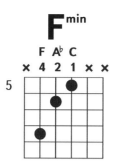

Fmin
F Ab C
× × × 3 2 1
8

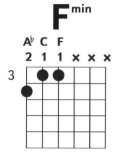

Fmin
Ab C F
2 1 1 × × ×
3

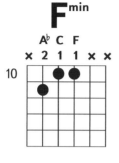

Fmin
Ab C F
× 2 1 1 × ×
10

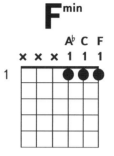

Fmin
Ab C F
× × 2 1 3 ×
5

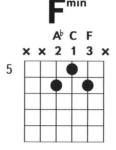

Fmin
Ab C F
× × × 1 1 1
1

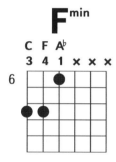

Fmin
C F Ab
3 4 1 × × ×
6

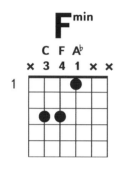

Fmin
C F Ab
× 3 4 1 × ×
1

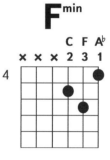

Fmin
C F Ab
× × 2 3 1 ×
9

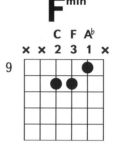

Fmin
C F Ab
× × × 2 3 1
4

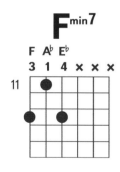

Fmin7
F Ab Eb
3 1 4 × × ×
11

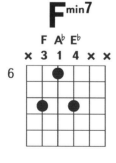

Fmin7
F Ab Eb
× 3 1 4 × ×
6

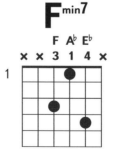

Fmin7
F Ab Eb
× × 3 1 4 ×
1

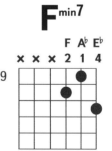

Fmin7
F Ab Eb
× × × 2 1 4
9

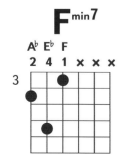

Fmin7
Ab Eb F
2 4 1 × × ×
3

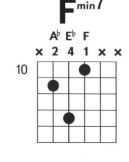

Fmin7
Ab Eb F
× 2 4 1 × ×
10

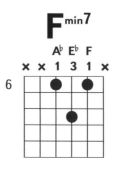

Fmin7
Ab Eb F
× × 1 3 1 ×
6

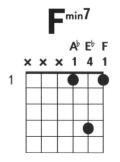

Fmin7
Ab Eb F
× × × 1 4 1
1

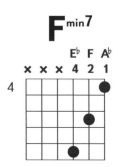

Fmin7
Eb F Ab
× × × 4 2 1
4

CHORDS WITH ROOT F 181

COMPACT
MINOR (CONT.)

Fmin7♭5
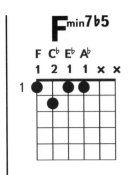

Fmin7♭5
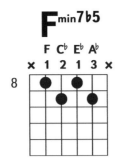

Fmin7♭9
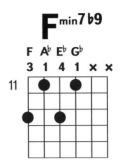

Fmin7♭9
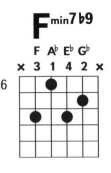

COMPACT
DOMINANT

F7
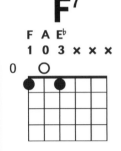

F7
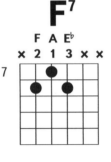

F7
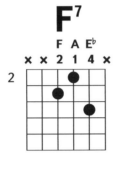

F7
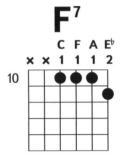

F7
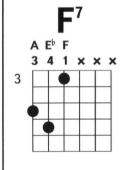

F7
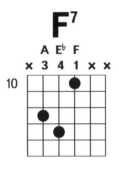

F7
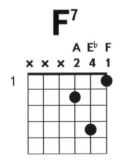

F7
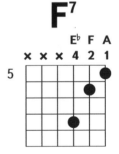

F7#5
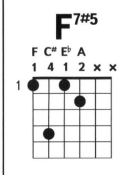

F7#5
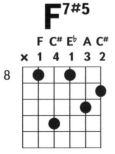

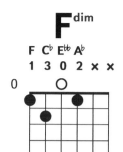

Fdim

F C♭ E♭♭ A♭
1 3 0 2 × ×
0

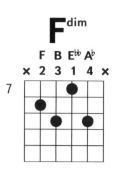

Fdim

F B E♭♭ A♭
× 2 3 1 4 ×
7

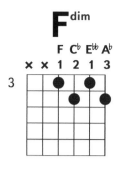

Fdim

F C♭ E♭♭ A♭
× × 1 2 1 3
3

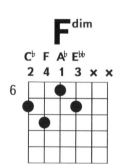

Fdim

A♭ E♭♭ F C♭
2 4 1 3 × ×
3

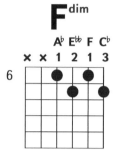

Fdim

A♭ E♭♭ F B
× 2 3 1 4 ×
10

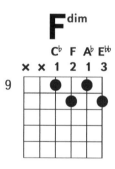

Fdim

A♭ E♭♭ F C♭
× × 1 2 1 3
6

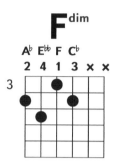

Fdim

C♭ F A♭ E♭♭
2 4 1 3 × ×
6

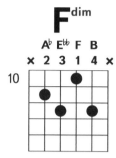

Fdim

B F A♭ E♭♭
× 2 3 1 4 ×
1

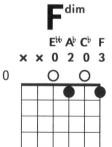

Fdim

C♭ F A♭ E♭♭
× × 1 2 1 3
9

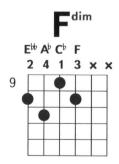

Fdim

E♭♭ A♭ C♭ F
2 4 1 3 × ×
9

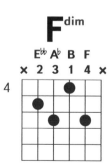

Fdim

E♭♭ A♭ B F
× 2 3 1 4 ×
4

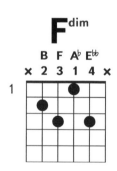

Fdim

E♭♭ A♭ C♭ F
× × 0 2 0 3
0

COMPACT
DIMINISHED (CONT.)

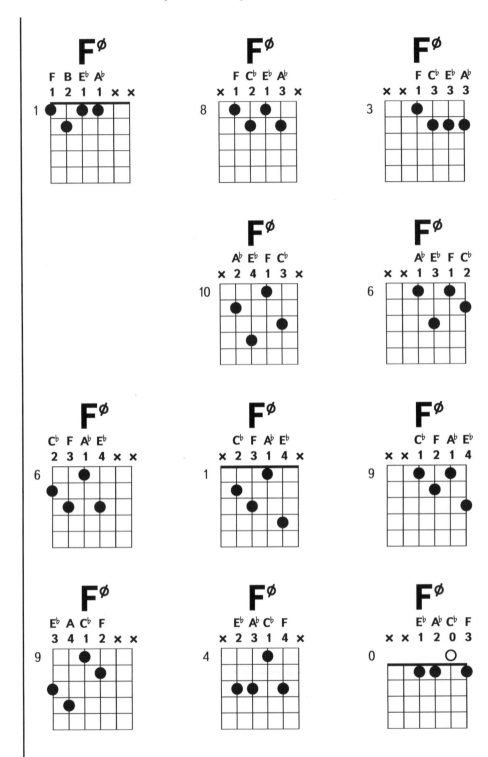

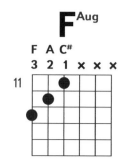
F^{Aug}
F A C#
3 2 1 × × ×
11

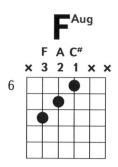
F^{Aug}
F A C#
× 3 2 1 × ×
6

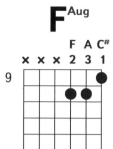
F^{Aug}
F A C#
× × 2 1 1 ×
2

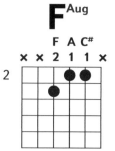
F^{Aug}
F A C#
× × × 2 3 1
9

COMPACT
AUGMENTED

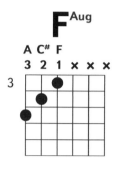
F^{Aug}
A C# F
3 2 1 × × ×
3

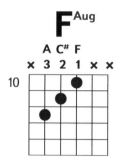
F^{Aug}
A C# F
× 3 2 1 × ×
10

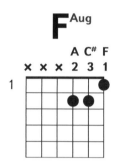
F^{Aug}
A C# F
× × 3 2 1 ×
6

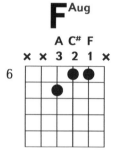
F^{Aug}
A C# F
× × × 2 3 1
1

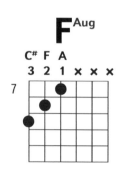
F^{Aug}
C# F A
3 2 1 × × ×
7

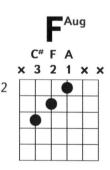
F^{Aug}
C# F A
× 3 2 1 × ×
2

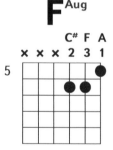
F^{Aug}
C# F A
× × 2 1 1 ×
10

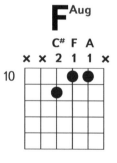
F^{Aug}
C# F A
× × × 2 3 1
5

COMPACT
STACKED 5THS

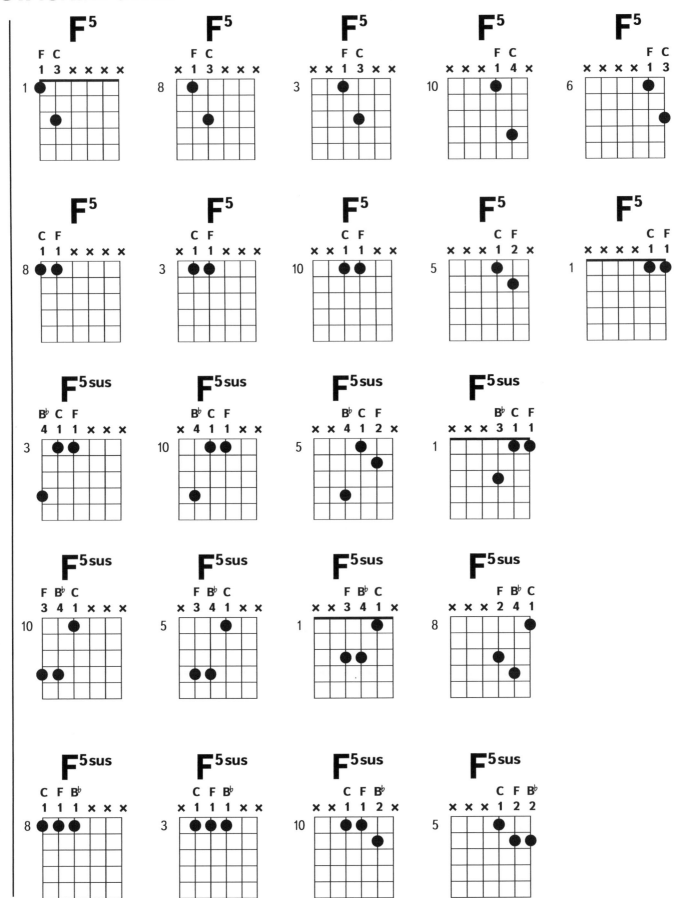

F⁵ᵃᵈᵈ⁹

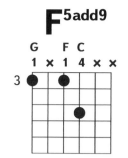

F⁵ᵃᵈᵈ⁹

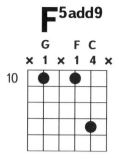

F⁵ᵃᵈᵈ⁹

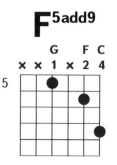

F⁵ᵃᵈᵈ⁹

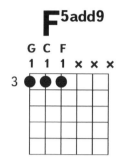

F⁵ᵃᵈᵈ⁹

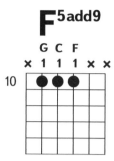

F⁵ᵃᵈᵈ⁹

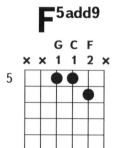

F⁵ᵃᵈᵈ⁹

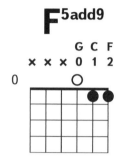

F⁵ᵃᵈᵈ⁹

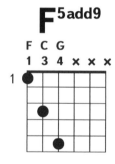

F⁵ᵃᵈᵈ⁹

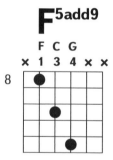

F⁵ᵃᵈᵈ⁶/⁹

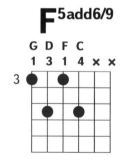

F⁵ᵃᵈᵈ⁶/⁹

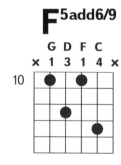

F⁵ᵃᵈᵈ⁶/⁹

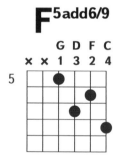

F⁵ᵃᵈᵈ⁶/⁹

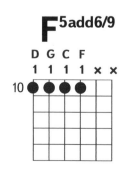

F⁵ᵃᵈᵈ⁶/⁹

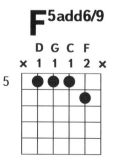

F⁵ᵃᵈᵈ⁶/⁹

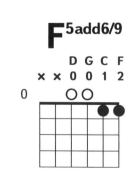

F△7

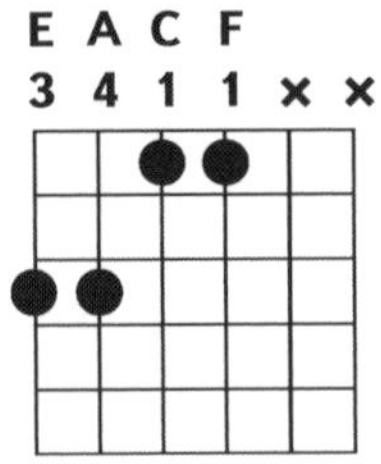

E A C F
3 4 1 1 × ×
10

F△7

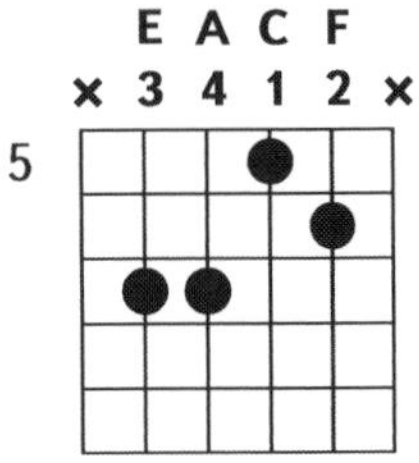

E A C F
× 3 4 1 2 ×
5

F△7

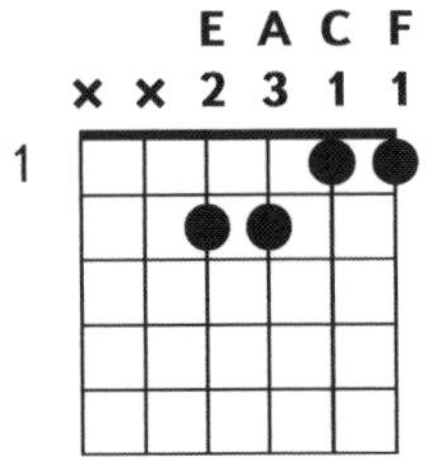

E A C F
× × 2 3 1 1
1

F△9

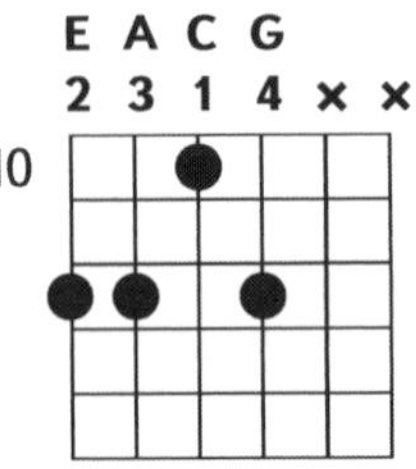

E A C G
2 3 1 4 × ×
10

F△9

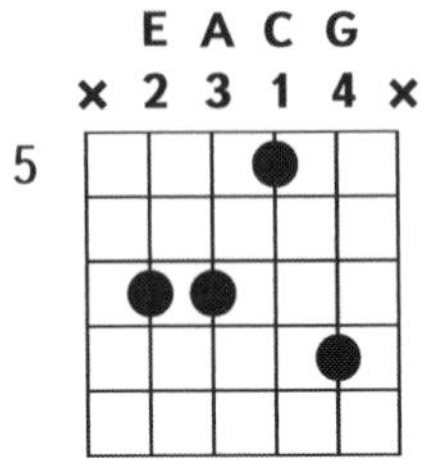

E A C G
× 2 3 1 4 ×
5

F△9

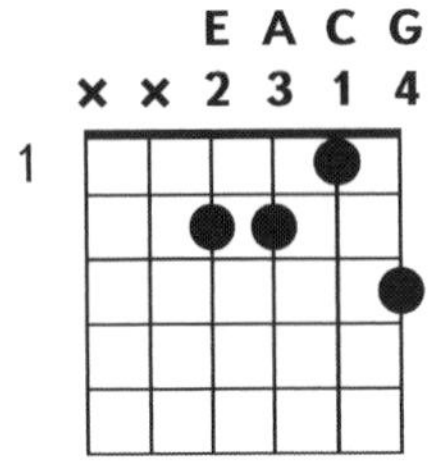

E A C G
× × 2 3 1 4
1

F6/9

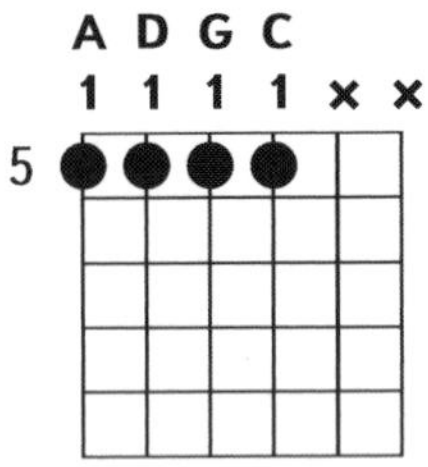

A D G C
1 1 1 1 × ×
5

F6/9

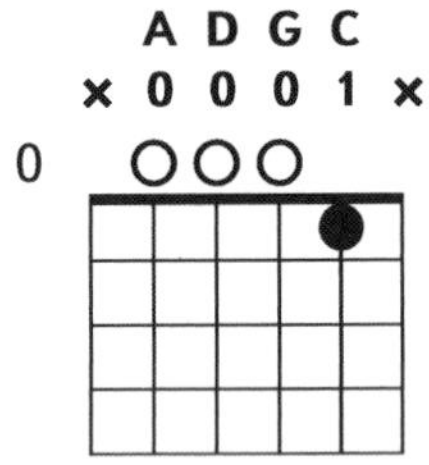

A D G C
× 0 0 0 1 ×
0

F6/9

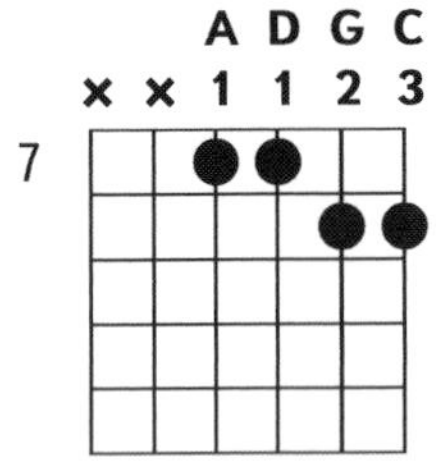

A D G C
× × 1 1 2 3
7

F6/9

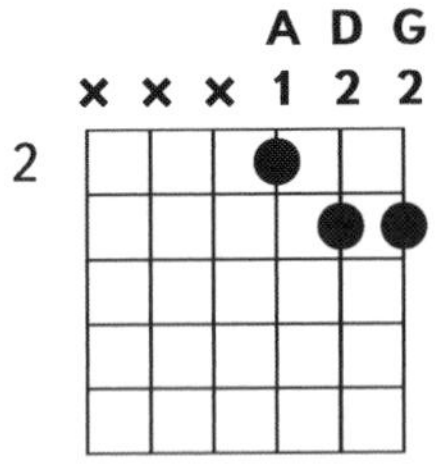

A D G
× × × 1 2 2
2

F6/9

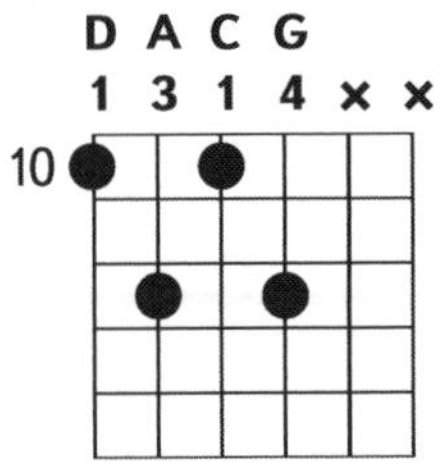

D A C G
1 3 1 4 × ×
10

F6/9

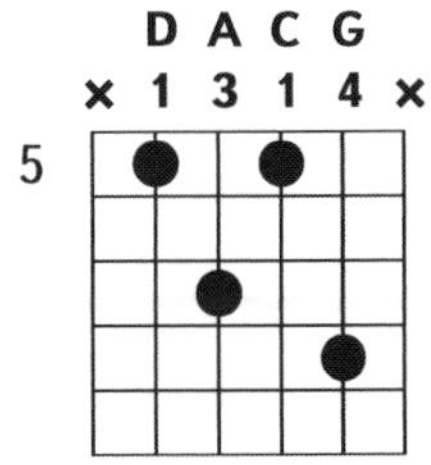

D A C G
× 1 3 1 4 ×
5

F6/9

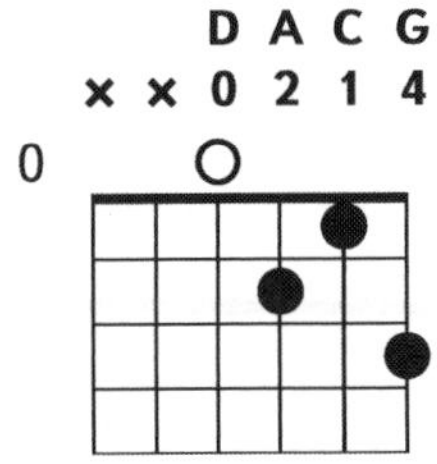

D A C G
× × 0 2 1 4
0

F△7#11

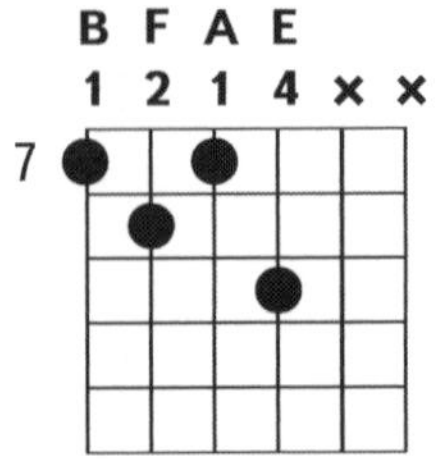

B F A E
1 2 1 4 × ×
7

F△7#11

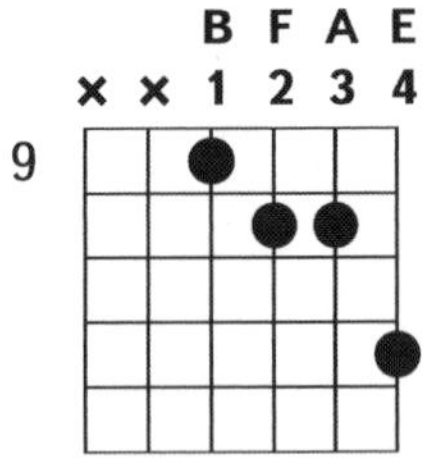

B F A E
× × 1 2 3 4
9

188 GUITAR CHORDS ENCYCLOPEDIA: A SEEING MUSIC METHOD BOOK

VIVID
MINOR

F△7#11

F B E A
1 2 3 4 × ×

1

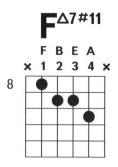

F△7#11

F B E A
× 1 2 3 4 ×

8

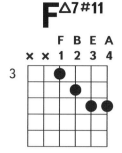

F△7#11

F B E A
× × 1 2 3 4

3

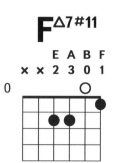

F△7#11

E A B F
× × 2 3 0 1

0

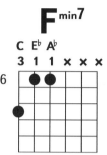

Fmin7

C E♭ A♭
3 1 1 × × ×

6

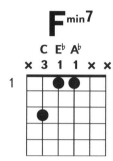

Fmin7

C E♭ A♭
× 3 1 1 × ×

1

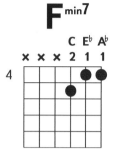

Fmin7

C E♭ A♭
× × 3 1 2 ×

8

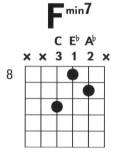

Fmin7

C E♭ A♭
× × × 2 1 1

4

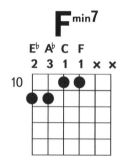

Fmin7

E♭ A♭ C F
2 3 1 1 × ×

10

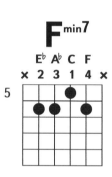

Fmin7

E♭ A♭ C F
× 2 3 1 4 ×

5

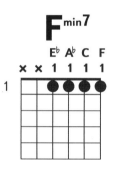

Fmin7

E♭ A♭ C F
× × 1 1 1 1

1

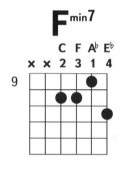

Fmin7

C F A♭ E♭
× × 2 3 1 4

9

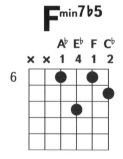

Fmin7♭5

A♭ E♭ F C♭
× 2 4 1 3 ×

10

Fmin7♭5

A♭ E♭ F C♭
× × 1 4 1 2

6

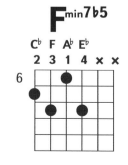

Fmin7♭5

C♭ F A♭ E♭
2 3 1 4 × ×

6

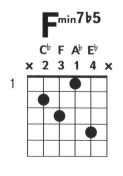

Fmin7♭5

C♭ F A♭ E♭
× 2 3 1 4 ×

1

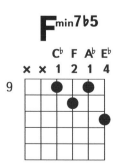

Fmin7♭5

C♭ F A♭ E♭
× × 1 2 1 4

9

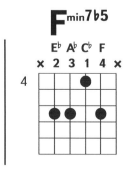

Fmin7♭5

E♭ A♭ C♭ F
× 2 3 1 4 ×

4

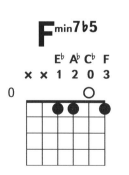

Fmin7♭5

E♭ A♭ C♭ F
× × 1 2 0 3

0

CHORDS WITH ROOT F 189

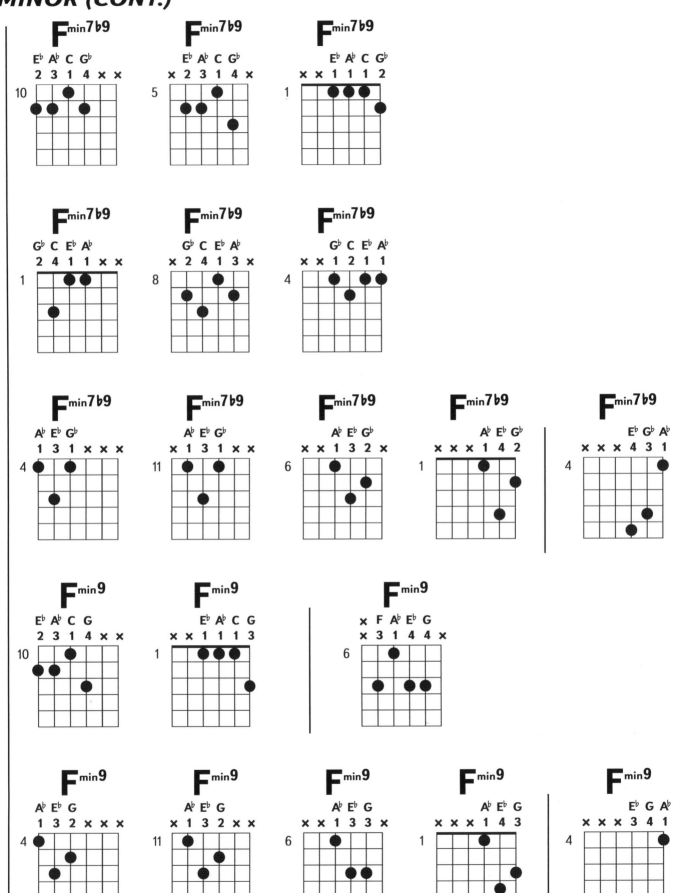

Fmin**9**

G C E♭ A♭
2 3 1 1 × ×

1

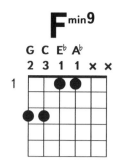

Fmin**9**

× 3 4 1 2 ×

8

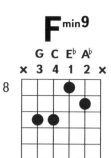

Fmin**9**

× × 2 3 1 1

4

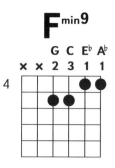

Fmin△**7**

A♭ C E
3 2 1 × × ×

2

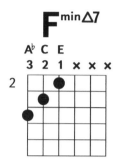

Fmin△**7**

× 3 2 1 × ×

9

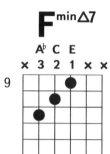

Fmin△**7**

× × 2 1 1 ×

5

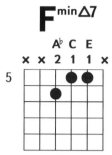

Fmin△**7**

× × × 2 3 1

0

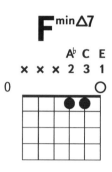

Fmin△**7**

C E A♭
3 2 1 × × ×

6

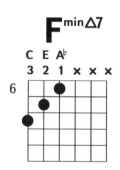

Fmin△**7**

× 3 2 1 × ×

1

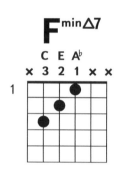

Fmin△**7**

× × 2 1 1 ×

9

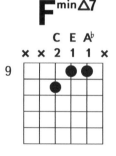

Fmin△**7**

× × 2 3 1

4

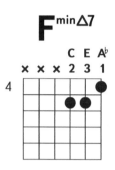

Fmin△**7**

E A♭ C F
3 2 1 1 × ×

10

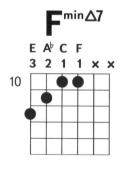

Fmin△**7**

× 4 2 1 3 ×

5

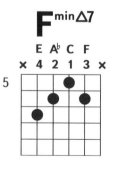

Fmin△**7**

E A♭ C F
× × 2 1 1 1

1

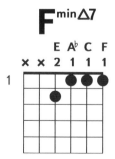

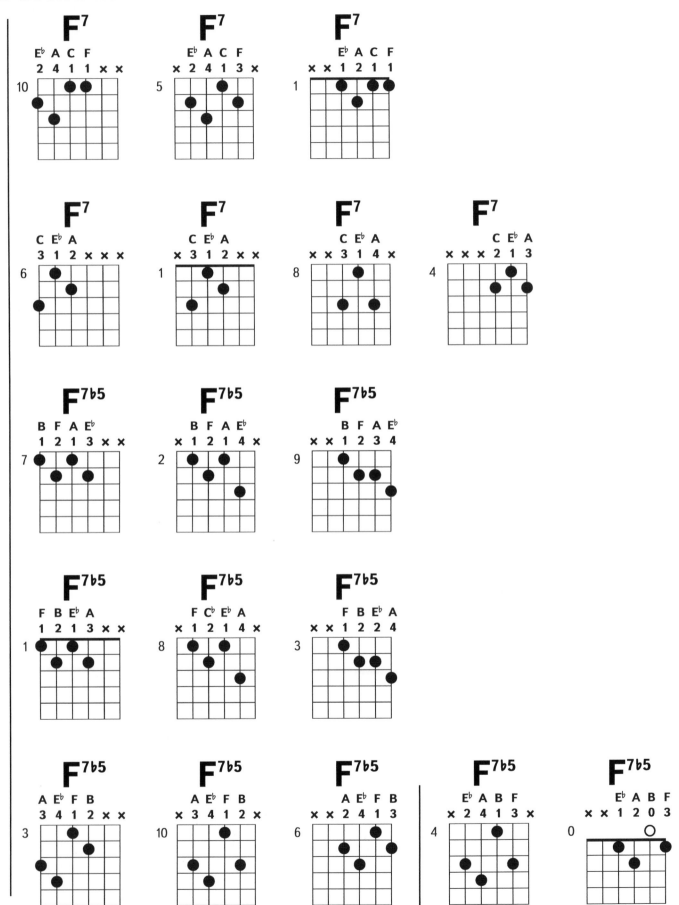

F$^{7\#5}$

C# F A E♭
4 2 1 3 × ×
7
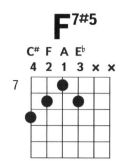

F$^{7\#5}$

C# F A E♭
× 3 2 1 4 ×
2
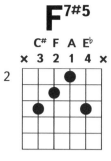

F$^{7\#5}$

C# F A E♭
× × 2 1 1 3
10
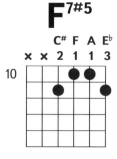

F$^{7\#5}$

E♭ A C# F
2 4 3 1 × ×
10
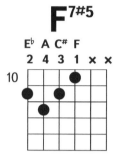

F$^{7\#5}$

E♭ A C# F
× 1 2 1 1 ×
6
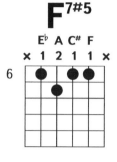

F$^{7\#5}$

E♭ A C# F
× × 1 2 3 1
1
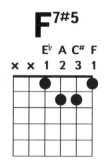

F$^{7♭9}$

E♭ A C G♭
2 4 1 3 × ×
10
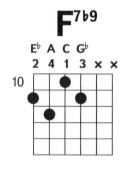

F$^{7♭9}$

E♭ A C G♭
× × 1 2 1 3
1
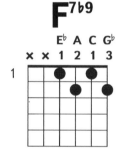

F$^{7♭9}$

F A E♭ G♭
× 2 1 3 1 ×
7
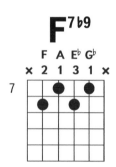

F$^{7♭9}$

F A E♭ G♭
× × 2 1 3 1
2
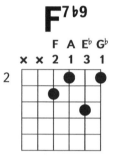

F$^{7♭9}$

G♭ C E♭ A
2 4 1 3 × ×
1
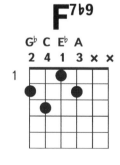

F$^{7♭9}$

G♭ C E♭ A
× 2 3 1 4 ×
8
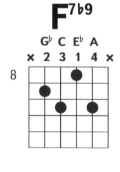

F$^{7♭9}$

G♭ C E♭ A
× × 2 3 1 4
4
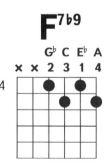

F$^{7♭9}$

A E♭ G♭
2 3 1 × × ×
4
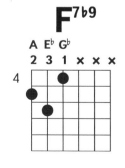

F$^{7♭9}$

A E♭ G♭
× 2 4 1 × ×
11
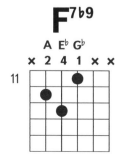

F$^{7♭9}$

A E♭ G♭
× × × 2 4 1
2
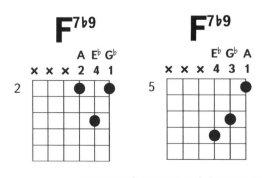

F$^{7♭9}$

E♭ G♭ A
× × × 4 3 1
5

CHORDS WITH ROOT F 193

F⁹
A E♭ G
1 2 1 x x x
5
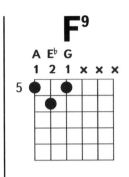

F⁹
x 1 2 1 x x
0
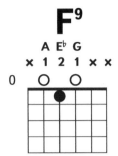

F⁹
A E♭ G
x x 1 2 3 x
7
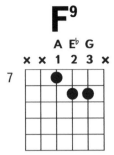

F⁹
A E♭ G
x x x 2 4 3
2
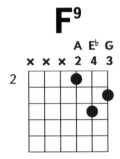

F⁹
E♭ G A
x x x 3 4 1
5
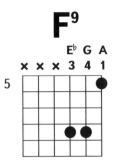

F⁹
E♭ A C G
2 3 1 4 x x
10
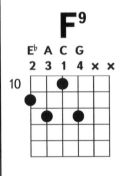

F⁹
E♭ A C G
x x 1 2 1 3
1
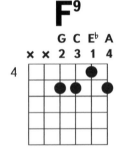

F⁹
G C E♭ A
3 4 1 2 x x
1
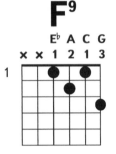

F⁹
G C E♭ A
x 2 3 1 4 x
8
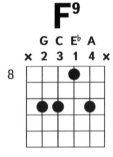

F⁹
G C E♭ A
x x 2 3 1 4
4
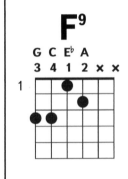

F⁷#⁹
A E♭ G#
1 2 2 x x x
5
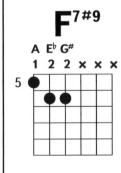

F⁷#⁹
A E♭ G#
x 0 1 1 x x
0
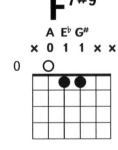

F⁷#⁹
A E♭ G#
x x 1 2 3 x
7
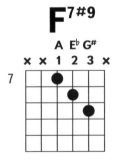

F⁷#⁹
A E♭ G#
x x x 1 3 4
2
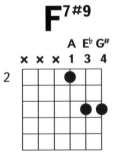

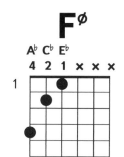

F^ø

A♭ C♭ E♭
4 2 1 × × ×
1

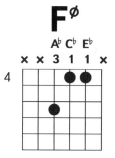

F^ø

A♭ C♭ E♭
× 4 2 1 × ×
8

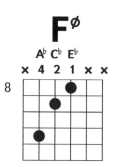

F^ø

A♭ C♭ E♭
× × 3 1 1 ×
4

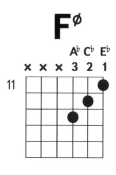

F^ø

A♭ C♭ E♭
× × × 3 2 1
11

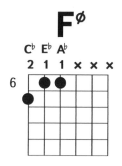

F^ø

C♭ E♭ A♭
2 1 1 × × ×
6

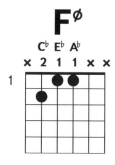

F^ø

C♭ E♭ A♭
× 2 1 1 × ×
1

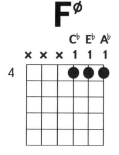

F^ø

C♭ E♭ A♭
× × 2 1 3 ×
8

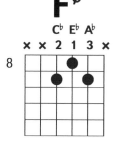

F^ø

C♭ E♭ A♭
× × × 1 1 1
4

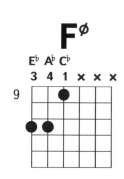

F^ø

E♭ A♭ C♭
3 4 1 × × ×
9

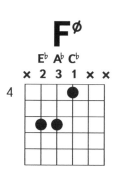

F^ø

E♭ A♭ C♭
× 2 3 1 × ×
4

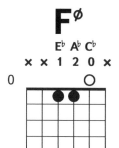

F^ø

E♭ A♭ C♭
× × 1 2 0 ×
0

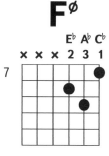

F^ø

E♭ A♭ C♭
× × × 2 3 1
7

F

VIVID
DIMINISHED

BIG
MAJOR

F#/Gb Maj
Gb Db Gb Bb Db Gb
F# C# F# A# C# F#
1 3 4 2 1 1
2
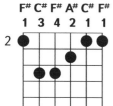

F#/Gb Maj
Gb Db Gb Bb
F# C# F# A#
× 1 3 3 3 ×
9
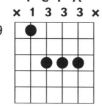

F#/Gb △7
Gb Db F Bb
F# C# E# A#
× 1 3 2 4 ×
9
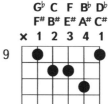

F#/Gb △7#11
Gb C Bb Db
F# B# E# A# C#
× 1 2 3 4 1
9
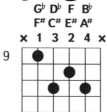

F#/Gb 6/9
Gb   Bb Eb Ab
F#   A# D# G#
1 × × 2 4 4
2
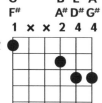

F#/Gb 6/9
Gb Bb Eb Ab
F# A# D# G#
× 2 1 1 3 ×
8
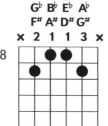

F#/Gb add9
Gb   Bb Db Ab
F#   A# C# G#
1 × × 2 1 4
2
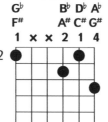

BIG
MINOR

F#/Gb min
Gb Db Gb Bb Db Gb
F# C# F# A C# F#
1 3 4 1 1 1
2
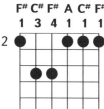

F#/Gb min
Gb Db Gb Bbb Db
F# C# F# A C#
× 1 3 4 2 1
9

F#/Gb min7
Gb Db F Bbb Db Gb
F# C# E A C# F#
1 3 1 1 1 1
2

F#/Gb min7b5
Gb Db Gb Dbb Fb Bbb
F# B# F# B# E A
1 2 3 4 4 4
2

F#/Gb min7b9
Gb   Fb Bbb Db Abb
F#   E A C# G
1 × 1 1 1 2
2

F#/Gb min9
Gb Db F Bbb Db Ab
F# C# E A C# G#
1 3 1 1 1 4
2

F#/Gb min△7
Gb Db F Bbb Db
F# C# E# A C#
× 1 4 2 3 1
9
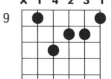

F#/Gb⁷

Gb Db Fb Bb Db Gb
F# C# E A# C# F#
1 3 1 2 1 1
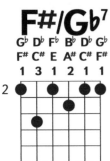
2

F#/Gb⁷

Gb Db Fb Bb Db
F# C# E A# C#
× 1 3 1 4 1
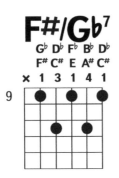
9

F#/Gb⁷b⁵

Gb Db Fb Bb
F# C E A#
× × 1 2 2 4
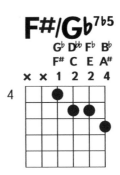
4

F#/Gb⁷#⁵

Gb Bb Fb Bb D
F# A# E A# C##
1 2 3 4 4 ×
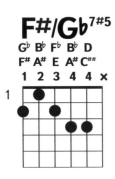
1

F#/Gb⁷#⁵

Gb D Fb Bb D
F# C## E A# C##
× 1 4 1 3 2
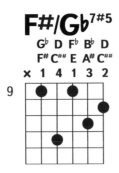
9

F#/Gb⁷b⁹

Gb   Fb Bb Db Ab
F#   E A# C# G
1 × 1 2 1 3
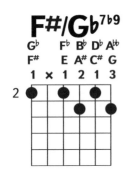
2

F#/Gb⁹

Gb Db Fb Bb Db Ab
F# C# E A# C# G#
1 3 1 2 1 4
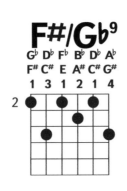
2

F#/Gb⁹

Gb Bb Fb Ab
F# A# E G#
× 2 1 3 4 ×
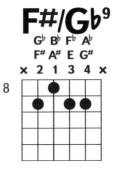
8

F#/Gb⁷#⁹

Gb   Fb Bb Fb A
F#   E A# E G##
1 × 1 2 4 4
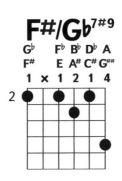
2

F#/Gb⁷#⁹

Gb   Fb Bb Db A
F#   E A# C# G##
1 × 1 2 1 4
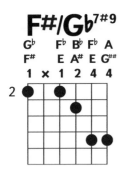
2

F#/Gb⁷#⁹

Gb Bb Fb A
F# A# E G##
× 2 1 3 4 ×
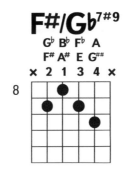
8

F#/Gb⁷#⁹

Gb Bb Fb A
F# A# E G##
× × 2 1 4 4
3

BIG
AUGMENTED

F#/Gb^{Aug}

Gb Bb D Gb
F# A# C## F#
4 3 2 1 × ×
11
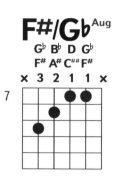

F#/Gb^{Aug}

Gb Bb D Gb
F# A# C## F#
× 3 2 1 1 ×
7
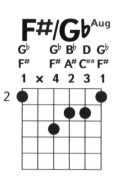

F#/Gb^{Aug}

Gb   Gb Bb D Gb
F#   F# A# C## F#
1 × 4 2 3 1
2
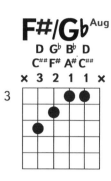

F#/Gb^{Aug}

D Gb Bb D
C## F# A# C##
× 3 2 1 1 ×
3

F#/Gb^{Aug}

Bb D Gb Bb
A# C## F# A#
× 3 2 1 1 ×
11
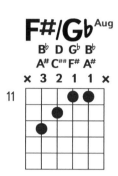

BIG
DIMINISHED

F#/Gb^ø

Gb Dbb Gb Dbb Fb Bbb
F# B# F# B# E A
1 2 3 4 4 4
2
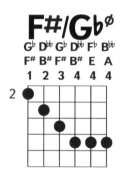

F#/Gb^{dim}

Gb   Fbb Bbb Dbb Gb
F#   Eb A B# F#
2 × 1 3 1 4
1
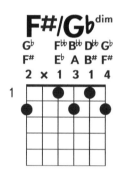

BIG
STACKED 5THS

F#/Gb^{5 sus}

Gb Db Gb Cb
F# C# F# B
× 1 3 4 1 ×
9
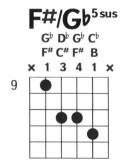

F#/Gb^{5 add9}

Gb Db Ab Db
F# C# G# C#
× 1 3 4 1 1
9
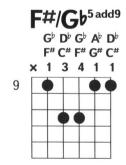

F#/Gb^{add6/9}

Gb Db   Ab Eb
F# C#   G# D#
× 1 3 × 1 4
9
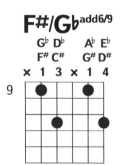

COMPACT
MAJOR

F#/Gb^{Maj}
Gb Bb Db
F# A# C#
4 3 1 × × ×
11
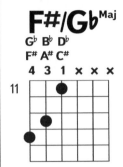

F#/Gb^{Maj}
Gb Bb Db
F# A# C#
× 4 3 1 × ×
6
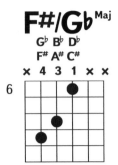

F#/Gb^{Maj}
Gb Bb Db
F# A# C#
× × 3 2 1 ×
2
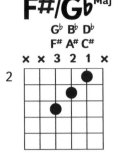

F#/Gb^{Maj}
Gb Bb Db
F# A# C#
× × × 2 3 1
9
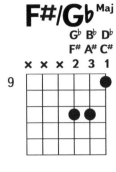

F#/Gb^{Maj}
Db Gb Bb
C# F# A#
2 3 1 × × ×
8
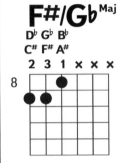

F#/Gb^{Maj}
Db Gb Bb
C# F# A#
× 2 3 1 × ×
3
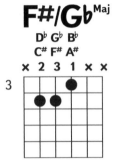

F#/Gb^{Maj}
Db Gb Bb
C# F# A#
× × 1 1 1 ×
11
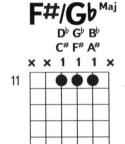

F#/Gb^{Maj}
Db Gb Bb
C# F# A#
× × × 1 3 2
6
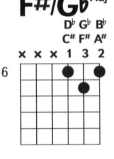

F#/Gb^{Maj}
Bb Db Gb
A# C# F#
3 1 1 × × ×
4
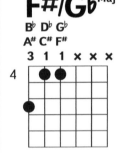

F#/Gb^{Maj}
Bb Db Gb
A# C# F#
× 3 1 1 × ×
11
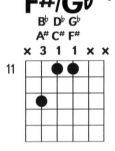

F#/Gb^{Maj}
Bb Db Gb
A# C# F#
× × 3 1 2 ×
6
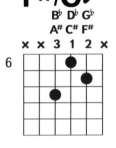

F#/Gb^{Maj}
Bb Db Gb
A# C# F#
× × × 2 1 1
2
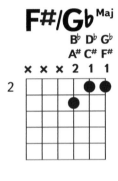

F#/Gb^{△7}
Gb Bb F
F# A# E#
2 1 4 × × ×
1
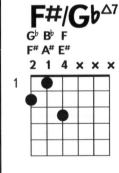

F#/Gb^{△7}
Gb Bb F
F# A# E#
× 2 1 4 × ×
8
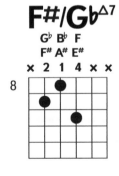

F#/Gb^{△7}
Gb Bb F
F# A# E#
× × 2 1 4 ×
3
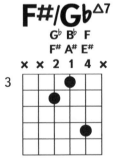

F#/Gb^{△7}
Db Gb Bb F
C# F# A# E#
× × 1 1 1 4
11
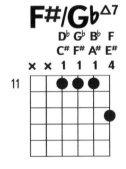

F#/Gb^{add9}
Gb Bb Db Ab
F# A# C# G#
× × 3 2 1 4
2
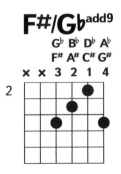

COMPACT
MINOR

F#/G♭^{min}
G♭ B♭♭ D♭
F♯ A C♯
4 2 1 × × ×
11
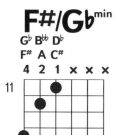

F#/G♭^{min}
G♭ B♭♭ D♭
F♯ A C♯
× 4 2 1 × ×
6
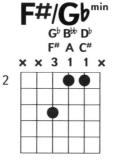

F#/G♭^{min}
G♭ B♭♭ D♭
F♯ A C♯
× × 3 1 1
2
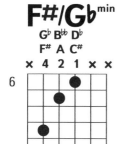

F#/G♭^{min}
G♭ B♭♭ D♭
F♯ A C♯
× × × 3 2 1
9
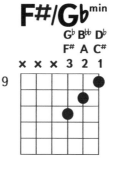

F#/G♭^{min}
B♭♭ D♭ G♭
A C♯ F♯
2 1 1 × × ×
4
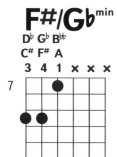

F#/G♭^{min}
B♭♭ D♭ G♭
A C♯ F♯
× 2 1 1 × ×
11
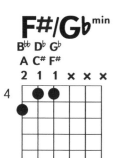

F#/G♭^{min}
B♭♭ D♭ G♭
A C♯ F♯
× × 2 1 3 ×
6
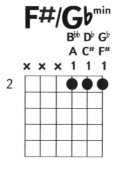

F#/G♭^{min}
B♭♭ D♭ G♭
A C♯ F♯
× × × 1 1 1
2
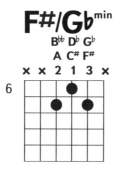

F#/G♭^{min}
D♭ G♭ B♭♭
C♯ F♯ A
3 4 1 × × ×
7
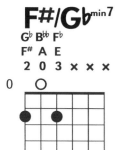

F#/G♭^{min}
D♭ G♭ B♭♭
C♯ F♯ A
× 3 4 1 × ×
2
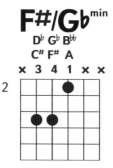

F#/G♭^{min}
D♭ G♭ B♭♭
C♯ F♯ A
× × 2 3 1 ×
10
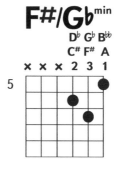

F#/G♭^{min}
D♭ G♭ B♭♭
C♯ F♯ A
× × × 2 3 1
5
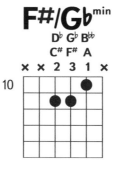

F#/G♭^{min7}
G♭ B♭♭ F♭
F♯ A E
2 0 3 × × ×
0
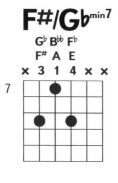

F#/G♭^{min7}
G♭ B♭♭ F♭
F♯ A E
× 3 1 4 × ×
7
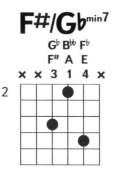

F#/G♭^{min7}
G♭ B♭♭ F♭
F♯ A E
× × 3 1 4 ×
2
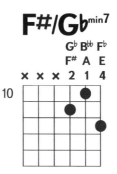

F#/G♭^{min7}
G♭ B♭♭ F♭
F♯ A E
× × × 2 1 4
10
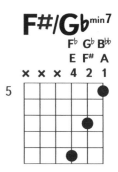

F#/G♭^{min7}
B♭♭ F♭ G♭
A E F♯
2 4 1 × × ×
4
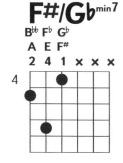

F#/G♭^{min7}
B♭♭ F♭ G♭
A E F♯
× 2 4 1 × ×
11
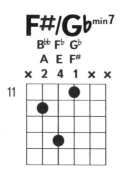

F#/G♭^{min7}
B♭♭ F♭ G♭
A E F♯
× × 1 3 1 ×
7
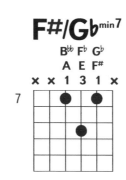

F#/G♭^{min7}
B♭♭ F♭ G♭
A E F♯
× × × 1 4 1
2
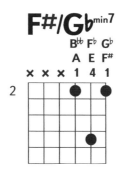

F#/G♭^{min7}
F♭ G♭ B♭♭
E F♯ A
× × × 4 2 1
5

CHORDS WITH ROOT F SHARP - G FLAT 201

COMPACT
MINOR (CONT.)

F#/Gbmin7b5
Gb Dbb Fb Bbb
F# C E A
1 2 1 1 × ×
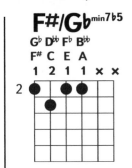
2

F#/Gbmin7b5
Gb Dbb Fb Bbb
F# C E A
× 1 2 1 3 ×
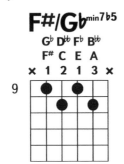
9

F#/Gbmin7b9
Gb Bbb Fb Abb
F# A E G
1 0 3 0 × ×
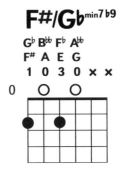
0

F#/Gbmin7b9
Gb Bbb Fb Abb
F# A E G
× 3 1 4 2 ×
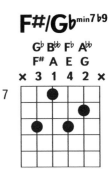
7

COMPACT
DOMINANT

F#/Gb7
Gb Bb Fb
F# A# E
2 1 3 × × ×
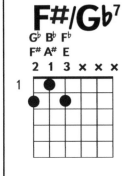
1

F#/Gb7
Gb Bb Fb
F# A# E
× 2 1 3 × ×
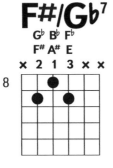
8

F#/Gb7
Gb Bb Fb
F# A# E
× × 2 1 4 ×
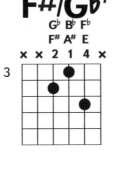
3

F#/Gb7
Db Gb Bb Fb
C# F# A# E
× × 1 1 1 2
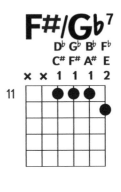
11

F#/Gb7
Bb Fb Gb
A# E F#
3 4 1 × × ×
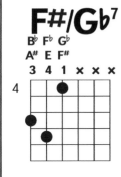
4

F#/Gb7
Bb Fb Gb
A# E F#
× 3 4 1 × ×
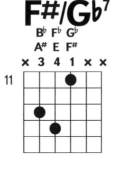
11

F#/Gb7
Bb Fb Gb
A# E F#
× × × 2 4 1
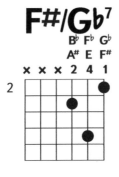
2

F#/Gb7
Fb Gb Bb
E F# A#
× × × 4 2 1
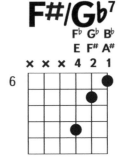
6

F#/Gb7#5
Gb D Fb Bb
F# C## E A#
1 4 1 2 × ×
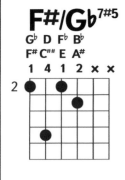
2

F#/Gb7#5
Gb D Fb Bb D
F# C## E A# C##
× 1 4 1 3 2
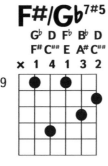
9

202 GUITAR CHORDS ENCYCLOPEDIA: A SEEING MUSIC METHOD BOOK

COMPACT
DIMINISHED

F#/G♭dim
G♭ D♭♭ F♭♭ B♭♭
F# B# E♭ A
2 4 1 3 × ×
1
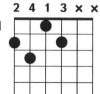

F#/G♭dim
G♭ D♭♭ F♭♭ B♭♭
F# C E♭ A
× 2 3 1 4 ×
8
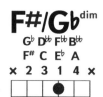

F#/G♭dim
G♭ D♭♭ F♭♭ B♭♭
F# C E♭ A
× × 1 2 1 3
4
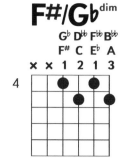

F#/G♭dim
B♭♭ F♭♭ G♭ D♭♭
A E♭ F# B#
2 4 1 3 × ×
4
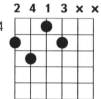

F#/G♭dim
B♭♭ F♭♭ G♭ D♭♭
A E♭ F# C
× 2 3 1 4 ×
11
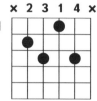

F#/G♭dim
B♭♭ F♭♭ G♭ D♭♭
A E♭ F# C
× × 1 2 1 3
7

F#/G♭dim
D♭♭ G♭ B♭♭ F♭♭
C F# A E♭
2 4 1 3 × ×
7
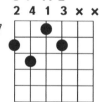

F#/G♭dim
D♭♭ G♭ B♭♭ F♭♭
C F# A E♭
× 2 3 1 4 ×
2
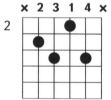

F#/G♭dim
D♭♭ G♭ B♭♭ F♭♭
C F# A E♭
× × 1 2 1 3
10
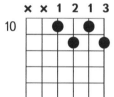

F#/G♭dim
F♭♭ B♭♭ D♭♭ G♭
E♭ A C F#
2 4 1 3 × ×
10
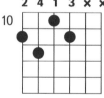

F#/G♭dim
F♭♭ B♭♭ D♭♭ G♭
E♭ A C F#
× 2 3 1 4 ×
5
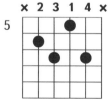

F#/G♭dim
F♭♭ B♭♭ D♭♭ G♭
E♭ A C F#
× × 1 2 1 3
1

CHORDS WITH ROOT F SHARP - G FLAT 203

COMPACT
DIMINISHED (CONT.)

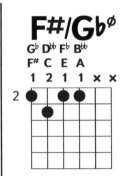

F#/Gb∅
Gb Dbb Fb Bbb
F# C E A
1 2 1 1 × ×

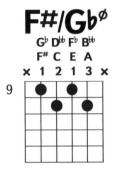

F#/Gb∅
Gb Dbb Fb Bbb
F# C E A
× 1 2 1 3 ×

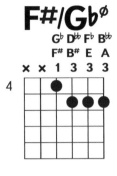

F#/Gb∅
Gb Dbb Fb Bbb
F# B# E A
× × 1 3 3 3

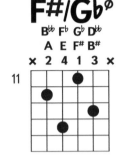

F#/Gb∅
Bbb Fb Gb Dbb
A E F# B#
× 2 4 1 3 ×

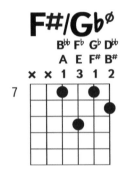

F#/Gb∅
Bbb Fb Gb Dbb
A E F# B#
× × 1 3 1 2

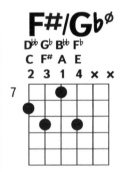

F#/Gb∅
Dbb Gb Bbb Fb
C F# A E
2 3 1 4 × ×

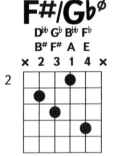

F#/Gb∅
Dbb Gb Bbb Fb
B# F# A E
× 2 3 1 4 ×

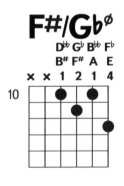

F#/Gb∅
Dbb Gb Bbb Fb
B# F# A E
× × 1 2 1 4

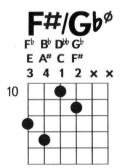

F#/Gb∅
Fb Bbb Dbb Gb
E A# C F#
3 4 1 2 × ×

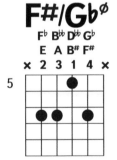

F#/Gb∅
Fb Bbb Dbb Gb
E A B# F#
× 2 3 1 4 ×

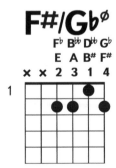

F#/Gb∅
Fb Bbb Dbb Gb
E A B# F#
× × 2 3 1 4

COMPACT
AUGMENTED

F#/Gb^Aug
Gb Bb D
F# A# C##
2 1 0 × × ×
0
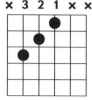

F#/Gb^Aug
Gb Bb D
F# A# C##
× 3 2 1 × ×
7
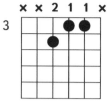

F#/Gb^Aug
Gb Bb D
F# A# C##
× × 2 1 1 ×
3
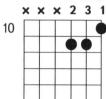

F#/Gb^Aug
Gb Bb D
F# A# C##
× × × 2 3 1
10
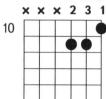

F#/Gb^Aug
Bb D Gb
A# C## F#
3 2 1 × × ×
4
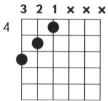

F#/Gb^Aug
Bb D Gb
A# C## F#
× 3 2 1 × ×
11
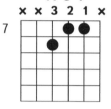

F#/Gb^Aug
Bb D Gb
A# C## F#
× × 3 2 1 ×
7

F#/Gb^Aug
Bb D Gb
A# C## F#
× × × 2 3 1
2
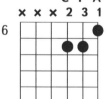

F#/Gb^Aug
D Gb Bb
C## F# A#
3 2 1 × × ×
8
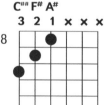

F#/Gb^Aug
D Gb Bb
C## F# A#
× 3 2 1 × ×
3
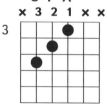

F#/Gb^Aug
D Gb Bb
C## F# A#
× × 2 1 1 ×
11
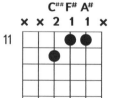

F#/Gb^Aug
D Gb Bb
C## F# A#
× × × 2 3 1
6

COMPACT
STACKED 5THS

F#/Gb⁵
Gb Db
F# C#
1 3 x x x
2
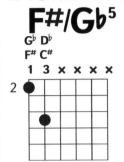

F#/Gb⁵
Gb Db
F# C#
x 1 3 x x
9
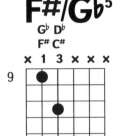

F#/Gb⁵
Gb Db
F# C#
x x 1 3 x
4
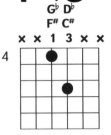

F#/Gb⁵
Gb Db
F# C#
x x x 1 4
11
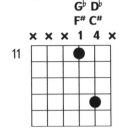

F#/Gb⁵
Gb Db
F# C#
x x x 1 3
7
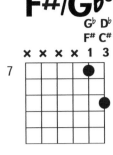

F#/Gb⁵
Db Gb
C# F#
1 1 x x x
9
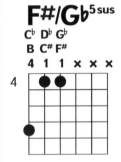

F#/Gb⁵
Db Gb
C# F#
x 1 1 x x
4
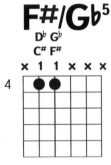

F#/Gb⁵
Db Gb
C# F#
x x 1 1 x
11
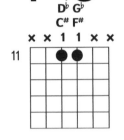

F#/Gb⁵
Db Gb
C# F#
x x x 1 2
6
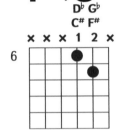

F#/Gb⁵
Db Gb
C# F#
x x x 1 1
2
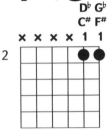

F#/Gb⁵ˢᵘˢ
Cb Db Gb
B C# F#
4 1 1 x x x
4
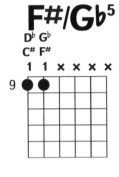

F#/Gb⁵ˢᵘˢ
Gb Cb Db
F# B C#
x x x 2 4 1
9
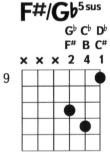

F#/Gb⁵ˢᵘˢ
Cb Db Gb
B C# F#
x x 4 1 2 x
6
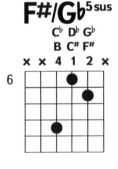

F#/Gb⁵ˢᵘˢ
Cb Db Gb
B C# F#
x x x 3 1 1
2
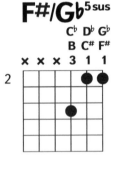

F#/Gb⁵ˢᵘˢ
Gb B Db
F# A## C#
3 4 1 x x x
11
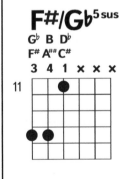

F#/Gb⁵ˢᵘˢ
Gb Cb Db
F# B C#
x 3 4 1 x x
6
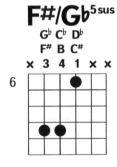

F#/Gb⁵ˢᵘˢ
Gb Cb Db
F# B C#
x x 3 4 1 x
2
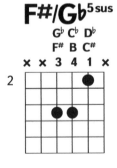

F#/Gb⁵ˢᵘˢ
Gb Cb Db
F# B C#
x x x 2 4 1
9
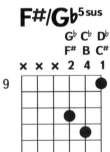

F#/Gb⁵ˢᵘˢ
Db Gb Cb
C# F# B
1 1 1 x x x
9
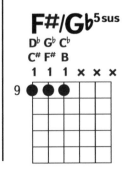

F#/Gb⁵ˢᵘˢ
Db Gb Cb
C# F# B
x 1 1 1 x x
4
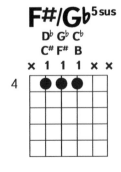

F#/Gb⁵ˢᵘˢ
Db Gb Cb
C# F# B
x x 1 1 2 x
11
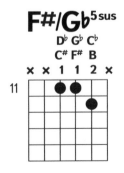

F#/Gb⁵ˢᵘˢ
Db Gb B
C# F# B
x x x 1 2 2
6
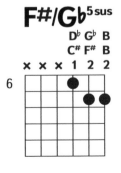

206 GUITAR CHORDS ENCYCLOPEDIA: A SEEING MUSIC METHOD BOOK

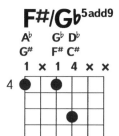

F#/Gb⁵ᵃᵈᵈ⁹

Ab   Gb Db
G#   F# C#
1 × 1 4 × ×
4

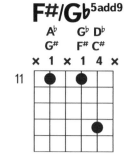

F#/Gb⁵ᵃᵈᵈ⁹

Ab   Gb Db
G#   F# C#
× 1 × 1 4 ×
11

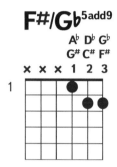

F#/Gb⁵ᵃᵈᵈ⁹

Ab   Gb Db
G#   F# C#
× × 1 × 2 4
6

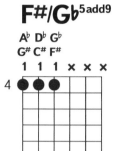

F#/Gb⁵ᵃᵈᵈ⁹

Ab Db Gb
G# C# F#
1 1 1 × × ×
4

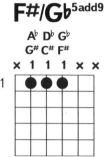

F#/Gb⁵ᵃᵈᵈ⁹

Ab Db Gb
G# C# F#
× 1 1 1 × ×
11

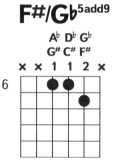

F#/Gb⁵ᵃᵈᵈ⁹

Ab Db Gb
G# C# F#
× × 1 1 2 ×
6

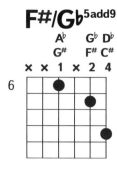

F#/Gb⁵ᵃᵈᵈ⁹

Ab Db Gb
G# C# F#
× × × 1 2 3
1

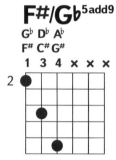

F#/Gb⁵ᵃᵈᵈ⁹

Gb Db Ab
F# C# G#
1 3 4 × × ×
2

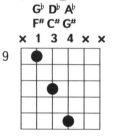

F#/Gbᵃᵈᵈ⁹

Gb Db Ab
F# C# G#
× 1 3 4 × ×
9

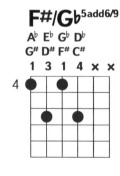

F#/Gb⁵ᵃᵈᵈ⁶/⁹

Ab Eb Gb Db
G# D# F# C#
1 3 1 4 × ×
4

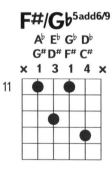

F#/Gb⁵ᵃᵈᵈ⁶/⁹

Ab Eb Gb Db
G# D# F# C#
× 1 3 1 4 ×
11

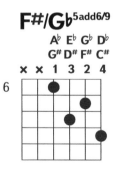

F#/Gb⁵ᵃᵈᵈ⁶/⁹

Ab Eb Gb Db
G# D# F# C#
× × 1 3 2 4
6

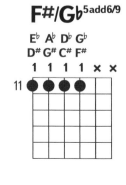

F#/Gb⁵ᵃᵈᵈ⁶/⁹

Eb Ab Db Gb
D# G# C# F#
1 1 1 1 × ×
11

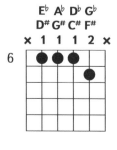

F#/Gb⁵ᵃᵈᵈ⁶/⁹

Eb Ab Db Gb
D# G# C# F#
× 1 1 1 2 ×
6

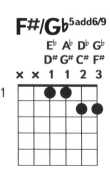

F#/Gb⁵ᵃᵈᵈ⁶/⁹

Eb Ab Db Gb
D# G# C# F#
× × 1 1 2 3
1

F#/Gb△7
F Bb Db Gb
E# A# C# F#
3 4 1 1 × ×
11
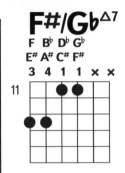

F#/Gb△7
F Bb Db Gb
E# A# C# F#
× 3 4 1 2 ×
6
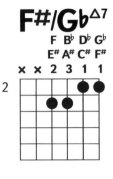

F#/Gb△7
F Bb Db Gb
E# A# C# F#
× × 2 3 1 1
2
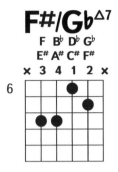

F#/Gb△9
F Bb Db Ab
E# A# C# G#
2 3 1 4 × ×
11
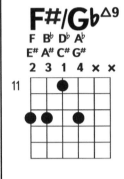

F#/Gb△9
F Bb Db Ab
E# A# C# G#
× 2 3 1 4 ×
6
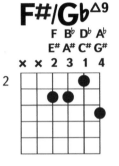

F#/Gb△9
F Bb Db Ab
E# A# C# G#
× × 2 3 1 4
2
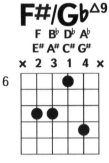

F#/Gb6/9
Bb Eb Ab Db
A# D# G# C#
1 1 1 1 × ×
6
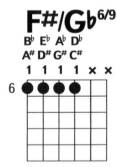

F#/Gb6/9
Bb Eb Ab Db
A# D# G# C#
× 1 1 1 2 ×
1
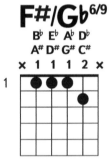

F#/Gb6/9
Bb Eb Ab Db
A# D# G# C#
× × 1 1 2 3
8
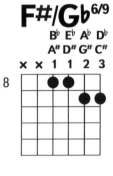

F#/Gb6/9
Bb Eb Ab
A# D# G#
× × × 1 2 2
3
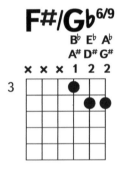

F#/Gb6/9
Eb Bb Db Ab
D# A# C# G#
1 3 1 4 × ×
11
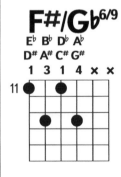

F#/Gb6/9
Eb Bb Db Ab
D# A# C# G#
× 1 3 1 4 ×
6
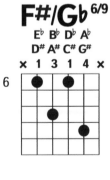

F#/Gb6/9
Eb Bb Db Ab
D# A# C# G#
× × 1 3 2 4
1
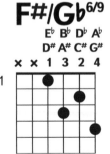

F#/Gb△7#11
C Gb Bb F
B# F# A# E#
1 2 1 4 × ×
8
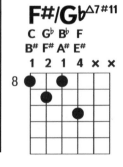

F#/Gb△7#11
C Gb Bb F
B# F# A# E#
× × 1 2 3 4
10
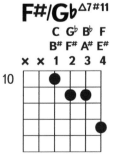

208 GUITAR CHORDS ENCYCLOPEDIA: A SEEING MUSIC METHOD BOOK

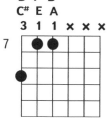

VIVID
MAJOR (CONT.)

VIVID
MINOR

F#/Gb△7#11
Gb C F Bb
F# B# E# A#
1 2 3 4 × ×
2

F#/Gb△7#11
Gb C F Bb
F# B# E# A#
× 1 2 3 4 ×
9

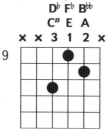

F#/Gb△7#11
Gb C F Bb
F# B# E# A#
× × 1 2 3 4
4

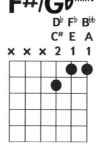

F#/Gb△7#11
F Bb C Gb
E# A# B# F#
× × 3 4 1 2
1

F#/Gbmin7
Db Fb Bbb
C# E A
3 1 1 × × ×
7

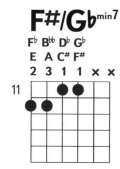

F#/Gbmin7
Db Fb Bbb
C# E A
× 3 1 1 × ×
2

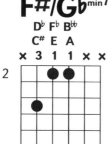

F#/Gbmin7
Db Fb Bbb
C# E A
× × 3 1 2 ×
9

F#/Gbmin7
Db Fb Bbb
C# E A
× × × 2 1 1
5

F#/Gbmin7
Fb Bbb Db Gb
E A C# F#
2 3 1 1 × ×
11

F#/Gbmin7
Fb Bbb Db Gb
E A C# F#
× 2 3 1 4 ×
6

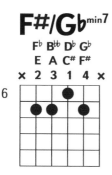

F#/Gbmin7
Fb Bbb Db Gb
E A C# F#
× × 1 1 1 1
2

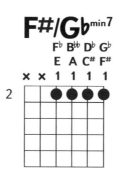

F#/Gbmin7
Db Gb Bbb Fb
C# F# A E
× × 2 3 1 4
10

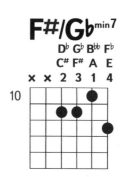

F#/Gbmin7b5
Bbb Fb Gb Dbb
A E F# C
× 2 4 1 3 ×
11

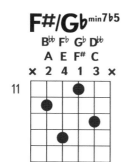

F#/Gbmin7b5
Bbb Fb Gb Dbb
A E F# B#
× × 1 4 1 2
7

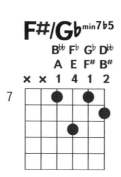

F#/Gbmin7b5
Dbb Gb Bbb Fb
B# F# A E
2 3 1 4 × ×
7

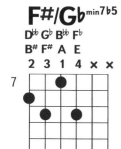

F#/Gbmin7b5
Dbb Gb Bbb Fb
B# F# A E
× 2 3 1 4 ×
2

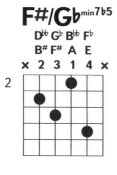

F#/Gbmin7b5
Dbb Gb Bbb Fb
C F# A E
× × 1 2 1 4
10

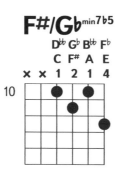

F#/Gbmin7b5
Fb Bbb Db Gb
E A C F#
× 2 3 1 4 ×
5

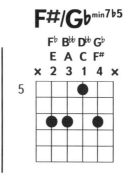

F#/Gbmin7b5
Fb Bbb Dbb Gb
E A C F#
× × 2 3 1 4
1

CHORDS WITH ROOT F SHARP - G FLAT 209

F#/Gb^{min7b9}

Fb Bbb Db Abb
E A C# G
2 3 1 4 × ×

11

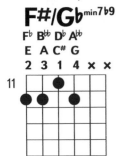

F#/Gb^{min7b9}

Fb Bbb Db Abb
E A C# G
× 2 3 1 4 ×

6

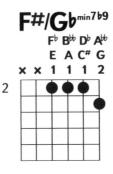

F#/Gb^{min7b9}

Fb Bbb Db Abb
E A C# G
× × 1 1 1 2

2

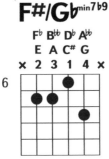

F#/Gb^{min7b9}

Abb Db Fb Bbb
G C# E A
2 4 1 1 × ×

2

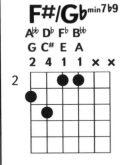

F#/Gb^{min7b9}

Abb Db Fb Bbb
G C# E A
× 2 4 1 3 ×

9

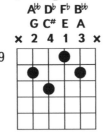

F#/Gb^{min7b9}

Abb Db Fb Bbb
G C# E A
× × 1 2 1 1

5

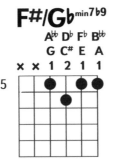

F#/Gb^{min7b9}

Bbb Fb Abb
A E G
1 3 1 × × ×

5

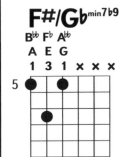

F#/Gb^{min7b9}

Bbb Fb Abb
A E G
× 0 2 0 × ×

0

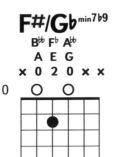

F#/Gb^{min7b9}

Bbb Fb Abb
A E G
× × 1 3 2 ×

7

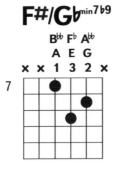

F#/Gb^{min7b9}

Bbb Fb Abb
A E G
× × × 1 4 2

2

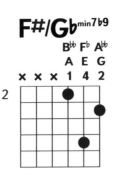

F#/Gb^{min7b9}

Fb Abb Bbb
E G A
× × × 4 3 1

5

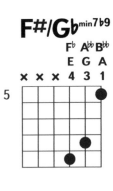

F#/Gb^{min9}

Fb Bbb Db Ab
E A C# G#
2 3 1 4 × ×

11

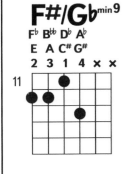

F#/Gb^{min9}

Fb Bbb Db Ab
E A C# G#
× × 1 1 1 3

2

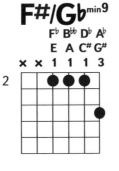

F#/Gb^{min9}

× Gb Bbb Fb Ab
× F# A E G#
× 3 1 4 4 ×

7

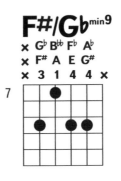

F#/Gb^{min9}

Bbb Fb Ab
A E G#
1 3 2 × × ×

5

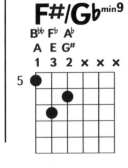

F#/Gb^{min9}

Bbb Fb Ab
A E G#
× 0 2 1 × ×

0

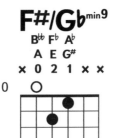

F#/Gb^{min9}

Bbb Fb Ab
A E G#
× × 1 3 3 ×

7

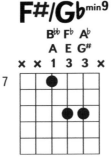

F#/Gb^{min9}

Bbb Fb Ab
A E G#
× × × 1 4 3

2

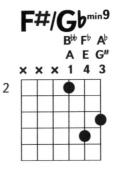

F#/Gb^{min9}

Fb Ab Bbb
E G# A
× × × 3 4 1

5

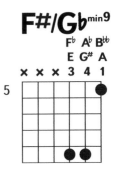

F#/Gbmin9
Ab Db Fb Bbb
G# C# E A
2 3 1 1 × ×
2
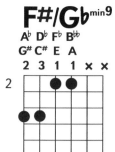

F#/Gbmin9
Ab Db Fb Bbb
G# C# E A
× 3 4 1 2 ×
9
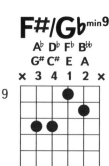

F#/Gbmin9
Ab Db Fb Bbb
G# C# E A
× × 2 3 1 1
5
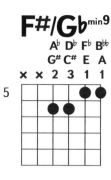

F#/Gbmin△7
Bbb Db F
A C# E#
3 2 1 × × ×
3
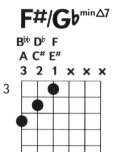

F#/Gbmin△7
Bbb Db F
A C# E#
× 3 2 1 × ×
10
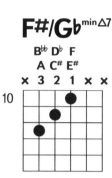

F#/Gbmin△7
Bbb Db F
A C# E#
× × 2 1 1 ×
6
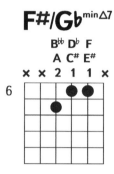

F#/Gbmin△7
Bbb Db F
A C# E#
× × × 2 3 1
1
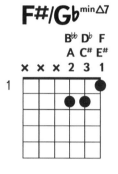

F#/Gbmin△7
Db F Bbb
C# E# A
3 2 1 × × ×
7
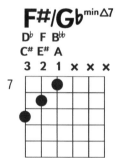

F#/Gbmin△7
Db F Bbb
C# E# A
× 3 2 1 × ×
2
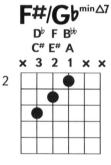

F#/Gbmin△7
Db F Bbb
C# E# A
× × 2 1 1 ×
10
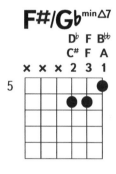

F#/Gbmin△7
Db F Bbb
C# F A
× × × 2 3 1
5
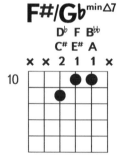

F#/Gbmin△7
F Bbb Db Gb
E# A C# F#
3 2 1 1 × ×
11
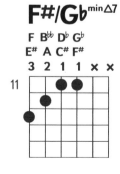

F#/Gbmin△7
F Bbb Db Gb
E# A C# F#
× 4 2 1 3 ×
6
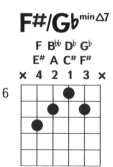

F#/Gbmin△7
F Bbb Db Gb
E# A C# F#
× × 2 1 1 1
2
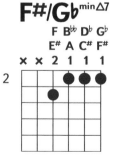

F#/Gb⁷

Fb Bb Db Gb
E A# C# F#
2 4 1 1 × ×
11

F#/Gb⁷

Fb Bb Db Gb
E A# C# F#
× 2 4 1 3 ×
6

F#/Gb⁷

Fb Bb Db Gb
E A# C# F#
× × 1 2 1 1
2

F#/Gb⁷

Db Fb Bb
C# E A#
3 1 2 × × ×
7

F#/Gb⁷

Db Fb Bb
C# E A#
× 3 1 2 × ×
2

F#/Gb⁷

Db Fb Bb
C# E A#
× × 3 1 4 ×
9

F#/Gb⁷

Db Fb Bb
C# E A#
× × × 2 1 3
5

F#/Gb⁷

Db Fb Bb
C# E A#
3 1 2 × × ×
7

F#/Gb⁷ᵇ⁵

Dbb Gb Bb Fb
B# F# A# E
× 1 2 1 4 ×
3

F#/Gb⁷

Db Fb Bb
C# E A#
× × 3 1 4 ×
9

F#/Gb⁷ᵇ⁵

Gb Dbb Fb Bb
F# C E A#
1 2 1 3 × ×
2

F#/Gb⁷ᵇ⁵

Gb Dbb Fb Bb
F# C E A#
× 1 2 1 4 ×
9

F#/Gb⁷ᵇ⁵

Gb Dbb Fb Bb
F# C E A#
× × 1 2 2 4
4

F#/Gb⁷ᵇ⁵

Bb Fb Gb Dbb
A# E F# C
3 4 1 2 × ×
4

F#/Gb⁷ᵇ⁵

Bb Fb Gb Dbb
A# E F# B#
× 3 4 1 2 ×
11

F#/Gb⁷ᵇ⁵

Bb Fb Gb Dbb
A# E F# C
× × 2 4 1 3
7

F#/Gb⁷ᵇ⁵

Fb Bb Db Gb
E A# C F#
× 2 4 1 3 ×
5

F#/Gb⁷

Fb Bb Db Gb
E A# C# F#
× × 1 2 1 1
2

F#/Gb⁷#⁵
D Gb Bb Fb
C## F# A# E
4 2 1 3 × ×
8
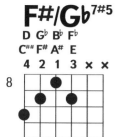

F#/Gb⁷#⁵
D Gb Bb Fb
C## F# A# E
× 3 2 1 4 ×
3
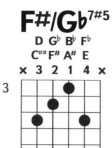

F#/Gb⁷#⁵
D Gb Bb Fb
C## F# A# E
× × 2 1 1 3
11
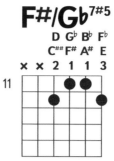

F#/Gb⁷#⁵
Fb Bb D Gb
E A# C## F#
2 4 3 1 × ×
11
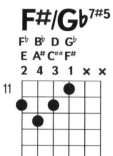

F#/Gb⁷#⁵
Fb Bb D Gb
E A# C## F#
× 1 2 1 1 ×
7
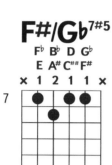

F#/Gb⁷#⁵
Fb Bb D Gb
E A# C## F#
× × 1 2 3 1
2
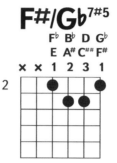

F#/Gb⁷b⁹
Fb Bb Db Abb
E A# C# G
2 4 1 3 × ×
11
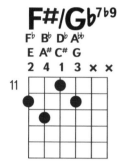

F#/Gb⁷b⁹
Fb Bb Db Abb
E A# C# G
× × 1 2 1 3
2
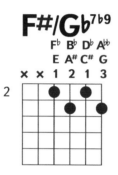

F#/Gb⁷b⁹
Gb Bb Fb Abb
F# A# E G
× 2 1 3 1 ×
8
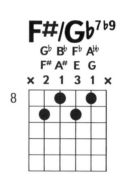

F#/Gb⁷b⁹
Gb Bb Fb Abb
F# A# E G
× × 2 1 3 1
3
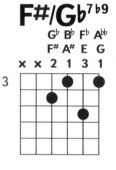

F#/Gb⁷b⁹
Abb Db Fb Bb
G C# E A#
2 4 1 3 × ×
2
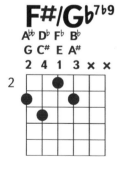

F#/Gb⁷b⁹
Abb Db Fb Bb
G C# E A#
× 2 3 1 4 ×
9
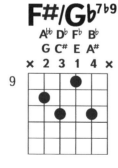

F#/Gb⁷b⁹
Abb Db Fb Bb
G C# E A#
× × 2 3 1 4
5
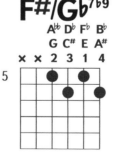

F#/Gb⁷b⁹
Bb Fb Abb
A# E G
2 3 1 × × ×
5
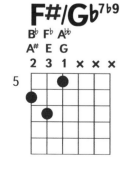

F#/Gb⁷b⁹
Bb Fb Abb
A# E G
× 2 4 1 × ×
0
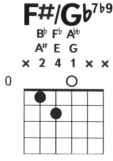

F#/Gb⁷b⁹
Bb Fb Abb
A# E G
× × × 2 4 1
3
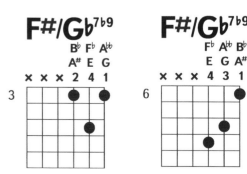

F#/Gb⁷b⁹
Fb Abb Bb
E G A#
× × × 4 3 1
6

VIVID
DOMINANT

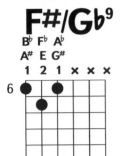

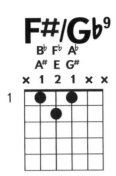

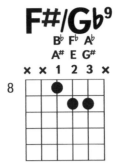

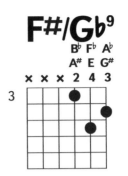

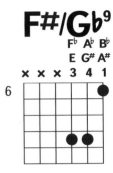

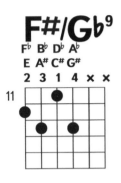

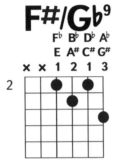

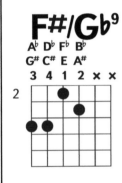

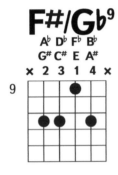

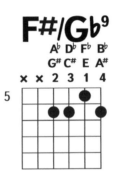

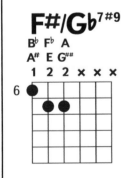

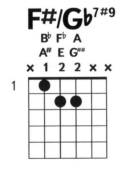

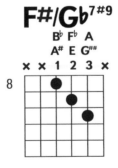

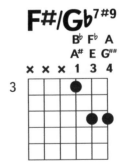

VIVID
DIMINISHED

F#/Gbø
Bbb Dbb Fb
A C E
4 2 1 × × ×
2

F#/Gbø
Bbb Dbb Fb
A C E
× 4 2 1 × ×
9

F#/Gbø
Bbb Dbb Fb
A B# E
× × 3 1 1 ×
5

F#/Gbø
Bbb Dbb Fb
A B# E
× × × 2 1 0
0

F#/Gbø
Dbb Fb Bbb
C E A
2 1 1 × × ×
7

F#/Gbø
Dbb Fb Bbb
B# E A
× 2 1 1 × ×
2

F#/Gbø
Dbb Fb Bbb
B# E A
× × 2 1 3 ×
9

F#/Gbø
Dbb Fb Bbb
C E A
× × × 1 1 1
5

F#/Gbø
Fb Bbb Dbb
E A C
3 4 1 × × ×
10

F#/Gbø
Fb Bbb Dbb
E A C
× 2 3 1 × ×
5

F#/Gbø
Fb Bbb Dbb
E A C
× × 2 3 1 ×
1

F#/Gbø
Fb Bbb Dbb
E A B#
× × × 2 3 1
8

GUITAR
CHORDS
ENCYCLOPEDIA

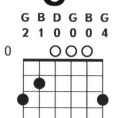

G^{Maj}

G B D G B G
2 1 0 0 0 4
0

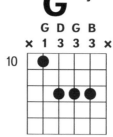

G^{Maj}

G D G B D G
1 3 4 2 1 1
3

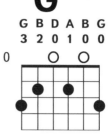

G^{Maj}

G D G B
× 1 3 3 3 ×
10

G^{add9}

G B D A B G
3 2 0 1 0 0
0

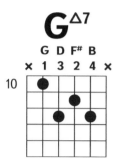

G^{△7}

G D F[#] B
× 1 3 2 4 ×
10

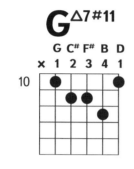

G^{△7#11}

G C[#] F[#] B D
× 1 2 3 4 1
10

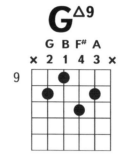

G^{△9}

G B F[#] A
× 2 1 4 3 ×
9

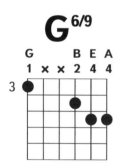

G^{6/9}

G B E A
1 × × 2 4 4
3

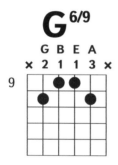

G^{6/9}

G B E A
× 2 1 1 3 ×
9

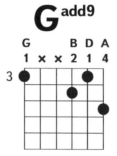

G^{add9}

G B D A
1 × × 2 1 4
3

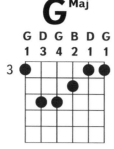

SEEING MUSIC
METHOD BOOKS

CHORDS WITH ROOT G 217

BIG
MINOR

G^{min}
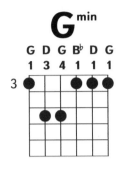

G^{min}
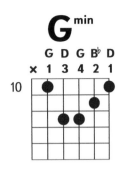

G^{min7}
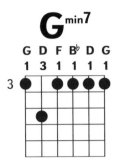

G^{min7♭5}
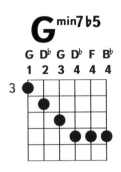

G^{min7♭9}
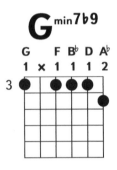

G^{min9}

G^{minΔ7}
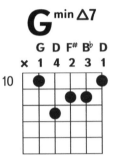

BIG
DOMINANT

G⁷
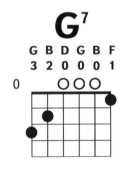

G⁷
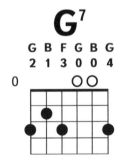

G⁷
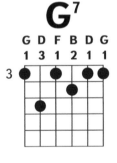

G⁷
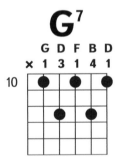

G^{7♭5}
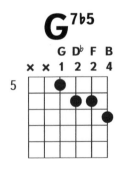

G^{7#5}
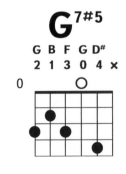

G^{7#5}
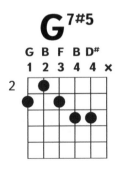

G^{7#5}
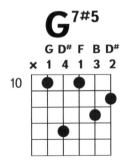

218 GUITAR CHORDS ENCYCLOPEDIA: A SEEING MUSIC METHOD BOOK

G⁷♭⁹

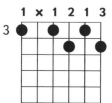

1 × 1 2 1 3
3

G⁹

G D F B D A
1 3 1 2 1 4
3

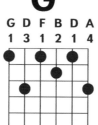

G⁹

G B F A
× 2 1 3 4 ×
9

G⁷#⁹

G F B F A#
1 × 1 2 4 4
3

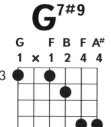

G⁷#⁹

G F B D A#
1 × 1 2 1 4
3

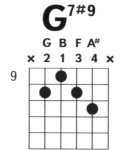

G⁷#⁹

G B F A#
× 2 1 3 4 ×
9

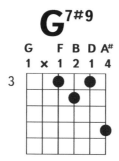

G⁷#⁹

G B F A#
× × 2 1 4 4
4

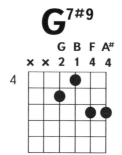

Gᴬᵘᵍ

G B D# G B G
3 2 1 0 0 4
0

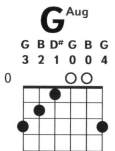

Gᴬᵘᵍ

G B D# G
× 3 2 1 1 ×
8

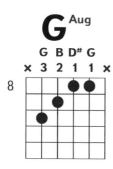

Gᴬᵘᵍ

G G B D# G
1 × 4 2 3 1
3

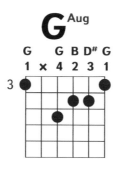

Gᴬᵘᵍ

E♭ G B D#
× 3 2 1 1 ×
4

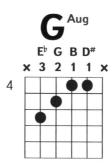

Gᴬᵘᵍ

B D# G B
× 2 1 0 0 ×
0

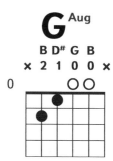

Gᵒ̸

G D♭ G D♭ F B♭
1 2 3 4 4 4
3

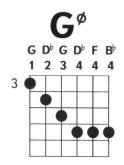

Gᵈⁱᵐ

G F♭ B♭ D♭ G
2 × 1 3 1 4
2

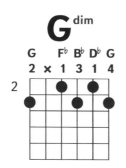

BIG
STACKED 5THS

G^{5sus}

G D G C
× 1 3 3 4 ×

10

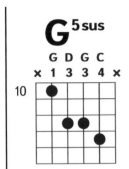

G^{5add9}

G D G A D
× 1 3 4 1 1

10

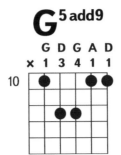

G^{add6/9}

G D A E
× 1 3 × 1 4

10

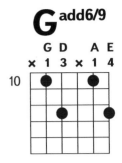

COMPACT
MAJOR

G^{Maj}

G B D
1 2 0 × × ×

0

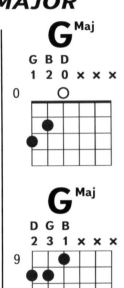

G^{Maj}

G B D
× 4 3 1 × ×

7

G^{Maj}

G B D
× × 3 2 1 ×

3

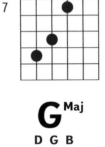

G^{Maj}

G B D
× × × 2 3 1

10

G^{Maj}

D G B
2 3 1 × × ×

9

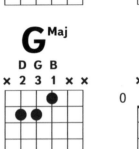

G^{Maj}

D G B
× 2 3 1 × ×

4

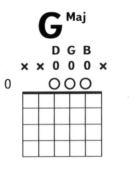

G^{Maj}

D G B
× × 0 0 0 ×

0

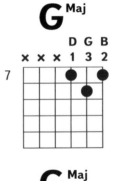

G^{Maj}

D G B
× × × 1 3 2

7

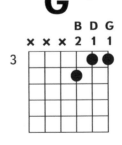

G^{Maj}

B D G
3 1 1 × × ×

5

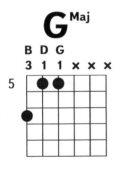

G^{Maj}

B D G
× 2 0 0 × ×

0

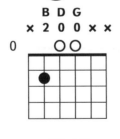

G^{Maj}

B D G
× × 3 1 2 ×

7

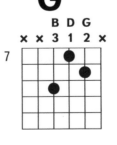

G^{Maj}

B D G
× × 2 1 1

3

G^{Δ7}

G B F#
2 1 4 × × ×

2

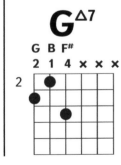

G^{Δ7}

G B F#
× 2 1 4 × ×

9

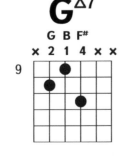

G^{Δ7}

G B F#
× × 2 1 4 ×

4

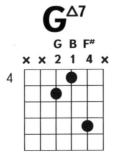

G^{Δ7}

D G B F#
× × 0 0 0 2

0

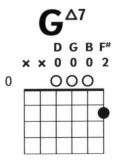

G^{add9}

G B D A
× × 3 2 1 4

3

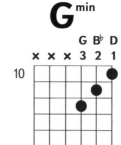

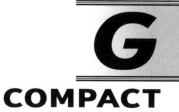

G
COMPACT
MINOR

Gmin
G B♭ D
3 1 0 × × ×
0
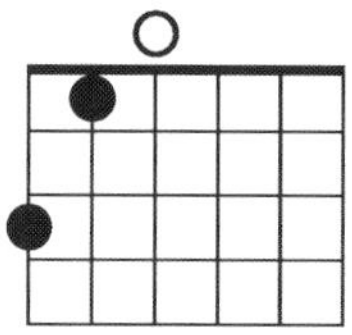

Gmin
G B♭ D
× 4 2 1 × ×
7
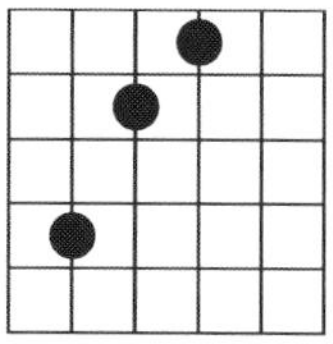

Gmin
G B♭ D
× × 3 1 1 ×
3
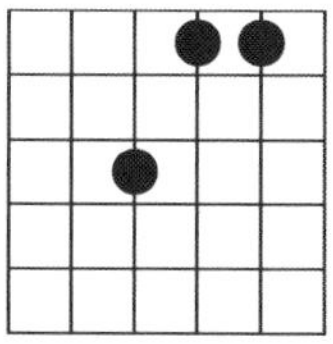

Gmin
G B♭ D
× × × 3 2 1
10
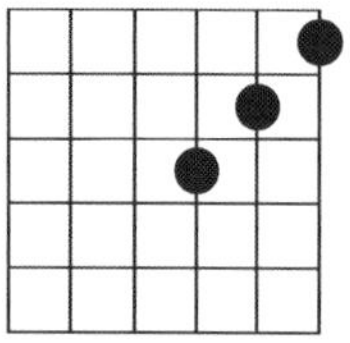

Gmin
B♭ D G
2 1 1 × × ×
5
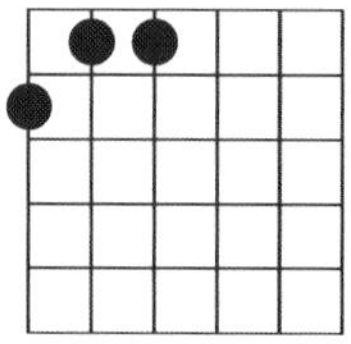

Gmin
B♭ D G
× 1 0 0 × ×
0
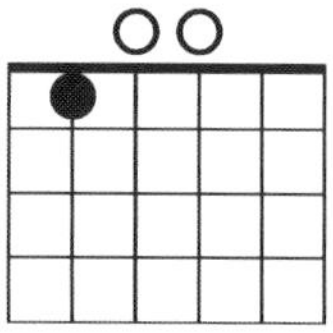

Gmin
B♭ D G
× × 2 1 3 ×
7
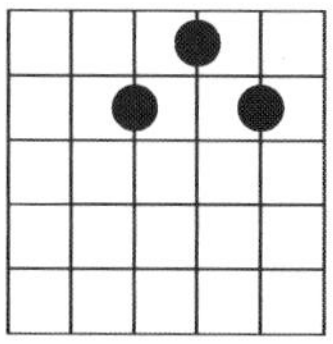

Gmin
B♭ D G
× × × 1 1 1
3
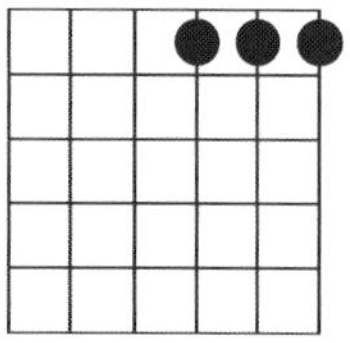

Gmin
D G B♭
3 4 1 × × ×
8
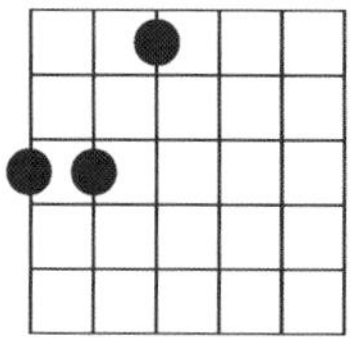

Gmin
D G B♭
× 3 4 1 × ×
3
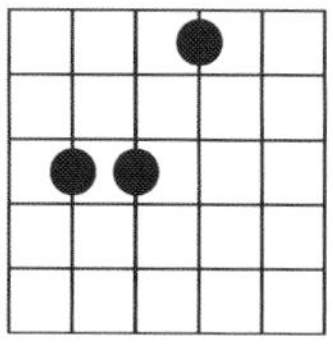

Gmin
D G B♭
× × 2 3 1 ×
11
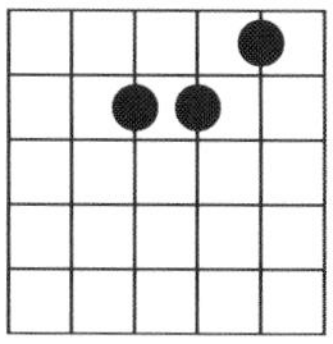

Gmin
D G B♭
× × × 2 3 1
6
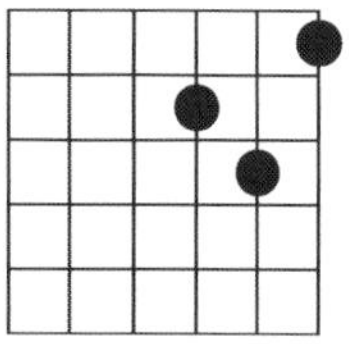

Gmin7
G B♭ F
3 1 4 × × ×
1
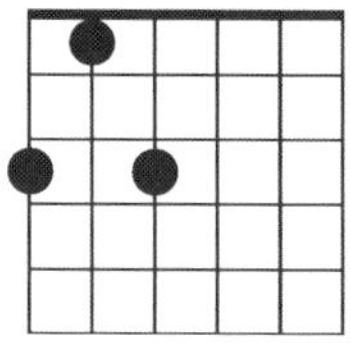

Gmin7
G B♭ F
× 3 1 4 × ×
8
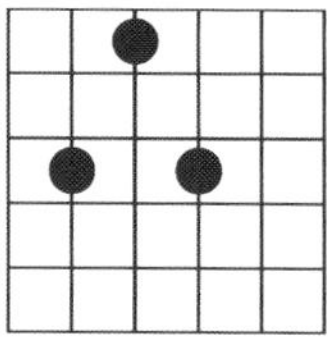

Gmin7
G B♭ F
× × 3 1 4 ×
3
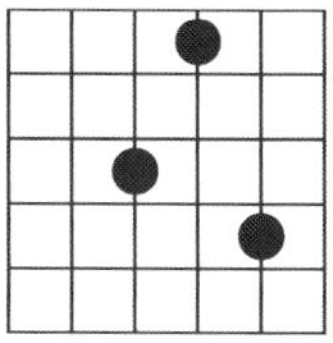

Gmin7
G B♭ F
× × × 2 1 4
11
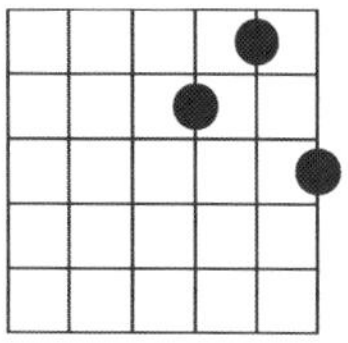

Gmin7
B♭ F G
2 4 1 × × ×
5
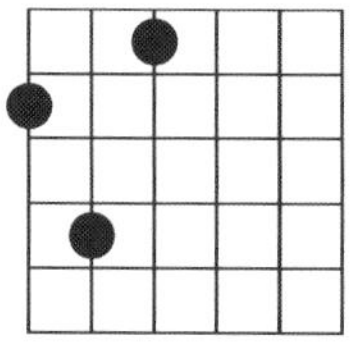

Gmin7
B♭ F G
× 1 4 0 × ×
0
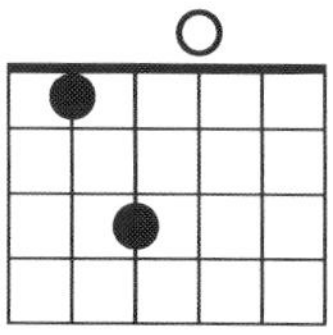

Gmin7
B♭ F G
× × 1 3 1 ×
8
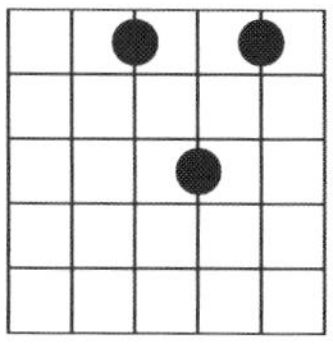

Gmin7
B♭ F G
× × × 1 4 1
3
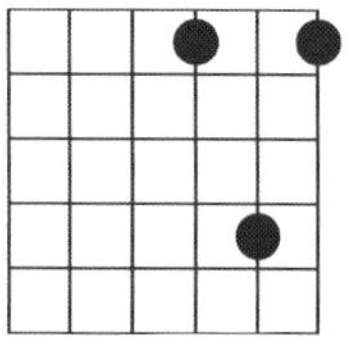

Gmin7
F G B♭
× × × 4 2 1
6
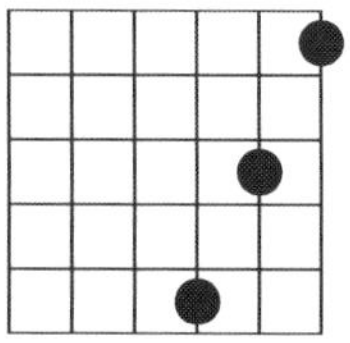

COMPACT
MINOR (CONT.)

Gmin7♭5
G D♭ F B♭
1 2 1 1 × ×
3
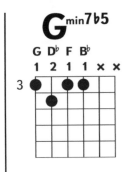

Gmin7♭5
G D♭ F B♭
× 1 2 1 3 ×
10
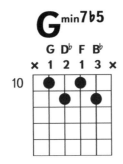

Gmin7♭9
G B♭ F A♭
3 1 4 1 × ×
1

Gmin7♭9
G B♭ F A♭
× 3 1 4 2 ×
8
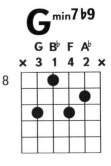

COMPACT
DOMINANT

G⁷
G B F
2 1 3 × × ×
2
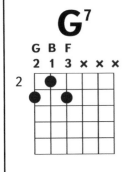

G⁷
G B F
× 2 1 3 × ×
9
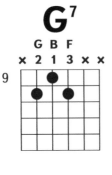

G⁷
G B F
× × 2 1 4 ×
4
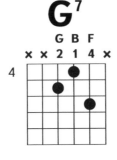

G⁷
D G B F
× × 0 0 0 1
0
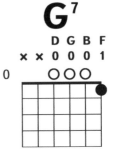

G⁷
B F G
3 4 1 × × ×
5
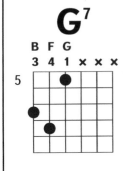

G⁷
B F G
× 2 3 0 × ×
0
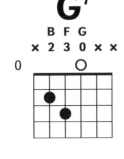

G⁷
B F G
× × × 2 4 1
3
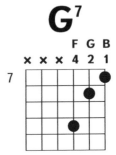

G⁷
F G B
× × × 4 2 1
7
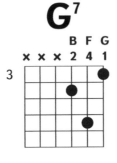

G⁷#⁵
G D# F B
1 4 1 2 × ×
3
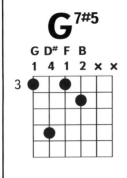

G⁷#⁵
G D# F B D#
× 1 4 1 3 2
10
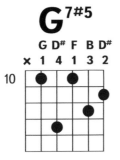

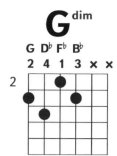

Gdim

G Db Fb Bb
2 4 1 3 × ×

2

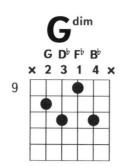

Gdim

G Db Fb Bb
× 2 3 1 4 ×

9

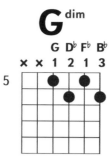

Gdim

G Db Fb Bb
× × 1 2 1 3

5

G

COMPACT
DIMINISHED

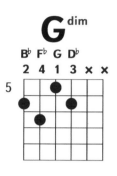

Gdim

Bb Fb G Db
2 4 1 3 × ×

5

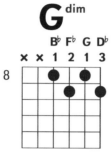

Gdim

Bb Fb G Db
× 1 2 0 4 ×

0

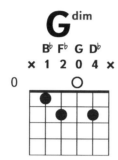

Gdim

Bb Fb G Db
× × 1 2 1 3

8

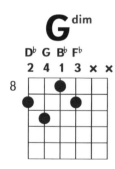

Gdim

Db G Bb Fb
2 4 1 3 × ×

8

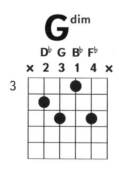

Gdim

Db G Bb Fb
× 2 3 1 4 ×

3

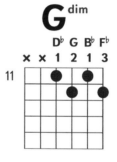

Gdim

Db G Bb Fb
× × 1 2 1 3

11

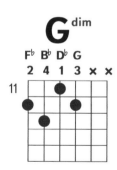

Gdim

Fb Bb Db G
2 4 1 3 × ×

11

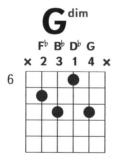

Gdim

Fb Bb Db G
× 2 3 1 4 ×

6

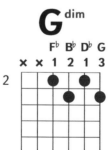

Gdim

Fb Bb Db G
× × 1 2 1 3

2

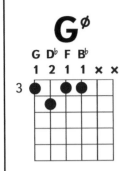

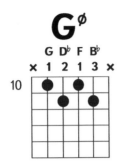

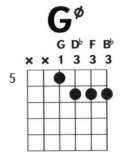

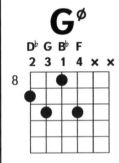

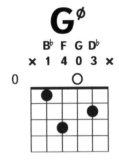

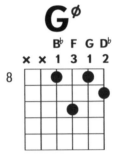

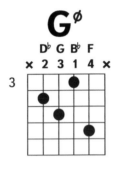

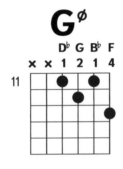

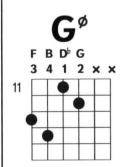

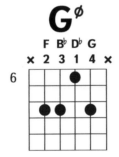

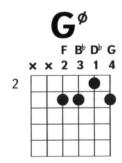

COMPACT *AUGMENTED*

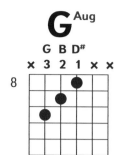

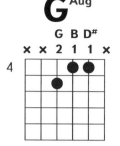

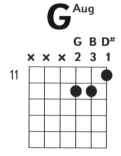

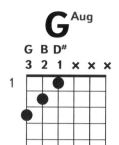

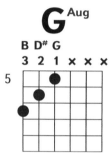

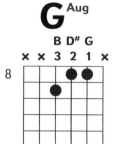

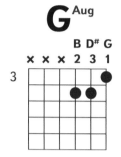

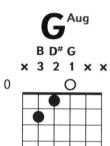

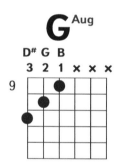

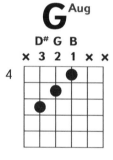

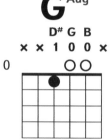

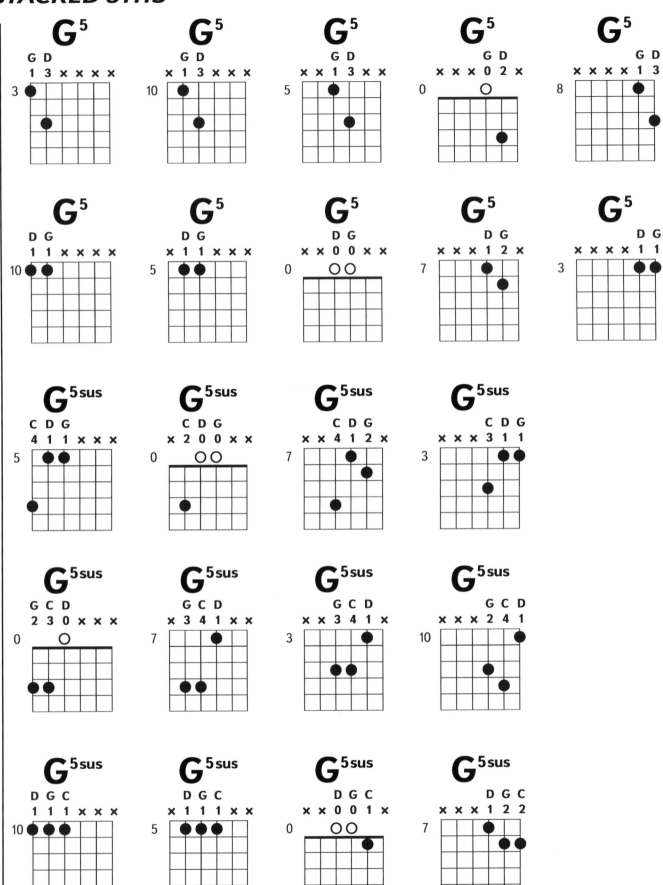

G^{5add9}

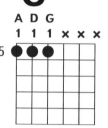

G^{5add9}

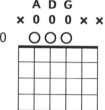

G^{5add9}

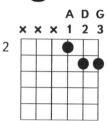

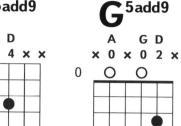

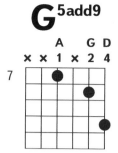

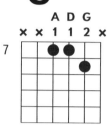

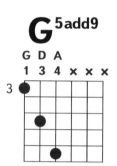

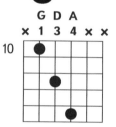

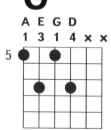

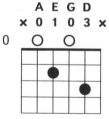

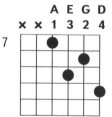

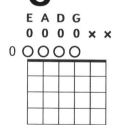

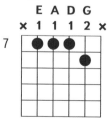

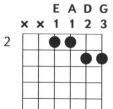

VIVID
MAJOR

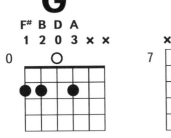

G△7

F# B D G
3 4 1 1 × ×
0

G△7

F# B D G
× 3 4 1 2 ×
7

G△7

F# B D G
× × 2 3 1 1
3

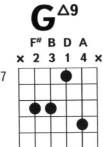
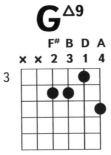

G△9

F# B D A
1 2 0 3 × ×
0

G△9

F# B D A
× 2 3 1 4 ×
7

G△9

F# B D A
× × 2 3 1 4
3

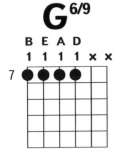
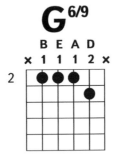
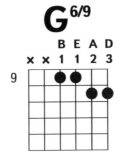
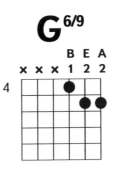

G6/9

B E A D
1 1 1 1 × ×
7

G6/9

B E A D
× 1 1 1 2 ×
2

G6/9

B E A D
× × 1 1 2 3
9

G6/9

B E A
× × × 1 2 2
4

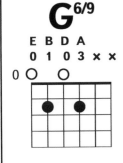
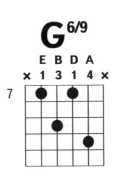
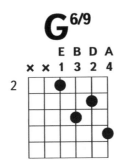

G6/9

E B D A
0 1 0 3 × ×
0

G6/9

E B D A
× 1 3 1 4 ×
7

G6/9

E B D A
× × 1 3 2 4
2

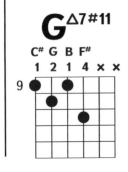
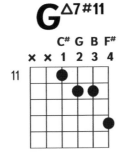

G△7#11

C# G B F#
1 2 1 4 × ×
9

G△7#11

C# G B F#
× × 1 2 3 4
11

228 GUITAR CHORDS ENCYCLOPEDIA: A SEEING MUSIC METHOD BOOK

G△7#11

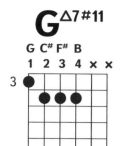

G C# F# B
1 2 3 4 × ×
3

G△7#11

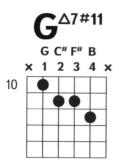

G C# F# B
× 1 2 3 4 ×
10

G△7#11

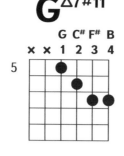

G C# F# B
× × 1 2 3 4
5

G△7#11

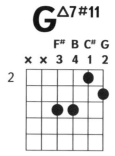

F# B C# G
× × 3 4 1 2
2

Gmin7

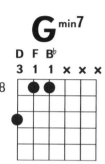

D F B♭
3 1 1 × × ×
8

Gmin7

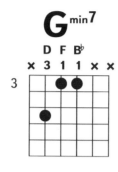

D F B♭
× 3 1 1 × ×
3

Gmin7

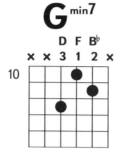

D F B♭
× × 3 1 2 ×
10

Gmin7

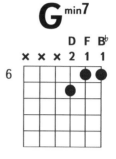

D F B♭
× × × 2 1 1
6

Gmin7

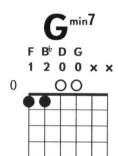

F B♭ D G
1 2 0 0 × ×
0

Gmin7

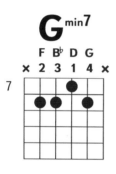

F B♭ D G
× 2 3 1 4 ×
7

Gmin7

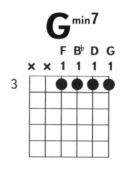

F B♭ D G
× × 1 1 1 1
3

Gmin7

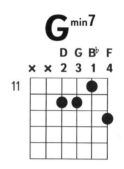

D G B♭ F
× × 2 3 1 4
11

Gmin7♭5

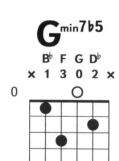

B♭ F G D♭
× 1 3 0 2 ×
0

Gmin7♭5

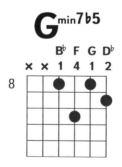

B♭ F G D♭
× × 1 4 1 2
8

Gmin7♭5

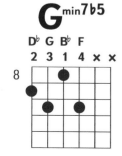

D♭ G B♭ F
2 3 1 4 × ×
8

Gmin7♭5

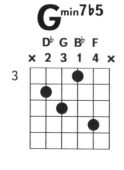

D♭ G B♭ F
× 2 3 1 4 ×
3

Gmin7♭5

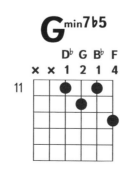

D♭ G B♭ F
× × 1 2 1 4
11

Gmin7♭5

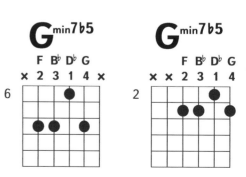

F B♭ D G
× 2 3 1 4 ×
6

Gmin7♭5

F B♭ D♭ G
× × 2 3 1 4
2

CHORDS WITH ROOT G 229

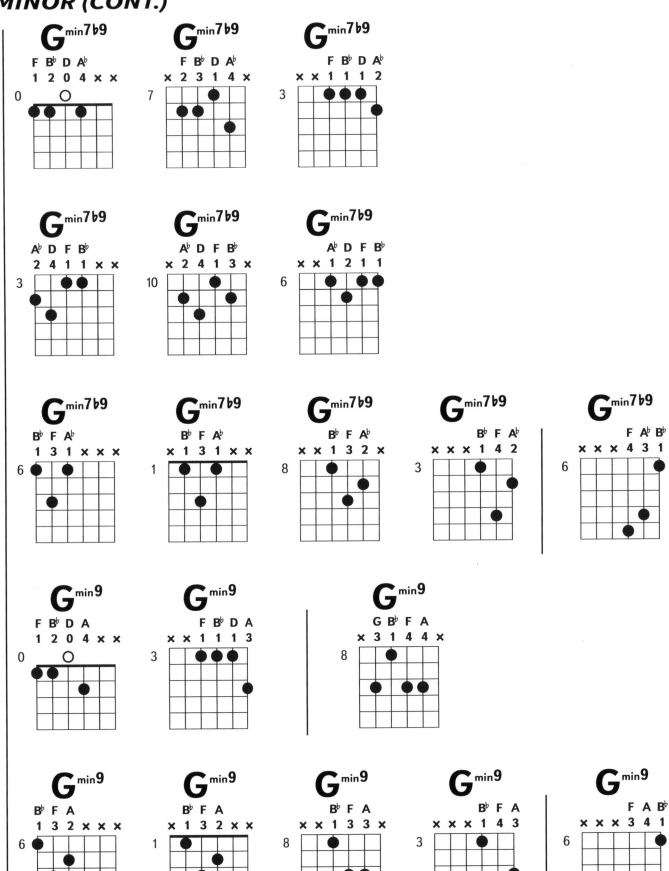

G^{min}**9**

A D F B♭
2 3 1 1 × ×

3

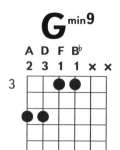

G^{min}**9**

A D F B♭
× 3 4 1 2 ×

10

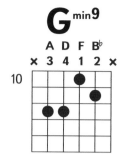

G^{min}**9**

A D F B♭
× × 2 3 1 1

6

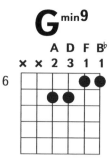

VIVID
MINOR (CONT.)

G^{min△7}

B♭ D F#
3 2 1 × × ×

4

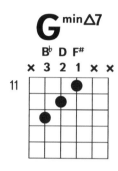

G^{min△7}

B♭ D F#
× 3 2 1 × ×

11

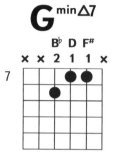

G^{min△7}

B♭ D F#
× × 2 1 1 ×

7

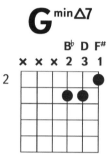

G^{min△7}

B♭ D F#
× × × 2 3 1

2

G^{min△7}

D F# B♭
3 2 1 × × ×

8

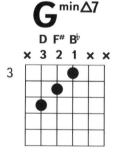

G^{min△7}

D F# B♭
× 3 2 1 × ×

3

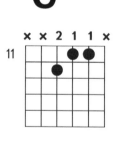

G^{min△7}

× × 2 1 1 ×

11

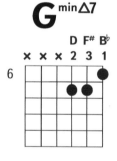

G^{min△7}

D F# B♭
× × × 2 3 1

6

G^{min△7}

F# B♭ D G
2 1 0 0 × ×

0

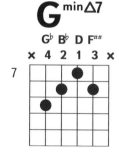

G^{min△7}

G♭ B♭ D F##
× 4 2 1 3 ×

7

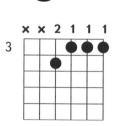

G^{min△7}

× × 2 1 1 1

3

VIVID
DOMINANT

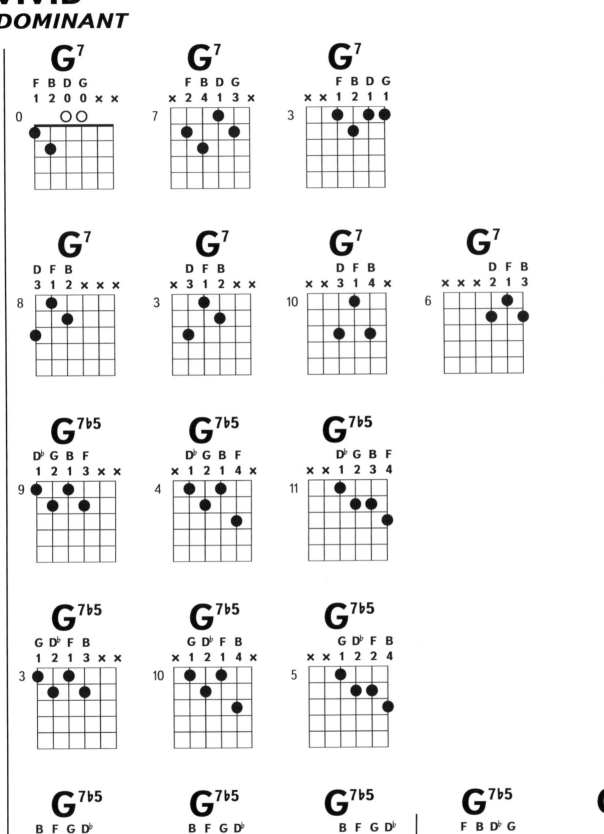

G⁷#⁵
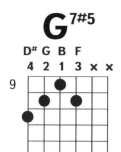

G⁷#⁵
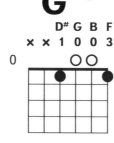

G⁷#⁵
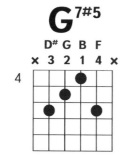

G⁷#⁵
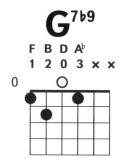

G⁷#⁵
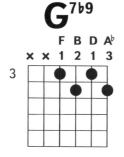

G⁷#⁵
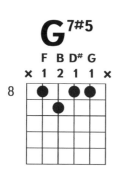

G⁷ᵇ⁹
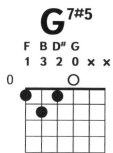

G⁷ᵇ⁹
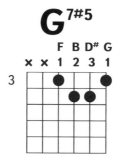

G⁷ᵇ⁹ **G**⁷ᵇ⁹
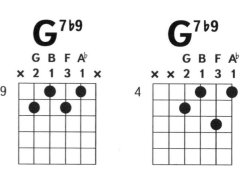

G⁷ᵇ⁹
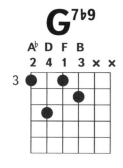

G⁷ᵇ⁹
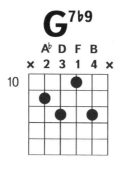

G⁷ᵇ⁹
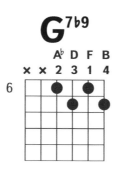

G⁷ᵇ⁹
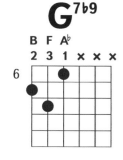

G⁷ᵇ⁹
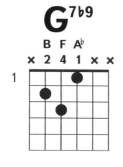

G⁷ᵇ⁹ **G**⁷ᵇ⁹
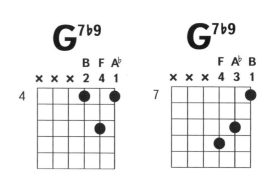

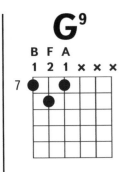

G⁹
B F A
1 2 1 × × ×
7

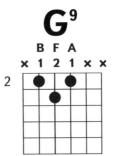

G⁹
× 1 2 1 × ×
2

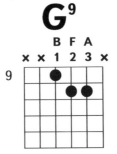

G⁹
× × 1 2 3 ×
9

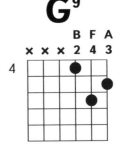

G⁹
× × 2 4 3
4

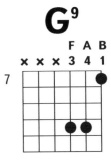

G⁹
F A B
× × × 3 4 1
7

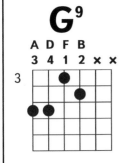

G⁹
F B D A
1 2 0 4 × ×
0

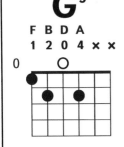

G⁹
F B D A
× × 1 2 1 3
3

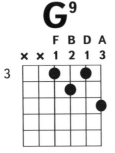

G⁹
A D F B
3 4 1 2 × ×
3

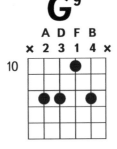

G⁹
A D F B
× 2 3 1 4 ×
10

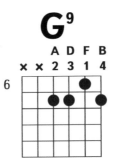

G⁹
A D F B
× × 2 3 1 4
6

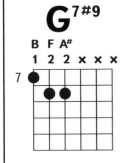

G⁷#⁹
B F A#
1 2 2 × × ×
7

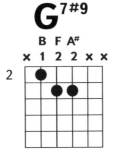

G⁷#⁹
B F A#
× 1 2 2 × ×
2

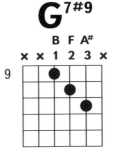

G⁷#⁹
B F A#
× × 1 2 3 ×
9

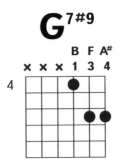

G⁷#⁹
B F A#
× × × 1 3 4
4

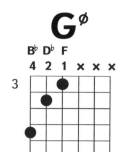

G∅
B♭ D♭ F
4 2 1 × × ×
3

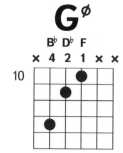

G∅
B♭ D♭ F
× 4 2 1 × ×
10

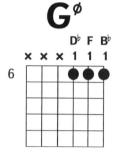

G∅
B♭ D♭ F
× × 3 1 1 ×
6

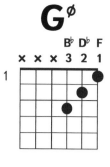

G∅
B♭ D♭ F
× × × 3 2 1
1

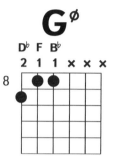

G∅
D♭ F B♭
2 1 1 × × ×
8

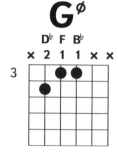

G∅
D♭ F B♭
× 2 1 1 × ×
3

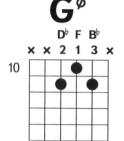

G∅
D♭ F B♭
× × 2 1 3 ×
10

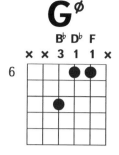

G∅
D♭ F B♭
× × × 1 1 1
6

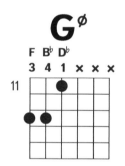

G∅
F B♭ D♭
3 4 1 × × ×
11

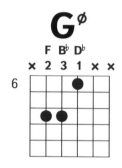

G∅
F B♭ D♭
× 2 3 1 × ×
6

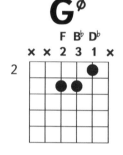

G∅
F B♭ D♭
× × 2 3 1 ×
2

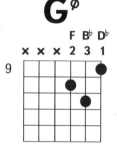

G∅
F B♭ D♭
× × × 2 3 1
9

236 GUITAR CHORDS ENCYCLOPEDIA: A SEEING MUSIC METHOD BOOK

BIG MAJOR

G#/Ab^Maj
Ab Eb Ab C Eb Ab
G# D# G# B# D# G#
1 3 4 2 1 1
4
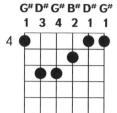

G#/Ab^Maj
Ab Eb Ab C
G# D# G# B#
× 1 3 3 3 ×
11
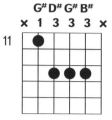

G#/Ab^△7
Ab Eb G C
G# D# F## B#
× 1 3 2 4 ×
11
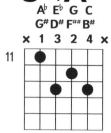

G#/Ab^△7#11
Ab D G C Eb
G# C## F## B# D#
× 1 2 3 4 1
11
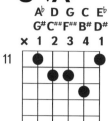

G#/Ab^6/9
Ab   C F Bb
G#   B# E# A#
1 × × 2 4 4
4
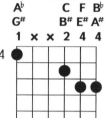

G#/Ab^6/9
Ab   C F Bb
G#   B# E# A#
× 2 1 1 3 ×
10
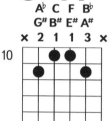

G#/Ab^add9
Ab   C Eb Bb
G#   B# D# A#
1 × × 2 1 4
4
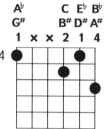

BIG MINOR

G#/Ab^min
Ab Eb Ab Cb Eb Ab
G# D# G# B D# G#
1 3 4 1 1 1
4
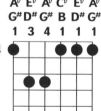

G#/Ab^min
Ab Eb Ab Cb Eb
G# D# G# B D#
× 1 3 4 2 1
11
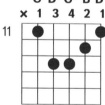

G#/Ab^min7
Ab Eb Gb Cb Eb Ab
G# D# F# B D# G#
1 3 1 1 1 1
4
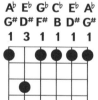

G#/Ab^min7b5
Ab Eb Ab Eb Gb Cb
G# D G# D F# B
1 2 3 4 4 4
4

G#/Ab^min7b9
Ab   Gb Cb Eb Bbb
G#   F# B D# A
1 × 1 1 1 2
4
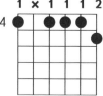

G#/Ab^min9
Ab Eb Gb Cb Eb Bb
G# D# F# B D# A#
1 3 1 1 1 4
4

G#/Ab^min△7
Ab Eb G Cb Eb
G# D# F## B D#
× 1 4 2 3 1
11

BIG
DOMINANT

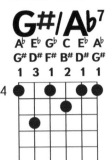

G#/Ab⁷
Ab Eb Gb C Eb Ab
G# D# F# B# D# G#
1 3 1 2 1 1
4

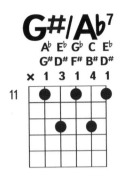

G#/Ab⁷
Ab Eb Gb C Eb
G# D# F# B# D#
× 1 3 1 4 1
11

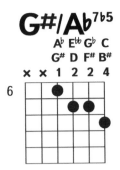

G#/Ab⁷b5
Ab Ebb Gb C
G# D F# B#
× × 1 2 2 4
6

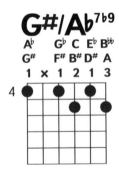

G#/Ab⁷#5
Ab C Gb C E
G# B# F# B# D##
1 2 3 4 4 ×
3

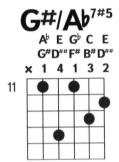

G#/Ab⁷#5
Ab E Gb C E
G# D## F# B# D##
× 1 4 1 3 2
11

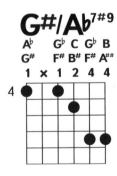

G#/Ab⁷b9
Ab Gb C Eb Bbb
G# F# B# D# A
1 × 1 2 1 3
4

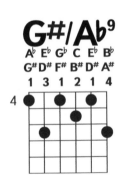

G#/Ab⁹
Ab Eb Gb C Eb Bb
G# D# F# B# D# A#
1 3 1 2 1 4
4

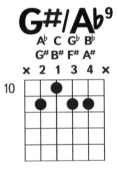

G#/Ab⁹
Ab C Gb Bb
G# B# F# A#
× 2 1 3 4 ×
10

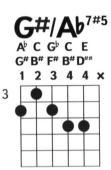

G#/Ab⁷#9
Ab Gb C Gb B
G# F# B# F# A##
1 × 1 2 4 4
4

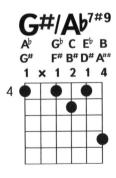

G#/Ab⁷#9
Ab Gb C Eb B
G# F# B# D# A##
1 × 1 2 1 4
4

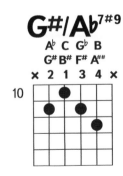

G#/Ab⁷#9
Ab C Gb B
G# B# F# A##
× 2 1 3 4 ×
10

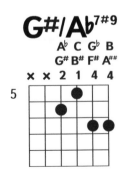

G#/Ab⁷#9
Ab C Gb B
G# B# F# A##
× × 2 1 4 4
5

238 GUITAR CHORDS ENCYCLOPEDIA: A SEEING MUSIC METHOD BOOK

BIG
AUGMENTED

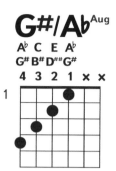

G#/Ab Aug
Ab C E Ab
G# B# D## G#
4 3 2 1 × ×
1

G#/Ab Aug
Ab C E Ab
G# B# D## G#
× 3 2 1 1 ×
9

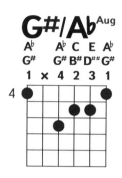

G#/Ab Aug
Ab   Ab C E Ab
G#   G# B# D## G#
1 × 4 2 3 1
4

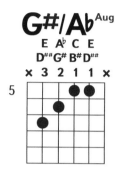

G#/Ab Aug
E A C E
D## G# B# D##
× 3 2 1 1 ×
5

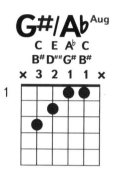

G#/Ab Aug
C E A C
B# D## G# B#
× 3 2 1 1 ×
1

BIG
DIMINISHED

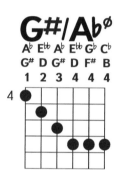

G#/Abø
Ab Ebb Ab Ebb Gb Cb
G# D G# D F# B
1 2 3 4 4 4
4

G#/Abdim
Ab   Gbb Cb Ebb Ab
G#   F B D G#
2 × 1 3 1 4
3

BIG
STACKED 5THS

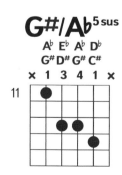

G#/Ab5sus
Ab Eb Ab Db
G# D# G# C#
× 1 3 4 1 ×
11

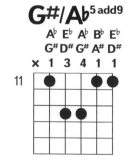

G#/Ab5add9
Ab Eb Ab Bb Eb
G# D# G# A# D#
× 1 3 4 1 1
11

G#/Abadd6/9
Ab Eb   Bb F
G# D#   A# E#
× 1 3 × 1 4
11

COMPACT
MAJOR

G#/Ab^Maj
Ab C Eb
G# B# D#
4 3 1 × × ×
1
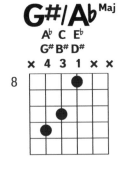

G#/Ab^Maj
Ab C Eb
G# B# D#
× 4 3 1 × ×
8
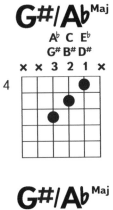

G#/Ab^Maj
Ab C Eb
G# B# D#
× × 3 2 1 ×
4
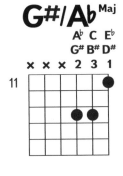

G#/Ab^Maj
Ab C Eb
G# B# D#
× × × 2 3 1
11
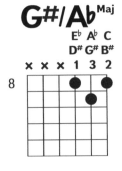

G#/Ab^Maj
Eb Ab C
D# G# B#
2 3 1 × × ×
10
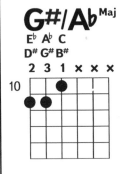

G#/Ab^Maj
Eb Ab C
D# G# B#
× 2 3 1 × ×
5
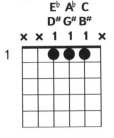

G#/Ab^Maj
Eb Ab C
D# G# B#
× × 1 1 1 ×
1
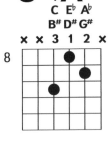

G#/Ab^Maj
Eb Ab C
D# G# B#
× × × 1 3 2
8
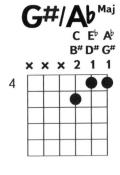

G#/Ab^Maj
C Eb Ab
B# D# G#
3 1 1 × × ×
6
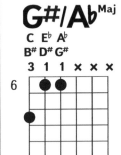

G#/Ab^Maj
C Eb Ab
B# D# G#
× 3 1 1 × ×
1
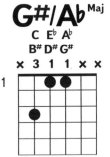

G#/Ab^Maj
C Eb Ab
B# D# G#
× × 3 1 2 ×
8
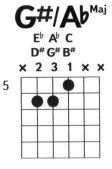

G#/Ab^Maj
C Eb Ab
B# D# G#
× × × 2 1 1
4
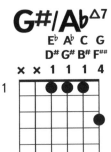

G#/Ab^△7
Ab C G
G# B# F##
2 1 4 × × ×
3
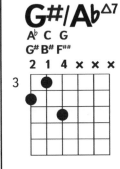

G#/Ab^△7
Ab C G
G# B# F##
× 2 1 4 × ×
10
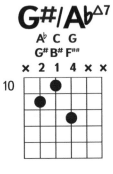

G#/Ab^△7
Ab C G
G# B# F##
× × 2 1 4 ×
5
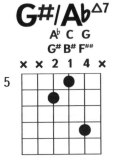

G#/Ab^△7
Eb Ab C G
D# G# B# F##
× × 1 1 1 4
1
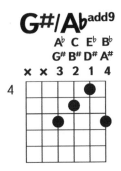

G#/Ab^add9
Ab C Eb Bb
G# B# D# A#
× × 3 2 1 4
4

COMPACT
MINOR

G#/A♭min
A♭ C♭ E♭
G# B D#
4 2 1 × × ×
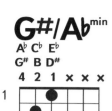
1

G#/A♭min
A♭ C♭ E♭
G# B D#
× 4 2 1 × ×
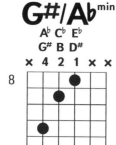
8

G#/A♭min
A♭ C♭ E♭
G# B D#
× × 3 1 1
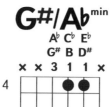
4

G#/A♭min
A♭ C♭ E♭
G# B D#
× × × 3 2 1
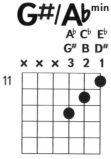
11

G#/A♭min
C♭ E♭ A♭
B D# G#
2 1 1 × × ×

6

G#/A♭min
C♭ E♭ A♭
B D# G#
× 2 1 1 × ×
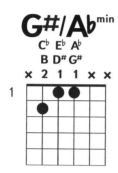
1

G#/A♭min
C♭ E♭ A♭
B D# G#
× × 2 1 3
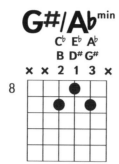
8

G#/A♭min
C♭ E♭ A♭
B D# G#
× × × 1 1 1
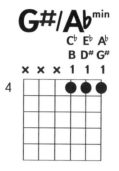
4

G#/A♭min
E♭ A♭ C♭
D# G# B
3 4 1 × × ×
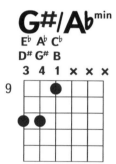
9

G#/A♭min
E♭ A♭ C♭
D# G# B
× 3 4 1 × ×
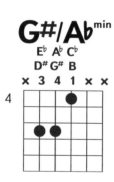
4

G#/A♭min
E♭ A♭ C♭
D# G# B
× × 1 2 0 ×
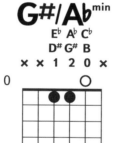
0

G#/A♭min
E♭ A♭ C♭
D# G# B
× × × 2 3 1
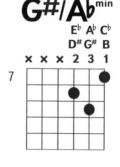
7

G#/A♭min7
A♭ C♭ G♭
G# B F#
3 1 4 × × ×
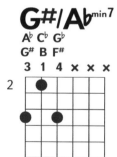
2

G#/A♭min7
A♭ C♭ G♭
G# B F#
× 3 1 4 × ×
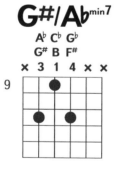
9

G#/A♭min7
A♭ C♭ G♭
G# B F#
× × 3 1 4 ×
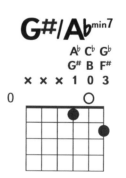
4

G#/A♭min7
A♭ C♭ G♭
G# B F#
× × × 1 0 3
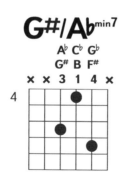
0

G#/A♭min7
C♭ G♭ A♭
B F# G#
2 4 1 × × ×
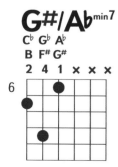
6

G#/A♭min7
C♭ G♭ A♭
B F# G#
× 2 4 1 × ×
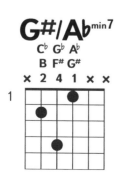
1

G#/A♭min7
C♭ G♭ A♭
B F# G#
× × 1 3 1 ×
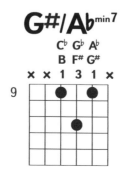
9

G#/A♭min7
C♭ G♭ A♭
B F# G#
× × × 1 4 1

4

G#/A♭min7
G♭ A♭ C♭
F# G# B
× × × 4 2 1
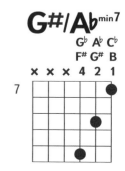
7

COMPACT
MINOR (CONT.)

G#/Ab min7b5
Ab Ebb Gb Cb
G# D F# B
1 2 1 1 × ×
4
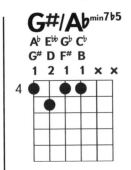

G#/Ab min7b5
Ab Ebb Gb Cb
G# D F# B
× 1 2 1 3 ×
11
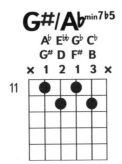

G#/Ab min7b9
Ab Cb Gb Bbb
G# B F# A
3 1 4 1 × ×
2
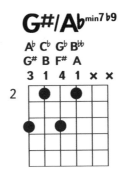

G#/Ab min7b9
Ab Cb Gb Bbb
G# B F# A
× 3 1 4 2 ×
9
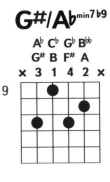

COMPACT
DOMINANT

G#/Ab 7
Ab C Gb
G# B# F#
2 1 3 × × ×
3
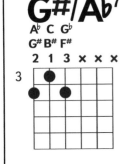

G#/Ab 7
Ab C Gb
G# B# F#
× 2 1 3 × ×
10
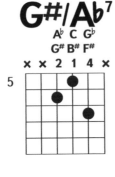

G#/Ab 7
Ab C Gb
G# B# F#
× × 2 1 4 ×
5
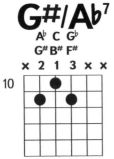

G#/Ab 7
Eb Ab C Gb
D# G# B# F#
× × 1 1 1 2
1
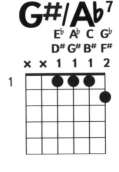

G#/Ab 7
C Gb Ab
B# F# G#
3 4 1 × × ×
6
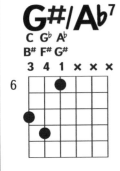

G#/Ab 7
C Gb Ab
B# F# G#
× 3 4 1 × ×
1
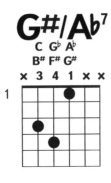

G#/Ab 7
C Gb Ab
B# F# G#
× × × 2 4 1
4
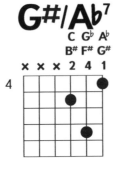

G#/Ab 7
Gb Ab C
F# G# B#
× × × 4 2 1
8
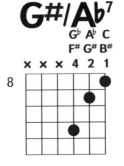

G#/Ab 7#5
Ab E Gb C
G# D## F# B#
1 4 1 2 × ×
4
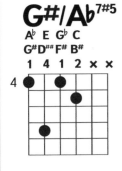

G#/Ab 7#5
Ab E Gb C E
G# D## F# B# D##
× 1 4 1 3 2
11
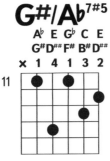

G#/A♭
COMPACT
DIMINISHED

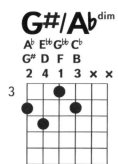

G#/A♭dim

A♭ E♭♭ G♭♭ C♭
G# D F B
2 4 1 3 × ×

3

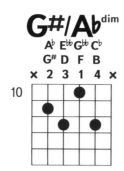

G#/A♭dim

A♭ E♭♭ G♭♭ C♭
G# D F B
× 2 3 1 4 ×

10

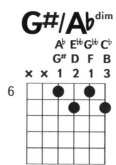

G#/A♭dim

A♭ E♭♭ G♭♭ C♭
G# D F B
× × 1 2 1 3

6

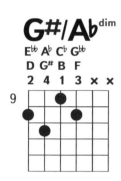

G#/A♭dim

C♭ G♭♭ A♭ E♭♭
B F G# D
2 4 1 3 × ×

6

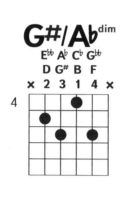

G#/A♭dim

C♭ G♭♭ A♭ E♭♭
B F G# D
× 2 3 1 4 ×

1

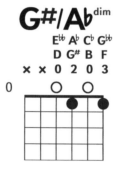

G#/A♭dim

C♭ G♭♭ A♭ E♭♭
B F G# D
× × 1 2 1 3

9

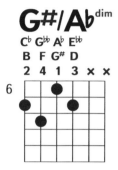

G#/A♭dim

E♭♭ A♭ C♭ G♭♭
D G# B F
2 4 1 3 × ×

9

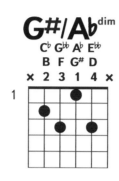

G#/A♭dim

E♭♭ A♭ C♭ G♭♭
D G# B F
× 2 3 1 4 ×

4

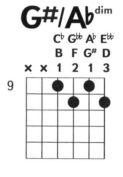

G#/A♭dim

E♭♭ A♭ C♭ G♭♭
D G# B F
× × 0 2 0 3

0

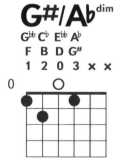

G#/A♭dim

G♭♭ C♭ E♭♭ A♭
F B D G#
1 2 0 3 × ×

0

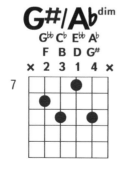

G#/A♭dim

G♭♭ C♭ E♭♭ A♭
F B D G#
× 2 3 1 4 ×

7

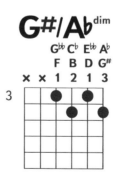

G#/A♭dim

G♭♭ C♭ E♭♭ A♭
F B D G#
× × 1 2 1 3

3

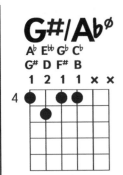

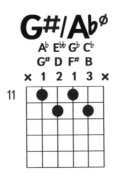

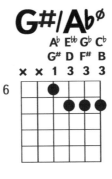

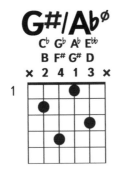

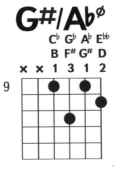

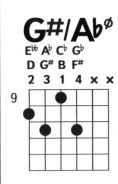

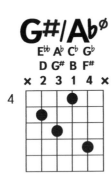

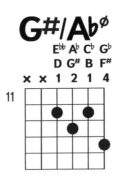

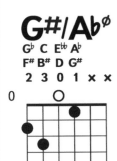

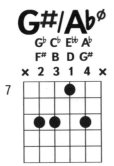

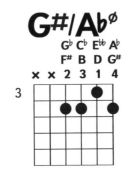

G#/Ab^{Aug}
Ab C E
G# B# D##
3 2 1 × × ×
2
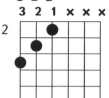

G#/Ab^{Aug}
Ab C E
G# B# D##
× 3 2 1 × ×
9
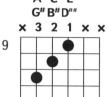

G#/Ab^{Aug}
Ab C E
G# B# D##
× × 2 1 1 ×
5
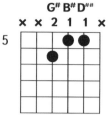

G#/Ab^{Aug}
Ab C E
G# B# D##
× × × 1 2 0
0
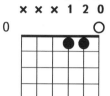

G#/Ab^{Aug}
C E Ab
B# D## G#
3 2 1 × × ×
6
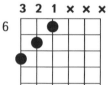

G#/Ab^{Aug}
C E Ab
B# D## G#
× 3 2 1 × ×
1
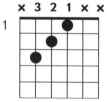

G#/Ab^{Aug}
C E Ab
B# D## G#
× × 3 2 1 ×
9
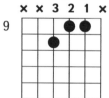

G#/Ab^{Aug}
C E Ab
B# D## G#
× × × 2 3 1
4
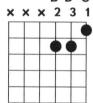

G#/Ab^{Aug}
E Ab C
D## G# B#
3 2 1 × × ×
10
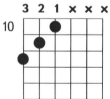

G#/Ab^{Aug}
E Ab C
D## G# B#
× 3 2 1 × ×
5
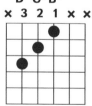

G#/Ab^{Aug}
E Ab C
D## G# B#
× × 2 1 1 ×
1
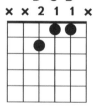

G#/Ab^{Aug}
E Ab C
D## G# B#
× × × 2 3 1
8
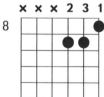

COMPACT
STACKED 5THS

G#/A♭⁵
A♭ E♭
G# D#
1 3 × × × ×
4

G#/A♭⁵
A♭ E♭
G# D#
× 1 3 × × ×
11
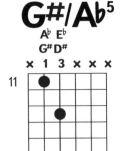

G#/A♭⁵
A♭ E♭
G# D#
× × 1 3 × ×
6
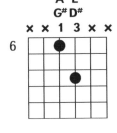

G#/A♭⁵
A♭ E♭
G# D#
× × × 1 4 ×
1
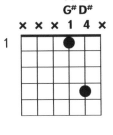

G#/A♭⁵
A♭ E♭
G# D#
× × × × 1 3
9
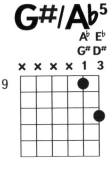

G#/A♭⁵
E♭ A♭
D# G#
1 1 × × × ×
11
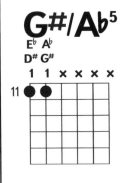

G#/A♭⁵
E♭ A♭
D# G#
× 1 1 × × ×
6
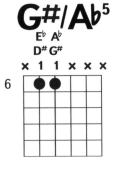

G#/A♭⁵
E♭ A♭
D# G#
× × 1 1 × ×
1
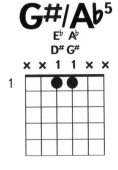

G#/A♭⁵
E♭ A♭
D# G#
× × × 1 2 ×
8
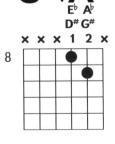

G#/A♭⁵
E♭ A♭
D# G#
× × × × 1 1
4
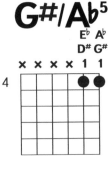

G#/A♭⁵ˢᵘˢ
D♭ E♭ A♭
C# D# G#
4 1 1 × × ×
6

G#/A♭⁵ˢᵘˢ
A♭ D♭ E♭
G# C# D#
× × 2 4 1
11
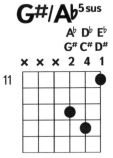

G#/A♭⁵ˢᵘˢ
D♭ E♭ A♭
C# D# G#
× × 4 1 2 ×
8
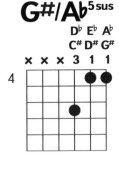

G#/A♭⁵ˢᵘˢ
D♭ E♭ A♭
C# D# G#
× × × 3 1 1
4
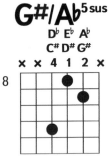

G#/A♭⁵ˢᵘˢ
A♭ D♭ E♭
G# C# D#
3 4 1 × × ×
1
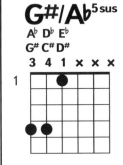

G#/A♭⁵ˢᵘˢ
A♭ D♭ E♭
G# C# D#
× 3 4 1 × ×
8
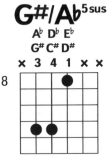

G#/A♭⁵ˢᵘˢ
A♭ D♭ E♭
G# C# D#
× × 3 4 1 ×
4
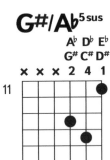

G#/A♭⁵ˢᵘˢ
A♭ D♭ E♭
G# C# D#
× × × 2 4 1
11
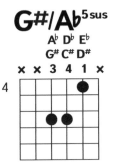

G#/A♭⁵ˢᵘˢ
E♭ A♭ D♭
D# G# C#
1 1 1 × × ×
11
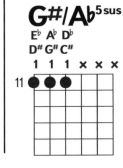

G#/A♭⁵ˢᵘˢ
E♭ A♭ D♭
D# G# C#
× 1 1 1 × ×
6
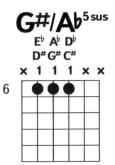

G#/A♭⁵ˢᵘˢ
E♭ A♭ D♭
D# G# C#
× × 1 1 2 ×
1
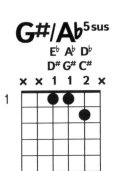

G#/A♭⁵ˢᵘˢ
E♭ A♭ D♭
D# G# C#
× × × 1 2 2
8
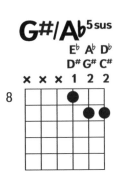

246 GUITAR CHORDS ENCYCLOPEDIA: A SEEING MUSIC METHOD BOOK

G#/Ab⁵ᵃᵈᵈ⁹

Bb   Ab Eb
A#   G# D#
1 × 1 4 × ×
6
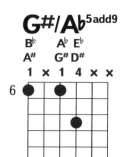

G#/Ab⁵ᵃᵈᵈ⁹

Bb   Ab Eb
A#   G# D#
× 1 × 1 4 ×
1
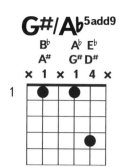

G#/Ab⁵ᵃᵈᵈ⁹

Bb   Ab Eb
A#   G# D#
× × 1 × 2 4
8
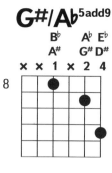

G#/Ab⁵ᵃᵈᵈ⁹

Bb E♭ Ab
A# D# G#
1 1 1 × × ×
6
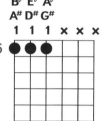

G#/Ab⁵ᵃᵈᵈ⁹

Bb Eb Ab
A# D# G#
× 1 1 1 × ×
1
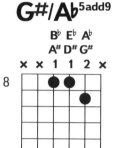

G#/Ab⁵ᵃᵈᵈ⁹

Bb Eb Ab
A# D# G#
× × 1 1 2 ×
8
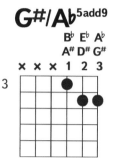

G#/Ab⁵ᵃᵈᵈ⁹

Bb Eb Ab
A# D# G#
× × × 1 2 3
3
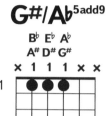

G#/Ab⁵ᵃᵈᵈ⁹

Ab Eb Bb
G# D# A#
1 3 4 × × ×
4
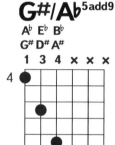

G#/Abᵃᵈᵈ⁹

Ab Eb Bb
G# D# A#
× 1 3 4 × ×
11
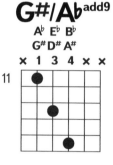

G#/Ab⁵ᵃᵈᵈ⁶/⁹

Bb F Ab Eb
A# E# G# D#
1 3 1 4 × ×
6
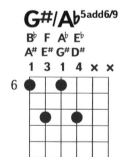

G#/Ab⁵ᵃᵈᵈ⁶/⁹

Bb F Ab Eb
A# E# G# D#
× 1 3 1 4 ×
1
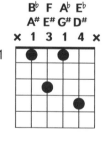

G#/Ab⁵ᵃᵈᵈ⁶/⁹

Bb F Ab Eb
A# E# G# D#
× × 1 3 2 4
8
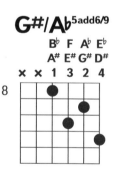

G#/Ab⁵ᵃᵈᵈ⁶/⁹

F Bb Eb Ab
E# A# D# G#
1 1 1 1 × ×
1
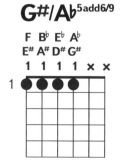

G#/Ab⁵ᵃᵈᵈ⁶/⁹

F Bb Eb Ab
E# A# D# G#
× 1 1 1 2 ×
8
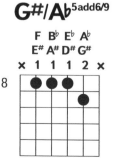

G#/Ab⁵ᵃᵈᵈ⁶/⁹

F Bb Eb Ab
E# A# D# G#
× × 1 1 2 3
3
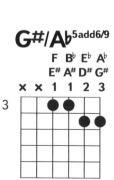

VIVID
MAJOR

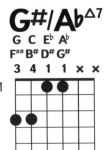

G#/Ab△7
G C Eb Ab
F## B D# G#
3 4 1 1 × ×
1

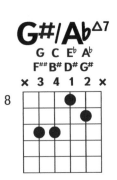

G#/Ab△7
G C Eb Ab
F## B D# G#
× 3 4 1 2 ×
8

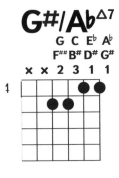

G#/Ab△7
G C Eb Ab
F## B D# G#
× × 2 3 1 1
4

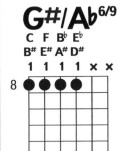

G#/Ab△9
G C Eb Bb
F## B D# A#
2 3 1 4 × ×
1

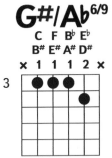

G#/Ab△9
G C Eb Bb
F## B D# A#
× 2 3 1 4 ×
8

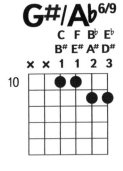

G#/Ab△9
G C Eb Bb
F## B D# A#
× × 2 3 1 4
4

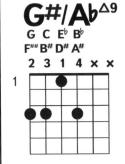

G#/Ab6/9
C F Bb Eb
B# E# A# D#
1 1 1 1 × ×
8

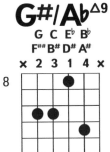

G#/Ab6/9
C F Bb Eb
B# E# A# D#
× 1 1 1 2 ×
3

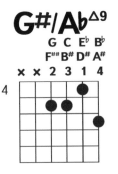

G#/Ab6/9
C F Bb Eb
B# E# A# D#
× × 1 1 2 3
10

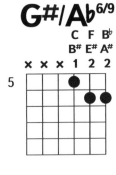

G#/Ab6/9
C F Bb
B# E# A#
× × × 1 2 2
5

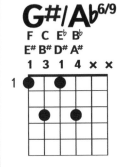

G#/Ab6/9
F C Eb Bb
E# B# D# A#
1 3 1 4 × ×
1

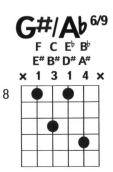

G#/Ab6/9
F C Eb Bb
E# B# D# A#
× 1 3 1 4 ×
8

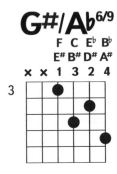

G#/Ab6/9
F C Eb Bb
E# B# D# A#
× × 1 3 2 4
3

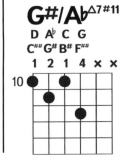

G#/Ab△7#11
D Ab C G
C## G# B# F##
1 2 1 4 × ×
10

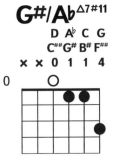

G#/Ab△7#11
D Ab C G
C## G# B# F##
× × 0 1 1 4
0

248 GUITAR CHORDS ENCYCLOPEDIA: A SEEING MUSIC METHOD BOOK

VIVID
MAJOR (CONT.)

VIVID
MINOR

G#/Ab△7#11
Ab D G C
G# C## F## B#
1 2 3 4 × ×
4

G#/Ab△7#11
Ab D G C
G# C## F## B#
× 1 2 3 4 ×
11

G#/Ab△7#11
Ab D G C
G# C## F## B#
× × 1 2 3 4
6

G#/Ab△7#11
G C D Ab
F## B# C## G#
× × 3 4 1 2
3

G#/Abmin7
Eb Gb Cb
D# F# B
3 1 1 × × ×
9

G#/Abmin7
Eb Gb Cb
D# F# B
× 3 1 1 × ×
4

G#/Abmin7
Eb Gb Cb
D# F# B
× × 3 1 2 ×
11

G#/Abmin7
Eb Gb Cb
D# F# B
× × 2 1 1
7

G#/Abmin7
Gb Cb Eb Ab
F# B D# G#
2 3 1 1 × ×
1

G#/Abmin7
Gb Cb Eb Ab
F# B D# G#
× 2 3 1 4 ×
8

G#/Abmin7
Gb Cb Eb Ab
F# B D# G#
× × 1 1 1 1
4

G#/Abmin7
Eb Ab Cb Gb
D# G# B F#
× × 1 2 0 3
0

G#/Abmin7b5
Cb Gb Ab Ebb
B F# G# D
× 2 4 1 3 ×
1

G#/Abmin7b5
Cb Gb Ab Ebb
B F# G# D
× × 1 4 1 2
9

G#/Abmin7b5
Ebb Ab Cb Gb
D G# B F#
2 3 1 4 × ×
9

G#/Abmin7b5
Ebb Ab Cb Gb
D G# B F#
× 2 3 1 4 ×
4

G#/Abmin7b5
Ebb Ab Cb Gb
D G# B F#
× × 0 2 0 4
0

G#/Abmin7b5
Gb Cb Ebb Ab
F# B D G#
× 2 3 1 4 ×
7

G#/Abmin7b5
Gb Cb Ebb Ab
F# B D G#
× × 2 3 1 4
3

G#/Ab min7b9
Gb Cb Eb Bbb
F# B D# A
2 3 1 4 × ×
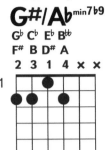
1

G#/Ab min7b9
Gb Cb Eb Bbb
F# B D# A
× 2 3 1 4 ×
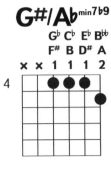
8

G#/Ab min7b9
Gb Cb Eb Bbb
F# B D# A
× × 1 1 1 2
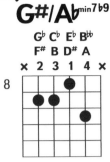
4

G#/Ab min7b9
Bbb Eb Gb Cb
A D# F# B
2 4 1 1 × ×
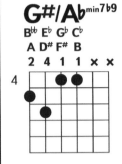
4

G#/Ab min7b9
Bbb Eb Gb Cb
A D# F# B
× 2 4 1 3 ×
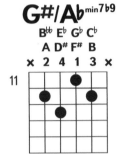
11

G#/Ab min7b9
Bbb Eb Gb Cb
A D# F# B
× × 1 2 1 1
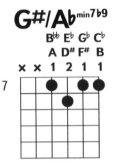
7

G#/Ab min7b9
Cb Gb Bbb
B F# A
1 3 1 × × ×
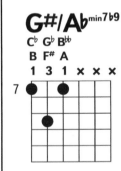
7

G#/Ab min7b9
Cb Gb Bbb
B F# A
× 1 3 1 × ×
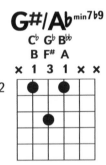
2

G#/Ab min7b9
Cb Gb Bbb
B F# A
× × 1 3 2 ×
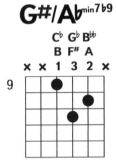
9

G#/Ab min7b9
Cb Gb Bbb
B F# A
× × × 1 4 2
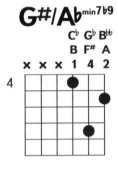
4

G#/Ab min7b9
Gb Bbb Cb
F# A B
× × × 4 3 1
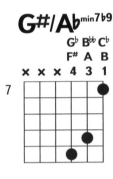
7

G#/Ab min9
Gb Cb Eb Bb
F# B D# A#
2 3 1 4 × ×
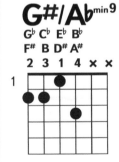
1

G#/Ab min9
Gb Cb Eb Bb
F# B D# A#
× × 1 1 1 3
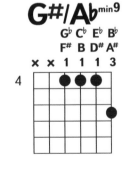
4

G#/Ab min9
Ab Cb Gb Bb
G# B F# A#
× 3 1 4 4 ×
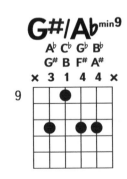
9

G#/Ab min9
Cb Gb Bb
B F# A#
1 3 2 × × ×
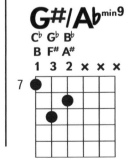
7

G#/Ab min9
Cb Gb Bb
B F# A#
× 1 3 2 × ×
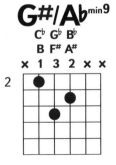
2

G#/Ab min9
Cb Gb Bb
B F# A#
× × 1 3 3 ×
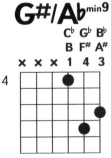
9

G#/Ab min9
Cb Gb Bb
B F# A#
× × × 1 4 3
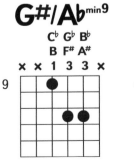
4

G#/Ab min9
Gb Bb Cb
F# A# B
× × × 3 4 1
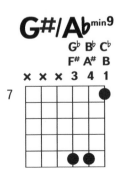
7

250 GUITAR CHORDS ENCYCLOPEDIA: A SEEING MUSIC METHOD BOOK

VIVID
MINOR (CONT.)

G#/A♭min9
B♭ E♭ G♭ C♭
A# D# F# B
2 3 1 1 × ×
4
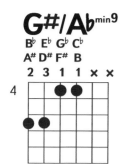

G#/A♭min9
B♭ E♭ G♭ C♭
A# D# F# B
× 3 4 1 2 ×
11
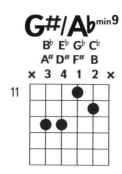

G#/A♭min9
B♭ E♭ G♭ C♭
A# D# F# B
× × 2 3 1 1
7
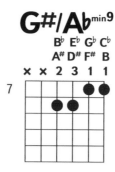

G#/A♭min△7
C♭ E♭ G
B D# F##
3 2 1 × × ×
5
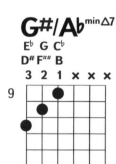

G#/A♭min△7
C♭ E♭ G
B D# F##
× 2 1 0 × ×
0
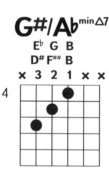

G#/A♭min△7
C♭ E♭ G
B D# F##
× × 2 1 1 ×
8
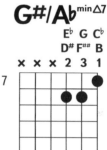

G#/A♭min△7
C♭ E♭ G
B D# F##
× × × 2 3 1
3
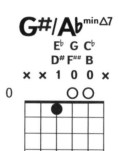

G#/A♭min△7
E♭ G C♭
D# F## B
3 2 1 × × ×
9
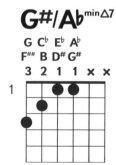

G#/A♭min△7
E♭ G B
D# F## B
× 3 2 1 × ×
4
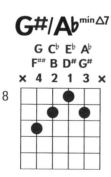

G#/A♭min△7
E♭ G C♭
D# F## B
× × 1 0 0 ×
0
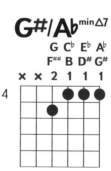

G#/A♭min△7
E♭ G C♭
D# F## B
× × × 2 3 1
7

G#/A♭min△7
G C♭ E♭ A♭
F## B D# G#
3 2 1 1 × ×
1

G#/A♭min△7
G C♭ E♭ A♭
F## B D# G#
× 4 2 1 3 ×
8

G#/A♭min△7
G C♭ E♭ A♭
F## B D# G#
× × 2 1 1 1
4

CHORDS WITH ROOT G SHARP - A FLAT 251

VIVID
DOMINANT

G#/Ab⁷
Gb C Eb Ab
F# B# D# G#
2 4 1 1 × ×
1
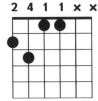

G#/Ab⁷
Gb C Eb Ab
F# B# D# G#
× 2 4 1 3 ×
8
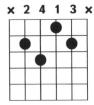

G#/Ab⁷
Gb C Eb Ab
F# B# D# G#
× × 1 2 1 1
4
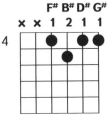

G#/Ab⁷
Eb Gb C
D# F# B#
3 1 2 × × ×
9
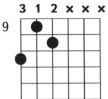

G#/Ab⁷
Eb Gb C
D# F# B#
× 3 1 2 × ×
4
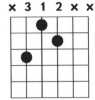

G#/Ab⁷
Eb Gb C
D# F# B#
× × 3 1 4 ×
11
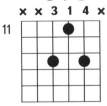

G#/Ab⁷
Eb Gb C
D# F# B#
× × × 2 1 3
7
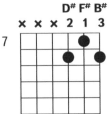

G#/Ab⁷
Eb Gb C
D# F# B#
3 1 2 × × ×
9
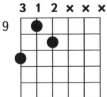

G#/Ab⁷b5
Ebb Ab C Gb
D G# B# F#
× 1 2 1 4 ×
5
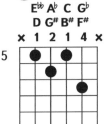

G#/Ab⁷
Eb Gb C
D# F# B#
× × 3 1 4 ×
11
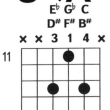

G#/Ab⁷b5
Ab Ebb Gb C
G# D F# B#
1 2 1 3 × ×
4

G#/Ab⁷b5
Ab Ebb Gb C
G# D F# B#
× 1 2 1 4 ×
11
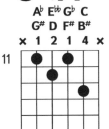

G#/Ab⁷b5
Ab Ebb Gb C
G# D F# B#
× × 1 2 2 4
6

G#/Ab⁷b5
C Gb Ab Ebb
B# F# G# D
3 4 1 2 × ×
6
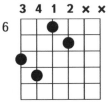

G#/Ab⁷b5
C Gb Ab Ebb
B# F# G# D
× 3 4 1 2 ×
1
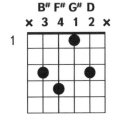

G#/Ab⁷b5
C Gb Ab Ebb
B# F# G# D
× × 2 4 1 3
9
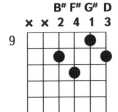

G#/Ab⁷b5
Gb C Ebb Ab
F# B# D G#
× 2 4 1 3 ×
7
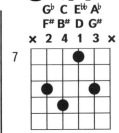

G#/Ab⁷
Gb C Eb Ab
F# B# D# G#
× × 1 2 1 1
4
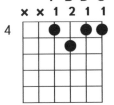

252 GUITAR CHORDS ENCYCLOPEDIA: A SEEING MUSIC METHOD BOOK

G#/A♭7#5
E A♭ C G♭
D## G# B# F#
4 2 1 3 × ×
10
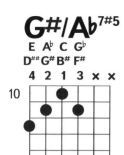

G#/A♭7#5
E A♭ C G♭
D## G# B# F#
× 3 2 1 4 ×
5
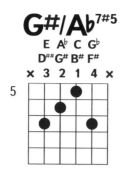

G#/A♭7#5
E A♭ C G♭
D## G# B# F#
× × 2 1 1 3
1
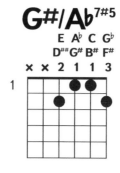

G#/A♭7#5
G♭ C E A♭
F# B# D## G#
2 4 3 1 × ×
1
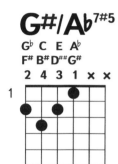

G#/A♭7#5
G♭ C E A♭
F# B# D## G#
× 1 2 1 1 ×
9
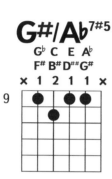

G#/A♭7#5
G♭ C E A♭
F# B# D## G#
× × 1 2 3 1
4
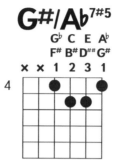

G#/A♭7♭9
G♭ C E♭ B♭♭
F# B# D# A
2 4 1 3 × ×
1
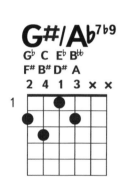

G#/A♭7♭9
G♭ C E♭ B♭♭
F# B# D# A
× × 1 2 1 3
4
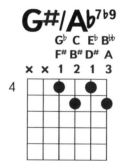

G#/A♭7♭9
A♭ C G♭ B♭♭
G# B# F# A
× 2 1 3 1 ×
10
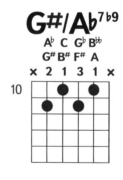

G#/A♭7♭9
A♭ C G♭ B♭♭
G# B# F# A
× × 2 1 3 1
5
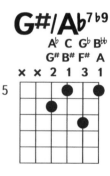

G#/A♭7♭9
B♭♭ E♭ G♭ C
A D# F# B#
2 4 1 3 × ×
4
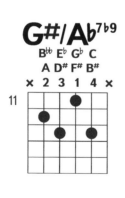

G#/A♭7♭9
B♭♭ E♭ G♭ C
A D# F# B#
× 2 3 1 4 ×
11
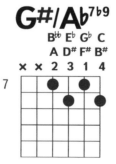

G#/A♭7♭9
B♭♭ E♭ G♭ C
A D# F# B#
× × 2 3 1 4
7

G#/A♭7♭9
C G♭ B♭♭
B# F# A
2 3 1 × × ×
7
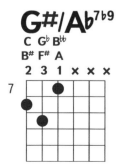

G#/A♭7♭9
C G♭ B♭♭
B# F# A
× 2 4 1 × ×
2
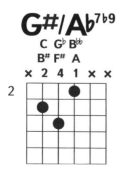

G#/A♭7♭9
C G♭ B♭♭
B# F# A
× × × 2 4 1
5

G#/A♭7♭9
G♭ B♭♭ C
F# A B#
× × × 4 3 1
8

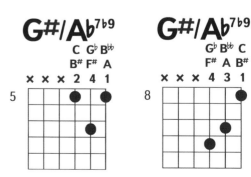

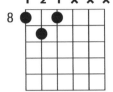

G#/Ab9
C Gb Bb
B# F# A#
1 2 1 × × ×
8

G#/Ab9
C Gb Bb
B# F# A#
× 1 2 1 × ×
3

G#/Ab9
C Gb Bb
B# F# A#
× × 1 2 3 ×
10

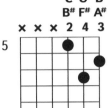

G#/Ab9
C Gb Bb
B# F# A#
× × × 2 4 3
5

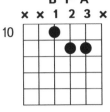

G#/Ab9
Gb Bb C
F# A# B#
× × × 3 4 1
8

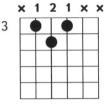

G#/Ab9
Gb C Eb Bb
F# B# D# A#
2 3 1 4 × ×
1

G#/Ab9
Gb C Eb Bb
F# B# D# A#
× × 1 2 1 3
4

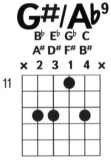

G#/Ab9
Bb Eb Gb C
A# D# F# B#
3 4 1 2 × ×
4

G#/Ab9
Bb Eb Gb C
A# D# F# B#
× 2 3 1 4 ×
11

G#/Ab9
Bb Eb Gb C
A# D# F# B#
× × 2 3 1 4
7

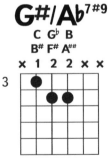
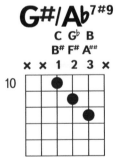

G#/Ab7#9
C Gb B
B# F# A##
1 2 2 × × ×
8

G#/Ab7#9
C Gb B
B# F# A##
× 1 2 2 × ×
3

G#/Ab7#9
C Gb B
B# F# A##
× × 1 2 3 ×
10

G#/Ab7#9
C Gb B
B# F# A##
× × × 1 3 4
5

G#/Ab⌀
Cb Ebb Gb
B D F#
4 2 1 × × ×
4
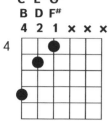

G#/Ab⌀
Cb Ebb Gb
B D F#
× 4 2 1 × ×
11
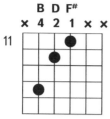

G#/Ab⌀
Cb Ebb Gb
B D F#
× × 3 1 1 ×
7
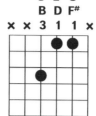

G#/Ab⌀
Cb Ebb Gb
B D F#
× × × 3 2 1
2
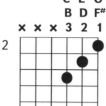

G#/Ab⌀
Ebb Gb Cb
D F# B
2 1 1 × × ×
9
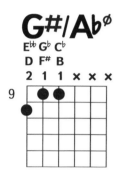

G#/Ab⌀
Ebb Gb Cb
D F# B
× 2 1 1 × ×
4
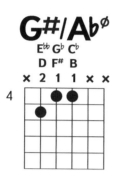

G#/Ab⌀
Ebb Gb Cb
D F# B
× × 2 1 3 ×
11
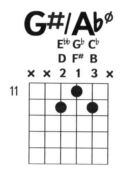

G#/Ab⌀
Ebb Gb Cb
C## F# B
× × × 1 1 1
7
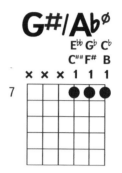

G#/Ab⌀
Gb Cb Ebb
F# B D
1 2 0 × × ×
0
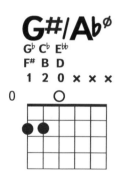

G#/Ab⌀
Gb Cb Ebb
F# B D
× 2 3 1 × ×
7
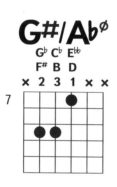

G#/Ab⌀
Gb Cb Ebb
F# B D
× × 2 3 1 ×
3
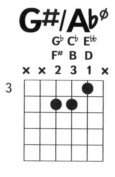

G#/Ab⌀
Gb Cb Ebb
F# B D
× × × 2 3 1
10
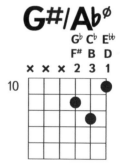

SEEING MUSIC
METHOD BOOKS

256 GUITAR CHORDS ENCYCLOPEDIA: A SEEING MUSIC METHOD BOOK

CHORD SYMBOL REFERENCE

The letter "X" is used to indicate the root of the chord (ex: A, B, C, etc..)

Augmented	X^{Aug}	X^{+}	
Diminished	X^{dim}	X^{O}	
Dominant 7th	X^{7}		
Dominant 7th plus Flat 9	$X^{7\flat 9}$		
Dominant 7th plus Sharp 9	$X^{7\#9}$		
Dominant 9th	X^{9}		
Half-Diminished	$X^{\emptyset}$		
Major	X^{Maj}	$X^{\triangle}$	X
Major 7	X^{Maj7}	$X^{\triangle 7}$	
Major 9	X^{Maj9}	$X^{\triangle 9}$	
Major Add 6, Add 9 (No 7th)	$X^{add6/9}$	$X^{6/9}$	
Major Add 9 (no 7th)	X^{add9}		
Major Suspended	X^{sus}		
Minor	X^{min}	X^{-}	x
Minor plus Major 7th	$X^{min\,Maj7}$	$X^{-\triangle 7}$	$x^{\triangle 7}$
Minor 7	X^{min7}	X^{-7}	x^{7}

Minor 7 plus Major 9th

Minor 7 plus Minor 9th

X^{min9} X^{-9} x^9

$X^{min♭9}$ $X^{-♭9}$ $x^{♭9}$

Printed in Great Britain
by Amazon